Bakhtin and cultural theory

edited by
Ken Hirschkop and David Shepherd

Bakhtin
and cultural theory

MANCHESTER
UNIVERSITY PRESS

Manchester and New York

distributed exclusively in the USA and Canada
by St. Martin's Press

Published by Manchester University Press, Oxford Road, Manchester M13 9PL, UK

and Room 400, 175 Fifth Avenue, New York, NY 10010, USA

Distributed exclusively in the USA and Canada
by St. Martin's Press, Inc.,
175 Fifth Avenue, New York, NY 10010, USA

Reprinted 1990, 1991

British Library cataloguing in publication data
Bakhtin and cultural theory
   1. Literature. Criticism. Bakhtin, M.
   (Mikhail), 1895-1975 – Critical studies
   I. Hirschkop, Ken II. Shepherd, David G.
   801'.95'0924

Library of Congress cataloging in publication data
Bakhtin and cultural theory   edited by Ken Hirschkop and David Shepherd
     p.   cm.
   Bibliography: p.
   Includes index.
   IBSN 0-7190-2615-6
   1. Bakhtin, M. M. (Mikhail Mikhailovich), 1895-1975
2. Criticism—History and criticism—20th century.
I. Hirschkop, Ken II. Shepherd, David (David G.)
PG2947.B3B3   1989
801'.95'0924—dc19   89-30358

ISBN 0 7190 2615 6 *paperback*

Printed in Great Britain
by Hartnolls Ltd., Bodmin, Cornwall

Contents

Preface

The reasons for assembling this collection of polemical essays on Bakhtin should be clear enough from the Introduction and the essays themselves to make any further explanation here superfluous. The arrangement of the contributions is intended to highlight both the range of issues which they raise and their shared concerns. Graham Pechey, Tony Crowley and David Shepherd focus predominantly upon the work of Bakhtin and the Bakhtin school from the 1920s and 1930s, showing how Bakhtinian theories of language, and in particular the notions of dialogism and heteroglossia, insistently require reference to a broad political and institutional context. Nancy Glazener is no less concerned with these issues, but also foregrounds their connection with the complex of questions centring on carnival and the treatment of the body which are addressed at greater length by Clair Wills, Ann Jefferson and Terry Eagleton. Crucial though the shared preoccupations of the contributions are to the volume's polemical thrust, our principal concern in editing them has been to respect their differences in approach and emphasis, and to ensure maximum clarity for each essay takes on its own, since it is clear that many readers may wish to consult individual chapters rather than the collection as a whole. Therefore, although every effort has been made to standardise the form of notes and references throughout the book, each essay retains its own peculiarities with respect to such matters as in-text references and modification of the standard translations of Bakhtin.

Bakhtin and Cultural Theory was to have included essays by Raymond Williams and Allon White, both of whom died in 1988. It is a much poorer volume without their contributions, as we are all poorer intellectually, politically and personally for their loss. They were exceptionally warm and decent people, and, though from different generations, and with véry different styles of work, they shared a commitment to theoretically informed historical analysis which is all too rare today. Their distinctive voices and projects, which were of immense value to our common work, will be greatly missed.

Acknowledgements

Graham Pechey's 'On the borders of Bakhtin' first appeared in the *Oxford Literary Review*, and David Shepherd's 'Bakhtin and the reader' contains some material first used in an article in *Poetics Today*; permission from both journals to re-publish is hereby gratefully acknowledged. We should also like to thank John Banks, our editor at Manchester University Press, for his unfailing encouragement, helpfulness and patience during the preparation of this volume.

Transliteration of Russian

Russian words are transliterated according to British Standard 2979 (1958), with the exception of some names which appear in their most familiar form (e.g. Gorky rather than Gor'kii).

Ken Hirschkop

Introduction: Bakhtin and cultural theory

The idea of a common language and the goal of a democratic society have long been linked. After the establishment of the modern nation-state, it was assumed that access to an arena of public vernacular discourse was equivalent to access to political power, in so far as it allowed one to participate in the deliberative process whereby social values and priorities were determined. This bourgeois illusion experienced a particularly hard landing in the early part of the twentieth century. The advent of 'mass' forms of politics, general literacy and 'mass' culture should have led to thoroughly democratic societies based on the discourse of an entire nation; in fact, as we well know, it led to anything but that. What had been thought of as a common language now appeared as a loose association of varying forms of social communication. Everyone may have spoken English, or French, or German but the substance of their linguistic life could differ dramatically. In practice, 'speech' could consist of private conversation, writing or reading a newspaper (very different uses of 'language'), political debate on the radio or preparing a bureaucratic document, and often these contexts entailed distinctions in grammar, syntax, accent and style. The common language turned out not to be the transparent and homogeneous ideal envisaged in the eighteenth century but a dense web of distinct linguistic practices, by means of which existing inequalities in political power could easily be maintained.

In 1940 Mikhail Bakhtin implied he accepted the illusion – 'We live, speak, and write', he claimed, 'in a world of free and democratised language' – but then continued his lifelong effort to describe and analyse the ways in which differences of form, genre and style within a shared national language could enforce or challenge political domination.[1] Together with Pavel Medvedev and Valentin Voloshinov, Bakhtin developed a body of work which purported to describe an already democratised language, one which was 'dialogical', 'hetero-glottic', at its better moments even 'carnivalesque'; but the very scale of their labours is the surest clue to the fact that their real business was the provision of tools for transforming a notionally popular language into an actually democratic one.

It would be a great, although not extraordinary, irony if the most interesting theorisation of the politics of national languages came from a country which was never a bourgeois nation-state, was overwhelmingly illiterate, and lacked the kind of mass culture typical of the industrial West. But there was another field in which a supposedly unified language was rethought as a battlefield of political forces: avant-garde and modernist literature, which had a very strong base in Russia and the Soviet Union. The Formalists and Futurists brought politics directly into the heart of linguistic culture when they divided it into competing literary, extraliterary and everyday forms of language. And although the Bakhtin circle disagreed sharply with many of their formulations, they took from these theorists the idea of a language riven by struggles between styles and forms, with 'literary' authority the prize.

These historical considerations make it appear more reasonable that the Left today should so enthusiastically embrace theorists who are regarded with equal awe across the political spectrum. When one of the contributors to this volume admitted to me that he thought Bakhtin's categories were empty but nevertheless crucial for us to 'keep', I knew exactly what he meant: they represent contemporary attempts by socialist theorists to analyse 'modernism' and modern 'democracy', historical realities which constitute part of the terrain for twentieth-century politics and culture. In the case of modernism, the works of the Bakhtin circle participate in the emphasis on linguistic 'material' so prevalent today, but give it, as it were, a socio-historical twist, associating avant-garde estrangement and shock with traditions of popular subversive discourse. Some current theorists have even gone so far as to offer Bakhtin as a kind of Left alternative to deconstruction, who provides a socio-historical basis for the latter's formal practice.[2]

The issue of democracy is a more complicated one. It was not always the case, of course, that Left, Right and Centre would line up so enthusiastically behind theorists advocating a 'free and democratised' language. Until very recently, the liberal middle classes, the bourgeoisie and the aristocracy frowned on democracy and its egalitarian pretensions, equating it with mob rule. But in the early twentieth century the terms of the argument shifted, as debates over whether democracy and popular rule were desirable gave way to debates about which forms and procedures were authentically democratic. It is no exaggeration to say that arguments over the concepts of the Bakhtin school are to a great extent arguments about democracy, and the kind of linguistic and cultural life it implies.

Thus the ease with which *everyone* can endorse the central elements of the Bakhtinian programme indicates that the hard work has not really begun. What is this 'dialogism' that so many celebrate as liberating and democratic: what are its actual cultural forms, its social or political preconditions, its participants, methods and goals? When we first meet this concept in Bakhtin's work it describes a certain relation between distinct 'voices' in a narrative text, in which each takes its shape as a conscious reaction to the ideological position of the other; but even then it is a metaphor for a broader principle of discourse. 'Heteroglossia', when first mentioned, is a description of stylistic and generic stratification and conflict within the confines of a national vernacular. But what are the consequences of this stratification? Do all such divisions have political significance? Is it a recipe for social diversity or the establishment of warring interest groups? 'Carnivalesque' works, in Bakhtin's parlance, use motifs, themes and generic forms drawn from a tradition of subversive medieval popular culture, a tradition linked to a very specific festive practice and to the significance of the body in medieval and Renaissance culture. How can these practices be translated into the very different kinds of popular culture one finds in modern capitalist societies? These are all questions which the Bakhtin circle left unanswered, but they pose in particularly acute form the problem of how to establish a democratic culture and language in modern societies.

It would be misleading, however, to suggest that the interpretation of the Bakhtin circle's work is a matter of arbitrary appropriation. Notions such as dialogism, heteroglossia, grotesque realism and the carnivalesque come to us already charged with social and political significance: they embody or identify distinct, though often complex and contradictory, impulses in a historical situation. The meaning of a concept like dialogism or carnival is a sedimentation of past usages, current and past social conflicts, the changing forms of ideological life; in short, these terms are themselves dialogical. Thus the word 'dialogism' is not only linked to a system of concepts but has a social force or implication as well, a socially 'concrete' meaning (to use Bakhtin's language) which could be expressed as the difference between imagining dialogism as a debate in the Houses of Parliament or as an open-air trade union meeting.

This social concreteness is a property of even the most theoretical text, but in the case of Bakhtin, Voloshinov and Medvedev, it is unusually explicit. As a number of interpreters have noted, there are concerns, problems and ideas which seem to float through the works of Bakhtin and his circle, surfacing in different contexts with markedly different inflections.[3] Take, for example, the concept of value. In Bakhtin's earliest works value means human intention and purpose of any kind, so that even scientific discourse can be said to have a value orientation, in so far as it is aimed at the achievement of truth, which would be a value on a par with beauty and the good. In his discussion of aesthetic issues, this purpose is defined as the emotional – volitional response of the creator or perceiver to the aesthetic object; a more restricted definition, which associates value specifically with will and desire. Medvedev, in *The Formal Method*, redefines value as 'social evaluation', understanding by this phrase a world-view or set of social beliefs characteristic of a particular group or social practice. By the time of 'Discourse in the novel' value has by and large ceded its place to the concepts of 'interest' and 'point of view' (*tochka zreniya*) or 'horizon' (*krugozor*), all of which take values to be sociological entities, which are comprehensible only from the perspective of a theory of social and historical change.

This conceptual movement is one of the more interesting features of the Bakhtin circle's work, but also the source of many difficulties of interpretation, for it is never quite clear which is the appropriate context for any particular element of their vocabulary. Should these terms be read in the context of neo-Kantian epistemological debate? The philosophy of language? Modernist literary theorising? Sociolinguistics? A great deal of the argument over Bakhtin has revolved around precisely this question (Clark and Holquist, and Todorov privileging the philosophical, Titunik and Morson the linguistic, White the sociological).[4] But the variety of interpretations can also be construed as the index of a very particular problem, which I will describe as the need to endow these concepts with both a 'transcendental' or philosophical significance and an analytical or empirical meaning. In retrospect we can see that there were good reasons for Bakhtin wanting to have a foot in the camps of both philosophy and empirical cultural analysis: the latter entails the specification of historical phenomena – heteroglossia versus monoglossia, or the different types of chronotope – while the philosophical edge of those same concepts, the sense in which heteroglossia and chronotope are the internal conditions of any language or culture whatsoever, made it possible for Bakhtin to approach those historical objects critically. If we say that 'language is heteroglottic', we mean that it is characteristic of language as such that it is made up of a number of disjunct and perhaps opposed stylistic forms of speech, which cannot be reduced to a linguistic system: this would be, as it were, a tenet in the philosophy of language. Yet it is also possible to say that 'a language is heteroglottic', in which case we are referring to a particular historical state of language, implying that the kind of internal division spoken of above was the product of particular historical circumstances, so that one could also speak of languages being monoglottic. The conflation of these meanings is bound to cause some confusion, even dismay. If all language is heteroglottic, then it is hard to see how and why certain languages have escaped this requirement: monoglossia appears to be explicable only as a language whose natural tendency is repressed or obstructed by some external force. As I will show below, this is a characteristic weakness of Bakhtin's historical analysis. But this form of dual definition also provides an implicit critique of monoglossia, in the light of which the latter appears as a systematisation of language which prevents language from doing its job, from realising the kind of social interaction which it should. Heteroglossia, like most of Bakhtin's other concepts, is both historical and normative.

By defining his objects of investigation philosophically, Bakhtin chose to describe culture not in the neutral terms of social science, but as an activity with political and moral ends and objectives. Each of his analytical concepts imputes a purpose or aim to the phenomenon it describes, a purpose which is both internal to the phenomenon and liable to ethico-political evaluation. The continuous tension in his conceptual language, whatever its limits, results in a kind of critical theorising about language and culture which renounces neither empirical analysis nor the ethico-political purposes of moral philosophy. Bakhtin will speak of syntactic forms, lexical choices and stylistic patterns, making use of the battery of formal linguistics, but without reducing language to a 'given', governed by natural-scientific lawfulness. Language appears not as an indifferent medium of social exchange but as a form of social exchange, susceptible to political and moral evaluation like any other. From this perspective heteroglossia or the chronotope figure as social and cultural achievements, while language in general becomes an activity which can be criticised and even improved. The frame which endows linguistic forms with a

purpose changes throughout Bakhtin's career – a philosophical belief
in moral responsibility within language gives way to conceptions of
discourse as an arena of social conflict – but the belief in the purposefulness of discourse always provides a critical edge to his discussion
of existing linguistic usage.[5]

Perhaps this conceptual ambiguity is most striking in the concept
of dialogism. Does it represent a principle from a philosophical anthropology, or denote a certain kind of language-use, found in novels and
particular forms of popular speech? Let us examine this case, in many
respects the central one, at some length. As it has been adopted in
formal literary analysis, dialogism designates a number of disparate
practices – parody, the use of socially marked languages in literary
texts (from Shakespeare's Porter to the Artful Dodger), collage, and
what Bakhtin calls stylisation, the pointed emphasis of socially distinct speech. Not only are these practices arguably very different in
form and effect, they are also typical of very dissimilar historical
moments. The argument of an essay like 'Discourse in the novel' is that
such practices are all varieties of dialogism, defined as the coexistence
in a single utterance of two intentionally distinct, identifiable voices.
The definition here is itself revealing. Why describe such stylistic
phenomena in terms of *voices,* with all the connotations of individuality this implies? It would seem more accurate to describe them as
social conventions – stylistic or generic – characteristic of particular
historical moments and situations. Bakhtin, of course, says as much,
and this essay is often cited, quite rightly, as evidence of a 'social' turn
in his work. But he nevertheless treats these varied stylistic and
generic patterns as indices of a deeper principle of language, that of
dialogism, which then must be redefined to accommodate its various
manifestations: as the constant mixing of intentions of speaker and
listener; as the way an utterance acquires meaning by inflecting past
utterances; as the need of each form of speech to position itself
stylistically among other existing forms. Dialogism at this level of
definition denotes a transcendental principle of discourse, the very
condition of communication and of the creation of meaningful utterances. And one can only assume that such a transcendental principle
applies equally to individual utterances and the more recognisably
'social' conventions of style, genre and the like. Redescribing language
in terms of 'voices' thus functions as an empirical shorthand for this
novel proposition about the dialogism of all utterances.

If we are to understand how styles and genres can come to be
characterised in terms of 'voices', we will have to retrace our steps,

and examine some of Bakhtin's essays of the early 1920s. In a short fragment, 'The architectonics of the deed', Bakhtin argues against what he calls 'theoreticism', that is, doctrines which entail 'the principled split between the content-meaning of an act and the historical reality of its being'.[6] Objects of experience, he claims, do not confront us as 'givens', defined through an abstract conceptuality, because 'to understand the object is to understand my intention in relation to it' (AP, p. 159). The consequences of not relating to objects as intended objects, defined by our purpose in relation to them, are very serious indeed. If we maintain a division between the products or objects of our culture and our purposeful activity or 'life', then the culture, here equivalent to the society, will develop 'immanently', in ways which may not please us: 'Logical clarity and necessary consequence, torn from the single, unique centre of a responsible consciousness, are dark and elemental forces, precisely because of the law of immanent necessity inherent in logic' (AP, p. 164). Without an intentional connection, social life cultivates its own logic and consequence, one seemingly alien to any human purpose. To these 'dark and elemental forces', presumably culpable for the destruction of Europe and the Soviet Union, Bakhtin can only oppose the 'responsible consciousness', which should already put us on our guard. The point, however, of this phenomenological argument, posed as a challenge to both abstract philosophy and positivistic science, is the need to find a mode of discourse which would convey the value-laden connection between the subject and its objects. Without this all the rules, norms and propositions which constitute a culture are 'document[s] without a signature, obligating no one to anything' (AP, p. 168).

What is interesting and perhaps distinctive about Bakhtin's argument is his conviction that these relevant purposes and intentions take their shape from the immediate 'event' or situation of experience. In Bakhtin's philosophising, situations and events take on an almost physical particularity, so that the 'life' with which logic must be reconnected appears to be composed of unique experiential moments.[7] Language – if one believes it to be composed of grammatical rules, agreed conventional lexis and the like – would seem to negate this uniqueness of experience, and with it any possibility of maintaining a connection with value and intention. And yet an escape route exists: intonation. For what distinguishes pragmatic from conceptual meaning in language, and what conveys, to Bakhtin's mind, the value relation of a speaking subject to his or her situation is precisely 'intonation', the links of which to 'voice' are too obvious to require discussion: '*Emotional–volitional tone flows all around the semantic content of the thought in the deed and relates it to the unique existence – event*' (AP, p. 165). In such early works as the 'Architectonics' essay, the study of the 'Author and hero in aesthetic activity' and Bakhtin's 1924 critique of Formalism ('The problem of content, material and form in verbal artistic creation') aesthetic experience is differentiated from cognitive and ethical activity in so far as it emphasises this element of 'intonation', and through it the situatedness of the utterance, its necessary binding to some human purpose. Aesthetic activity is even advanced as a superior form for moral discourse, one capable of transforming the abstractions of Kantian ethics into concretely obligating utterances.[8] In the context of arguments like these, Formalist theory, which abstracted intention from language almost as a first move, would appear as one more attempt to explain language in terms of an immanent logic. But however consistent Bakhtin might have been in his polemic with positivism and 'theoreticism', he clearly was affected by the theorising around him, for one can observe a notable transformation in his work. On the road from the early 1920s to the mid-1930s (a long and winding road in the Soviet Union) new concepts of the 'novel' and of 'style' were introduced as replacements or reworkings of the concepts of the aesthetic object and intonation respectively.

What might have triggered this shift is the Bakhtin circle's confrontation with Saussure, and his proposition that *langue* is a 'social fact' which, however, provides the categories which structure our experience. To some extent the new linguistics could be interpreted as an attempt by empirical social science to claim for itself ground which philosophers of Bakhtin's ilk had staked out for themselves. But the terms of this claim could only have horrified Bakhtin: the 'society' we find in Saussure is a disturbingly homogeneous collective. *Langue* describes a bureaucratised world we are only too familiar with, in which every subject behaves according to formal rules, to be obeyed without reference to ends, values or mitigating circumstances: 'for language furnishes the best proof that a law accepted by a community is a thing that is tolerated and not a rule to which all freely consent'.[9] How then to reinsert intention and value? The Formalists, with very different aims in mind, provided a possible answer by emphasising the analysis of *skaz*, the peculiar form of narration which signalled, for the educated Russian reader, an encounter with 'oral' storytelling. *Skaz* appears to offer an ideal compromise: a form which conveys 'intonation' and yet can be defined with the concepts of formal linguistics.

Whatever the inspiration, sometime in the middle or late 1920s Voloshinov and Bakhtin change their tack. Their new argument is that the diversity of actual intentions and values is expressed not by means of an individualising intonation, but by the varying styles of a language, the consistent patterns of usage which overlay a basic syntactic and grammatical structure. The adoption of the concept of style implies – and Bakhtin recognises that it does – that intentions and values, embodied in language, are social quantities, a notion which would represent a radical departure from the earlier doctrine. Bakhtin would seem to be claiming that the situatedness of an utterance can be expressed by the kind of abstract structures identified by linguistics; but he cannot quite bring himself to accept this position. So the original philosophical position rumbles along underneath, creating an ambiguity in the concept of dialogism. On the one hand, it is the relation between linguistically distinct styles; on the other hand, it is the relation between individual utterances, a formulation which preserves the belief in the uniqueness of each speech event. But even when endorsing the latter formulation, Bakhtin will accept that dialogism is only perceptible in very specific textual moments, when linguistic structures – syntactic, lexical, or generic – appear as the expression of particular, delimited 'points of view'.

But so far I have left out a crucial element of the argument: the proposition that 'value' is only perceptible in a collision of two of these points of view, i.e. in 'dialogue'. This omission is not quite as scandalous as it seems, for the emphasis on dialogism really follows from a particular conception and justification of aesthetic experience. In the earlier work aesthetic experience is prized as a place where we can become conscious of the value or intentional content of all experience, the assumption being that there one is disengaged from ethical and cognitive impulses which lead beyond language into action. Although language is conceived of as always anthropomorphised, embedded with intentions, containing therefore 'potential heroes', these intentions, according to Bakhtin, must be detached from the 'open event of being' (AH, p. 18) by means of aesthetic totalisation or 'finalisation', if they are to be manifested. Thus while 'the hero lives ethically and cognitively' so that 'his deed is oriented towards the open ethical event of life and the posited world of cognition', the intentions thereby generated must be recontextualised by the aesthetic activity of the author, who 'orients the hero and his cognitive-ethical position in a world of being which is finalised in principle' (AH, p. 16). The claim that reflection on the value-bearing properties of language requires some distance from an already constituted 'living' language is maintained in different forms throughout the works of the circle; it is not, needless to say, a necessarily radical idea. In 'Author and hero', an essay almost wholly devoted to exploring the subtleties of this proposition, the premiss of a necessary aesthetic distance corresponds, rather unsurprisingly, to an emphasis on the contemplative character of the aesthetic event. By establishing a typology of author–hero relations, Bakhtin hopes to define a specific balance between the author (reflection) and the hero (the living consciousness), which would make it possible for this sense of value to emerge. What is thereby established as a general principle is the idea that the relation between a reflective consciousness and a consciousness ensnared in the activity of everyday life is 'a relation of intense outsidedness' (AH, p. 18): it is only through reflection on an *alien* language that the right mix of distance and empathy can be achieved.

The 'Problem' essay of 1924 retains this schema, insisting on the necessity of refracting one consciousness through another (here ethical or cognitive consciousness through the aesthetic consciousness; not two different characters but two different principles); as in 'Author and hero' the dialogical collision is described in phenomenal rather than linguistic terms. But by the time of Medvedev's critique of Formalism (1928), this basic idea has been reformulated: literature as such is now distinguished from other kinds of ideology to the extent that it isolates, distances and reprocesses their forms, a notion which leads straight to the Tartu school's definition of literature as a secondary modelling system. In Voloshinov, and then later in 'Discourse in the novel', the question is framed as a linguistic one, so that quasi-direct discourse, the new embodiment of the reflective function of the author, somehow becomes the model for all artistic reworking of language. And even in the study of Rabelais it turns out that the aesthetic version of carnival is actually superior in force to the real thing. In many respects Bakhtin *et al.* are simply revising the Kantian definition of the beautiful as 'purposiveness without purpose', substituting for Kantian 'purpose' modern concepts of 'intention', 'value' and 'ideology'. But unlike Kant, Bakhtin is interested in the aesthetic as a form of activity rather than as a mode of experience, his concern is with the production and reproduction of aesthetic works. This means he must face a problem Kant did not have to face, the question of how to produce 'the form of purposiveness' from actually existing purposes. As a consequence, Bakhtin's initial formulations concern the relation between an 'aesthetic' finalising purpose and an 'object' purpose, a relation which Bakhtin will later translate into the belief that linguistic meaning of any kind arises from the recontextualising of one purpose by another. From such diverse roots arise the conflicts in the concept of dialogism which are played out today in critical discussion. Whether it is a relation among utterances or styles, or whether it is a relation between any two intentions or an 'authorial' and a 'heroic' one, are questions which make possible a great variety of interpretations. But a particularly significant focus of dispute has been and will be whether dialogism is a relation between individual utterances, and in that sense always in operation, or a more specifically historical phenomenon, depending on a confrontation between social conventions of style or genre. In line with the first interpretation, one can define dialogism as the contamination of 'conceptual' meaning by values, interests and desires: 'In actuality we never say or hear *words*, we say and hear what is true or false, good or bad, important or unimportant, pleasant or unpleasant, and so on.'[10] In this conception language is composed of unrepeatable performances, its entwinement with values wholly conditional on the recognition of the uniqueness of the utterance. In Bakhtin's now celebrated later works this definition of dialogism dominates: the utterance 'always creates something that had not been before, that is always new and nonreiterative, and that, moreover, always has a relation to values (truth, the good, the beautiful, etc.)'.[11] But there are other definitions available:

> double-voicedness draws its energy, its dialogized dual meaningfulness, not from individual voice differences, misunderstandings or contradictions (even if they are both tragic, and firmly based on individual destinies); in the novel, this double-voicedness sinks its roots deep into a fundamental socio-linguistic heteroglossia and hetero-languagedness.[12]

Dialogism, in a string of works from 1934 onwards, is defined as the unmasking of social languages. Cesare Segre has indicated a relevant confusion in Bakhtin's concept of polyphony (which he equates with dialogism) and in the accompanying account of the novel: 'Bakhtin, in separating the history of polyphonic procedures from that of narrative invention, brings together in the category of polyphony phenomena with very different origins and functions.'[13] Two different programmes are thereby conflated under the name polyphony: the separation of the author's voice from those of the characters, which makes narrative possible; and the representation of the linguistic stratification of a society. As Segre rather shrewdly notes, the Bakhtin of 'Discourse in the novel' searches for linguistic manifestations of a phenomenon, the differentiation of author and hero, which is not necessarily linguistic. And if we look but five years earlier we see the proof of this, for the study of Dostoevsky reveals polyphony in an otherwise stylistically homogeneous language. There would seem to be no neat correspondence between the differentiation of voices and the differentiation of a language into styles. Consequently, the novelistic techniques Bakhtin describes at length and, indeed, the general project of identifying speech forms with social groups or situations, may not be enough to provide that 'participatory description', uniting the content with the act of speech, that Bakhtin earlier felt was essential. In fact, many recent discussions of the 'reality effects' of the novel emphasise that novels only work because their discourse makes it possible for their readers to take up positions somehow analogous with that of a character or speaker.[14] So while Bakhtin could be right in thinking that 'Responsibility is possible not for meaning in itself but for its unique assertion or non-assertion' (AP, p. 168), and that therefore one has to turn to the world of speech acts and their contexts to understand how we act in language, this realm of dialogical relations, the object of what Bakhtin will call metalinguistics, is not identical with the world of heteroglossia vividly described in 'Discourse in the novel'. Between phenomenological and sociological descriptions of discourse there remains a significant gap.

Or it may be that in the realm of speech acts, things are not quite as unformalised and 'unique' as Bakhtin thinks. The resistance to those dark elemental forces for which no one is responsible, to that faceless pressure of modernity, in which one can't pin the blame for disasters on a particular landlord or king, is to be generated wholly by the 'responsible consciousness'. It may not recognise the phenomenal reality which confronts it as its own work, but it must be able to find the evidence of its own intentional, purposeful activity in that phenomenal world. What prevents this recognition, and so encourages a certain indifference to historical events, is a composite tendency Bakhtin calls 'rationalism', and in fighting it over the course of twenty-five years Bakhtin will make appeals to the materiality of the sign, the concrete context of discourse, the social conditions of a genre and the needs of the body. In his most interesting and daring move, Bakhtin will endow the plebeian masses with a kind of spontaneous materialist philosophy, a Falstaffian scepticism which recognises even the modern nation as an abstraction: 'The people never fully share the ruling truth. If the nation [*natsiya*, and not, significantly, *narod*, the people-nation] is threatened by danger, they do their duty and save it, but they never take seriously the patriotic slogans of the class state, their heroism retains a sober derisiveness towards the pathos of the ruling power and the ruling truth.'[15] At least in this case the distrust of rationalisations is grounded in a body which could more feasibly challenge the elemental forces. But popular scepticism is not quite the same thing as phenomenological self-reflection, and the kinds of response they suggest couldn't be much further apart.[16] The 'participatory description' which, in the early 1920s, is the preferred form of phenomenological self-reflection, promotes a heightened awareness of one's *immediate* situation: 'In the given unique point at which I am now located, no one else in the unique time and unique space of unique being can be located' (AP, pp. 167-8). What could be more individualistic? It seems odd that Bakhtin should so often define 'situation' as one's *place* in the most literal, physical sense of the word. There is, in fact, a kind of gross and vulgar materialism underlying the theoretical sophistication: after all the philosophical subtleties, everything depends on a concept of abstract space drawn undiluted from mechanical physics. Of course, Bakhtin himself will later provide an elaborate phenomenology of historical space, based on the chronotopes, the systems of time/space co-ordination, found in novelistic writing. But even within that phenomenology there exists a clearly normative progression from the primitive abstraction of the Greek romance to the dense historical space of the modern 'realistic' chronotope, which carefully differentiates each historical moment.

Why is there such a deep connection between the discovery of value and consciousness of exact physical placement? In one sense Bakhtin, in these earlier works, participates in the 'modernist' fetish of 'the material', which extracts physical qualities from specific historical embodiments and then proposes to investigate them as properties in their own right. He extends this fetishism to one's social situation, which then becomes something felt, tangible, physically sensible, and so subject to the mediation of human value. As has been pointed out, any such concentration on 'material' uses the concept metaphorically.[17] In the present case the emphasis is motivated in part by a certain utopianism: an ideal of communal relations in which people are connected by something more physical than principles or even shared morals. Although Bakhtin was clearly impressed by the pure form of 'I–Thou' relations enacted in Dostoevsky's aesthetic practice, he realised that this was at the cost of an unacceptable ideal of human community. Dostoevsky's characters 'are moved by the utopian dream of the creation of some kind of commune of people outside of existing social forms'.[18] As Bakhtin notes, 'It is as if society was voided of its real body. . .' (*PDP*, pp. 280-1), and he will pose an alternative to this version of community in his utopian description of the very bodily life of the medieval peasantry in his study of Rabelais. Somewhat ironically, the ultimate social image of community is found not in the intellectual circles of 1920s Leningrad but in the more genuinely communal life of the peasantry, in which the experience of working 'the land', and thus depending on natural conditions, serves to integrate one's conscious life fully with 'the material'.

In more strictly conceptual terms one could say the Bakhtin circle conflate the concrete with the immediate. Utterances may very well depend on such things as context and situation for their meaning, but, arguably, these too are formalised and conventional, and must be in any society. Voloshinov's emphasis on the 'concrete speech act in a concrete situation' is sometimes taken as an axiom of historical materialist thought, but it sounds as much like a reference to the work of J. L. Austin, an obviously less sociological thinker. Austin was interestingly ambiguous on the conditions which make speech acts possible: they consist in equal parts of conventional procedures, 'the particular persons and circumstances in a given case' and of sincere and good intentions.[19] Implicitly, he accepted the fact that social life is necessarily conventional, and yet he describes conventions less as shaping parameters of social life than as procedures or laws to be obeyed or ignored at will. As Jacques Derrida pointed out in his famous critique, 'Signature event context', in the final analysis, Austin defined the context controlling the force of the utterance in such a way that the sovereignty of the individual consciousness was always guaranteed. In Austin's work context is composed of circumstances one can see or at least be aware of. His typical speech acts – promising, warning, and getting married – are all acts whose force alters interpersonal relations of a very narrow kind, and they imply situations in which an individual could be held responsible for what he or she says. But, to take a different kind of example, under what conditions would an electoral candidate's promise to lower defence spending be 'felicitous'? If the answer is 'when he/she is sincere, knows the possibilities, and so forth' then the limits of Austin's paradigm, and its ideal model of controllable interpersonal situations, become clear. Could performative statements ever succeed, Derrida asks, if they 'were not identifiable as *conforming* to an iterable model, if therefore they were not identifiable in a way as "citation"'?[20] The contexts which make possible the force of speech acts entail conventions and conditions well beyond the control or consciousness of individual speakers, a kind of 'structural unconsciousness', as Derrida calls it, which suggests that context isn't something 'present' to the utterer. If this is so, then the immediate conditions of a speech act, the unique situation which Bakhtin appeals to, is not equivalent to the context which determines its values. One's place may be neither unique nor definable in the purely 'material' terms of time and space.

In one of the circle's first articles with a linguistic bearing, 'Discourse in life and discourse in poetry' (1926), Voloshinov describes the non-verbal context of an utterance and its relation to its particular intonation.[21] The model, a very telling one, is of a couple sitting in a room. The context consists, we are told, of the common knowledge of circumstances, common evaluation of the same and, most interestingly, a shared spatial horizon (what is visible to both in the room). The 'material' circumstances are limited to what is close at hand, and in so far as it is defined by what can be *seen*, Derrida's remarks about the connection of context and consciousness in Austin would seem to apply to Voloshinov's theory with equal force. And though the definition here is Voloshinov's, it doesn't differ from many offered by Bakhtin (who may have written the article anyhow: but that is another matter). In many passages the 'concrete' meaning of an utterance, intonation and all, is said to depend on a context which is first of all composed of an immediate speaker and an immediate listener; dialogue in a rather everyday sense is offered as a paradigm for all discourse. The sociological arguments of Medvedev and Voloshinov, often contrasted with Bakhtin, may appear to break with this model, but in many respects they simply enlarge the subjects of the dialogue without, however, deviating from the model of an immediate situation.[22] Needless to say, such a definition of social context doesn't have a lot to do with society as envisioned by historical materialism, although the notion of circumstances is so vague that it can still be turned to good use.

But there is another sense of context lurking in these texts, implying a very different concept of the dialogic. This other sense refers to the encounter of the utterance with the 'social heteroglossia surrounding the object' (DN, p. 278), the other languages against which it must define itself. The encounter is described in a marvellous passage from the opening of the second section of 'Discourse in the novel': 'The discourse directed at its object enters into this dialogically agitated and tense medium of alien words, evaluations and accents, it is entwined in their complex interrelationships, it merges with some, recoils from others and intersects with a third group' (DN, p. 276). This 'context' is in no sense immediate and would seem to resemble a rather more conflicted model of *langue*. Its historical dimension is striking; we are offered a vision of gradual historical change, in the shape of the continual reinflection of past, anonymous (in the literal sense) usages. But history also figures here as a kind of limit: the fact that speakers must work with an inheritance of 'concrete' styles, conventions and forms. While the earlier formulations suggested that through the mediation of an immediate situation the abstract possibilities of language were transformed into unique concrete actualities of speech, in the present model one's own context is assembled from the debris of the past.[23] 'Every word', Bakhtin tells us, 'tastes of the context and contexts in which it has lived its socially intense life' (DN, p. 293).

But at the same time context as it is defined in the 1930s is composed only of language; the rhetoric of immediate situations, in however curious a way, had the virtue of including the extra-linguistic world, 'real space and real time'. We are thus confronted with an awkward analytical choice: do we define context as the immediate material situation, through which are expressed the relevant social and historical factors, or do we define it as heteroglossia, a more spacious conception, but one which restricts context to the stuff of language?[24] Among Bakhtin's many descriptions of double-voiced discourse there are those which imply some combination of these two perspectives, and which may take us further: dialogism is also explained as a collision not of voices or intentions but of two or more *contexts* within a single utterance. This reassuring solution might only be interesting as wordplay, were it not for the fact that it alerts us to the specifically historical contours of dialogism, which seems predicated upon a very particular interplay of social isolation and contact. In order for dialogism to occur there must be different spheres of language: both 'local' contexts stable enough to generate differently inflected forms of language, and a public sphere in which these can meet and clash. Examining this formulation, one can understand why the 'public square' plays a leading role in Bakhtin's writing, for the market town is precisely a context or place where other contexts, or their representatives, meet.

Thus it might be more sensible to think of context as a set of largely invisible pressures and purposes, stemming from the social location of a speech act, which often are conflicting or contradictory. Indeed, this would seem to describe more accurately the typical forms of linguistic conflict in modern societies, where a common natural language is dialogised by its various inflections, so that the glue of allegiance to an ideal purpose like 'democracy' holds together the aspirations and needs of very diverse social groups.

Yet it is important to acknowledge that these linguistic subgroups are themselves, in Benedict Anderson's terms, 'imagined communities', integrated not by the literal fact of speaking together, but by occupying similar social 'locations' in a complex and divided society.[25] As Francis Mulhern has put it, 'If communities are notoriously hard to find it is because they are everywhere – not *places* but *practices* of collective identification'.[26] One characteristic of the universalising impetus of modern capitalist societies is the increasingly abstract nature of these communities, so that people actually physically remote from each other may none the less feel themselves to be part of a significant community, perhaps even an international one. The social cement of these communities can hardly be personal contact or a shared physical environment, but it may well be communicative contact of an obviously modern kind, embodied in the 'mass' media, or a belief in the comparability of their physical or material circumstances. Given this increasingly typical form of collective identification, a decision to define context in terms of a visible place appears curious. In a condition in which social locations are themselves abstractions, tied to concepts of class, nation, profession and the like, Bakhtin's appeal to the concrete, and his hope that 'responsibility' would follow from attention to one's immediate situation, sounds rather hollow. There are social pressures, physical limits, available definitions of need and purpose, but determining what these are 'concretely' is a rather more laborious task than Bakhtin implies. Indeed, some of the most significant shifts of value and intention may come from a redefinition of one's own context.

This raises the question of Bakhtin's own model of language in society, heteroglossia. In the essay 'From the prehistory of novelistic discourse' Bakhtin distinguishes between three discursive situations. In monoglossia, there is a shared language and a corresponding sense of ideological cohesion. Bakhtin's model for this is ancient Greek society, a choice which implies agreement at some level with German idealisations of the ancient Greek *Gemeinschaft*. This is succeeded by polyglossia, characteristic of Imperial Rome and the medieval period, in which different natural languages coexist in a single society. In both instances one language sees itself through the eyes of another (Latin through Greek, or church Latin and the vernaculars) and the result is a high degree of stylisation in literary production. According to

Bakhtin, heteroglossia is the language form of modern society, defined as everything which follows on the triumph of the vernaculars in the Renaissance. A condition of heteroglossia is characterised by unification of the society at the level of language and division at the level of style. This modern language situation makes possible the novel, a genre caught between its literary vocation and its desire to incorporate the stratified and typical styles of 'everyday life'.[27]

Much could be said about this hypothesis of heteroglossia. Even today, it doesn't square with many societies; and the notion that the major social forms of discourse have not changed since the Renaissance seems, to say the least, a little suspect. But as I remarked earlier in this essay, it is a concept balanced somewhere between evaluation and empirical description. As the former, it is the ideal of a society in which language is constantly productive, throwing out new forms and styles, developing and re-accentuating and differentiating itself. As empirical description it might best be thought of in connection with Bakhtin's description of nineteenth-century Russia in *Problems of Dostoevsky's Poetics*. There the combination of centripetal and centrifugal forces appears not as the normal course of modern society but as a condition resulting from the 'catastrophic' character of Russian capitalism, which brought together groups in an urban society before it could weld them into a cohesive urban, modern culture (*PDP*, pp. 19-20).[28] When previously separated and independent social groups are thrown together by the sudden onset of capitalism and its urbanising effects, the result is that coexistence of distinct languages which seems to define heteroglossia. Against that, what seems most striking about the advanced capitalist societies is the emergence of homogenising public linguistic forms, although many of these forms involve only the homogeneous reception of language. This is not to ignore the coexistence of powerful sub- and counter-currents, or to underestimate the degree to which a 'unified' public language may be dialogically processed and experienced by those on the receiving end. Even this, however, isn't the same as heteroglossia, which requires that socially different experiences be articulated *as language* (i.e. by means of the creation of distinct, ideologically charged syntactic, grammatical and lexical forms). When, for a variety of reasons, social pressures and conflicts cannot be translated into a coherent language or even ideology, they may find expression by other means: as 'nonsensical' ruptures in the normal language of society, or as a turning away from language altogether, to retreat into silence or resort to physical force. In the terms of Habermas, it is when the opportunities for communicative action – the discursive definition of identities, needs and interests – are lacking that groups have recourse to non-linguistic means for asserting their interests.[29]

Is our culture not, then, heteroglottic? Against the obvious signs of homogenisation one must set the extreme differentiation of the advanced societies, and the proliferation of jargon, technical terms, and styles of discourse that accompanies it. There is another way, however, of interpreting this phenomenon, which comes from Lukács rather than Bakhtin: proliferating specialised languages are a symptom of reification, the separating off and technicisation of human powers.[30] Perhaps these developing jargons and modes of discourse don't express anything as coherent, or even interesting, as a point of view or way of life? Must a distinct mode of speech convey something like a 'point of view'?

To consider this question properly we should turn once again to the changes in Bakhtin's polemic with positivism and other forms of 'rationalism' between the early 1920s and the 1930s. In the early phenomenological period, he insisted that objects of experience were only possible in the context of an intention or value, binding the subject to the object (recall the metaphor of the signed document). In the later 1920s the idea that language includes within itself a moment of value is replaced by the idea that languages embody a point of view. The crucial stops on this journey are Medvedev's book of 1928, which subtly changes the everpresentness of value into the everpresentness of social evaluation (a great change, and more or less the result of a new context: proof, if it were needed, of the power of re-accentuation), and Voloshinov's book on linguistics, which argues for the coincidence of the sign and ideology. Whereas the earlier concept of value implied only that language was always intentional or purposeful in relation to its object, the concept of ideology implies a system of connected ideas, a general perspective or 'world-view'. Most importantly, it implies a subject, a bearer of this world-view or ideology, whose identity *as a whole* is bound up with this ideology. This is not the person divided into different functions – labourer, member of a family, member of a community, consumer – whom Lukács would recognise (and who appears as, of all things, a peasant in a notable passage in 'Discourse in the novel'), but an individual with a coherent and singular social identity. Evidence of this supposition is to be found in a work which bridges the gap between Voloshinov–Medvedev and 'Discourse in the novel', *Problems of Dostoevsky's Art*, in which language and personhood are rendered inextricable: 'He [Dostoevsky] tried to perceive and formulate each thought in such a way that a whole person was expressed and began to sound in it' (*PDP*, p. 93).[31] Language now means not merely value or situation but person, voice, point of view. And if the linguistic world is divided into seemingly endless variations, this can only be because there is a corresponding number of points of view:

> Between these 'languages' of heteroglossia there are the most profound methodological distinctions; at the base of each lies a completely different principle of differentiation and formation (in some cases functional, in others content-thematic, in yet others properly socio-dialectological). Therefore these languages do not exclude one another but intersect in a variety of ways ... It might seem that, given this state of affairs, the very word 'language' loses all meaning for there is not, it would appear, a single plane for comparison of all these languages.
>
> In actual fact, this common plane, methodologically justifying our comparison, exists: all the languages of heteroglossia, no matter what the principle lying at the base of their specification, are specific points of view on the world, forms for its verbal interpretation, particular referentio-semantic and evaluative horizons (DN, pp. 291-2).

If each language is a voice, then society is a welter of intersecting groups and different ideologies, more or less the vision of society on offer from liberalism. And yet things are in a way even worse than that. For each point of view is also described as an *interested* point of view: it embodies not just a perspective but a set of values or desires.

Were not values at the base of all language and experience, even in 1924? Yes, but then *value* had a very different meaning. It referred to intentions of all different kinds – cognitive, ethical, aesthetic, so that, for instance, it would make no sense to speak of a distinction between fact and value. To say truth is a value in that context does not mean that truths are the products of arbitrary desires, but simply that truth is something one aims at in discourse. It is similar to what Habermas describes as the 'knowledge-constitutive interests': not interests which separate us, but purposes built into linguistic activity.[32] This is a rather dangerous little ambiguity, and it is one which abets some otherwise odd interpretations. If all languages are points of view, and all points of view embody values (for which read: desires or interests), one presumably is free to assume that differences in language reflect differences in interest, which can at best be 'balanced', 'accommo-dated' or 'tolerated'.[33] Through this line of argument Bakhtin becomes liberalism's, or, if you prefer, liberal pluralism's, best friend.

However, it could be argued that this confuses distinctive prin-ciples of linguistic differentiation. Not all social differentiation is political or even politically significant differentiation. Unless one is a primitive communist, a high degree of complexity and differentiation has to be accepted as characteristic of any modern society, even a socialist one, and in its wake one will find distinctive vocabularies, new and specialised forms of syntax and so on. Thus, while every language may involve intention, value and purpose, it doesn't follow that in every case these constitute a political ideology which must be iron-ised, dialogised or carnivalised. Conversely, it may be the case that significant ideological structures don't manifest themselves in the form of a recognisable voice, a point to which we shall return.

In short, the bond between style and ideology is not quite as secure as Bakhtin had hoped. Within Bakhtin's terminology, style is precisely the form of ideologies, which tells us something quite important about them: that they exist in social, semiotic form, and that they are dialogical in nature, defined by their necessary relation to opposing and alternative ideologies. But does that mean ideology is reducible to or determined by linguistic forms?[34] Are styles definable in linguistic terms? On the one hand, clearly not: the object of Bakhtin's meta-linguistics is the utterance, which we are repeatedly told is not a linguistic form. Sentences identical from the perspective of linguistics may be entirely different as utterances. But on the other hand, maybe: for if ideologies were not expressed at all in terms of particular linguistic structures (Bakhtin's habit is to describe those forms as sedimentations, or deposits, of ideological impulses), then one's choice of linguistic forms, the style of the utterance, would cease to be socially significant. We would return to a situation in which style was an individuation of language, not a mode of expressing social relations and ideologies. Once more, the attempt to integrate social, linguistic and philosophical concerns leads to significant ambiguities in Bakhtin's position. But here what succeeds only partly is the equation between linguistic form and ideology, an equation which none the less suggests a more properly social concept of interest and value. There is value, ideology and therefore dialogism in all discourse, but must it always have a linguistic expression? This is less clear.

But there remains another problem with this vision of a world of swarming intersecting styles. Any utterance or set of utterances can doubtless be located at the intersection of a number of circumstances: nation or region, class, gender, profession, age, historical moment, leisure or labour. What then legitimates the classification of an utter-ance as an instance of 'modern bureaucratic style', 'the discourse of the middle-class male intellectual', 'the language of the peasant under modernisation'?[35] That abstractions such as these must be justified by some sort of empirical demonstration is an ordinary enough demand, but the fact that a style cannot be identified with this or that set of linguistic practices makes this a far more precarious undertaking. The task increases in complexity: one must both find formal structures that define a socio-ideological language and also demonstrate that these structures carry a specifically political or ideological weight. To label a style is to identify a relevant context, but this process, as we learned above, is no simple matter. Rather than looking at the immediate situation we have to argue for the definition of a context or a style. Peasants in economies undergoing capitalist modernisation are also much more than that: they are French, Russian or Italian, Orthodox, Catholic or atheist, male, female; the list is potentially endless. A serious sociological stylistics (and this is Bakhtin's term for the discipline, not Medvedev's or Voloshinov's) will have to show that their political interests precisely as peasants were expressed in linguistic or generic structures, and it is by no means obvious that this will always be the case.[36]

Or put it another way: one will have to write novels. The novel's task is defined as the 'artistic representation of language', for which it must find the means to construct 'the image of a language':

> Typical moments, characteristic or even symbolically essential, are selected. A deviation from the empirical actuality of a represented language, not only in the sense of the biased selection and exaggeration of moments present in the given language but also in the sense of the free creation of moments in the spirit of a given language, which are empirically completely alien to it, can be in this case very important (DN, pp. 336-7).

From this passage we can derive two important lessons. Firstly, the image of a language is not simply an example of it, but an exhibition of its 'spirit', its ideological structure. In fact, simply to portray it as a language means to enforce some kind of abstraction on the speech presented: for how else are we to know that the significance of some cited discourse is that it is 'in the style of the déclassé intellectual' or whatever? However much Bakhtin may have polemicised against Saussure, he here indicates a debt to him. For by 'language' Bakhtin can only mean some formal deep structure which can be evidenced in particular instances of speech. In an essay on intertextuality, Laurent Jenny asks whether this phenomenon designates references to specific works alone or to generic structures as well.[37] In Bakhtin's case the answer is unequivocal, for speech is only represented as an index of a more abstract structure, the 'socio-ideological language'.

The second lesson is that one represents discourse for some definite purpose; it will only be against the backcloth of a certain story one wants to tell that represented speech will become the image of a language. Bakhtin speaks of the 'biased' selection and exaggeration of moments, not because all authors are necessarily prejudiced, but because they must approach the object language with some task, project, or aim in mind if speech is to exhibit its ideological structure. With the wisdom of hindsight, we can recognise the seeds of this idea as far back as the essay on the 'Author and hero'. Although author and hero are both purpose-laden subjects in the aesthetic process, their subjectivity manifests itself in dissimilar ways: so different are the roles they are assigned that it would be foolhardy to picture their interaction in the form of a conversational dialogue. None the less, the author, whose job it is to make an aesthetic object of the hero, can only do so by bringing his or her own values and purposes into play: 'An aesthetic event can only be realised given two participants, it presupposes two non-coincident consciousnesses' (AH, p. 25). As aesthetic contemplation remains, for Bakhtin, an 'activity', the existence of authorial values stands as a prerequisite for the achievement of what he will still call 'aesthetic objectivity' (AH, p. 17). Once again, there emerges a clear difference between value or purpose and the prevailing liberal concept of 'interest'; whereas the latter can only prejudice a representation, the former is an obvious prerequisite for any representation of language, whether it is describing a language for a textbook, analysing it as part of some scientific endeavour, or recounting a colourful turn of phrase for a friend.

Bakhtin's idealised novelist, however, elevates 'linguistic moments to symbols of a language' (DN, p. 337), and this seems a very different kind of achievement from that of, say, the writer of textbooks or the teller of anecdotes. Unlike the latter, the novelist is interested in language precisely in so far as it is coterminous with a specifically socio-ideological structure. If the 'novel' in the works of the 1930s takes on some of the functions of philosophy (in exchange for which Socratic dialogue becomes its earliest predecessor), it also becomes a kind of surrogate sociology, which redescribes language-use as a kind of social action, and defines and classifies its major types (as 'socio-ideological languages' or 'speech genres'). The crucial essays, 'Discourse in the novel' and 'From the prehistory of novelistic discourse' both devote a great deal of space to tracing, in works by Dickens, Turgenev and Pushkin, the precise methods by which novelists are able to reveal the social physiognomy of languages drawn from heteroglossia.[38]

One will note, however, that these are, as it were, stylistic microanalyses, which at no point address the question of whether a framing narrative structure is a necessary moment in the creation of an 'image of a language'. Given the fact that modern socio-historical identities are to a great extent dependent on some kind of historical narrative, be it national, private, or world-historical, this omission has to strike us as odd. At this point we should remind ourselves of Cesare Segre's comment that Bakhtin confused questions of narrative with questions of linguistic stratification, and then consider the difficulty Bakhtin critics have had integrating those works emphasising polyphony or dialogism (*Problems of Dostoevsky's Art*, 'Discourse in the novel', 'From the prehistory of novelistic discourse', 'Problems of speech genres') with works on narrative proper ('Forms of time and of the chronotope in the novel' and 'The *Bildungsroman* and its significance in the history of realism'). Symptomatically, in the text in which he first presents the idea of a dialogical novel, *Problems of Dostoevsky's Art* (i.e. the 1929 edition of this book), Bakhtin remarks on the fact that the narrative or evolutionary impulse is reduced in Dostoevsky's works, which strive 'to see everything as coexisting, to perceive and show all things side by side and simultaneous, as if they existed in space and not in time' (*PDP*, p. 28). The point is a fair one in one respect: works like *Crime and Punishment* exhibit a peculiar form of dream-like narrative logic, in which the movement of events appears to be motivated by the conflicts of Raskolnikov's mind rather than by the dark and elemental force of sociological or historical consequence. And Bakhtin himself regarded Dostoevsky's downgrading of narrative in favour of simultaneity as 'his greatest strength but his greatest weakness as well' (*PDP*, p. 30). But Bakhtin's argument goes much further than that, attempting to disconnect completely the narrative structure of such novels from the dialogue of ideologically charged languages within them. 'Plot itself', he argues, 'is subordinated to this task: the coordination and mutual exposure of languages' (DN, p. 365). Lurking behind this claim one can see, without much difficulty, an appeal to the Formalist distinction of motivation and device attacked by Medvedev six years earlier: the device is the dialogical confrontation of languages, for which the conventions of plot provide the mere motivation.[39] The dialogical interrelation of languages, it would seem, depends on narration intruding itself as little as possible into the matter at hand.

This assertion is relatively mild, however, compared with those moments when Bakhtin contrasts the very idea of dialogue with the idea of narration, an opposition which would have momentous and unhappy consequences, were it sustainable. Despite Bakhtin's professed belief in the importance and usefulness of the monologic genres (a category which seems to include all we would consider traditionally narrative), it appears that he considers narrative forms fundamentally unsuited to the depiction of 'the thinking human consciousness' (PDP, p. 271).

If narratives cite the speech of characters, and treat that speech as a trait or psychological fact to be explained rather than interpreted, they are engaged in the reduction of social events to natural-scientific phenomena, a reduction which denies the intentional or value-bearing character of the cited discourse. In as much as it implies that human action is only comprehensible from the perspective of an external observer, and that, correspondingly, subjectively held aims and motivations are irrelevant to our understanding of such action, the narrative method is presented as fundamentally at odds with the ideal of individual human freedom, as a textual practice which turns human voices into 'mute, voiceless objects of the author's discourse' (PDP, p. 63). Hence Bakhtin's insistence that 'a discourse truly adequate for the depiction of an ideological world can only be its own discourse, although not alone, but in combination with authorial discourse' (DN, p. 335).

Attractive as that last comment is, it effectively evades the central problem, which is the need to specify and describe this peculiar 'combination' of discourses, rather than pass it off as a 'dialogue' in some metaphorical sense. If the 'voices' of a novel are to become images of social languages, they must be combined with an authorial discourse which is different in kind, and not just in content. Mere disagreement with a position does not necessarily tell you anything important about its 'directionality' or its imbrication in the social world. In order to fulfil the task of describing discourse as some kind of 'located' social and historical action, novels have typically made some effort to represent 'history' and 'society'. The ideal of dialogism as an unending conversation, every utterance finely balanced between two personalised voices, between being represented and representing, is obviously a pipe-dream, but even if such works could be found, they would have little to do with what Bakhtin seems to have had in mind. The novelistic texts he presents as exemplars would have to be deemed only partially or inadequately dialogical, if we expected dialogism to entail the suspension of all social description and explanation. The ambiguity in the concept of dialogism I described above is embodied once again in the difference between this ideal notion of dialogue as multiple voices and the form of dialogism we are presented with in Bakhtin's chosen examples. In the nineteenth-century novels he draws from, narrative and cited discourse are combined in such a way as either to frame and demystify an authoritative language, or to test a 'cited' ideological position in a series of hypothetical narrative situations. Far from forgoing narrative consequence and historical explanation, they appear to regard it as a prerequisite for the creation of 'images of languages' with socio-historical identities.

The immediate objection will be that such texts are not examples of dialogism, but of narrative metalanguages accounting for cited discourse in characterological terms. Is it not the case that such narrative schemes provide authoritative frames for the interpretation of the utterances of characters? Certainly, one has to concede that a great many novels from the nineteenth and twentieth centuries adopt exactly that 'monologic' approach. But the significant question remaining is whether the dialogical writing Bakhtin aims at – that which is supposed to provide us with a sense of social concreteness, historical movement and discursive openness – can be achieved without some form of socio-historical narrative. And to resolve this question a distinction will have to be drawn between 'explaining' a discourse and 'testing' or 'experimenting' with it – a distinction which goes to the heart both of arguments about metalanguage and of interpretations of Bakhtin.

In our current theoretical climate it is axiomatic that social and historical understanding is itself dependent on textual and rhetorical procedures. What we often find, however, is that this important theoretical postulate is extrapolated to justify a very different assertion, the belief that all knowledge, especially social and historical knowledge, is somehow subjective, unstable or ungrounded. Whatever the claims of current theory, no such argument can be deduced from Bakhtin's texts. Instead, we find an emphasis on the need to combine different socio-historical 'languages' (and here the term must be understood loosely, for by language I mean both social dialects and the language of narrative) precisely in order to arrive at a more adequate knowledge of the historical world. If this knowledge is going to appear in the form of images of those 'socio-ideological languages', then one of the component languages of the dialogue will have to be that of social and historical explanation, which entails drawing on the resources of abstracting social theory, even if only indirectly. Thus Bakhtin's belief in the social dimension of all linguistic and rhetorical structures need not lead to some kind of thoroughgoing relativism, as he made amply clear: 'relativism and dogmatism equally exclude all argumentation, all authentic dialogue, by making it either unnecessary (relativism) or impossible (dogmatism)' (*PDP*, p. 69).[40]

Elsewhere in Bakhtin's texts an alternative line of argument is available, which suggests what may be a more balanced view of the relation between narrative and dialogism: 'The idea of the testing of the hero and his discourse may be the most fundamental organising idea of the novel' (DN, p. 388). Even in his most 'existentialist' literary study, the Dostoevsky book, Bakhtin points out that the former's characters are not just personalities but also *ideologues*, whose actions seem designed to test their speeches (*PDP*, p. 105). Dostoevsky's novels are, after all, composed not only of extended argument (though many might say: almost), but of argument punctuated with events which test the ideas, by submitting them to a kind of fictional experiment. Such narrative probing distinguishes the novelistic testing of ideas from the kind of purely argumentative resolution of disputes which Jürgen Habermas calls 'discourse'.[41] So far as Bakhtin is concerned, logical argument belongs to the world of rhetoric and direct discourse, a world inhabited by disembodied ideas. The novel's procedures, by contrast, present arguments in a different form, in the belief that this fictional experiment can reveal the import and significance of ideologies more adequately than could pure verbal disputation. One can find a similar justification for fictional experiment in the work of Raymond Williams, who argued (in relation to drama) that the re-emergence of a worthwhile realist project depended on the development of works written 'in the subjunctive mode', which would analyse conflicts between ideologies by portraying and evaluating, within a single work, the different courses of social action to which they led.[42]

In a seldom quoted passage Bakhtin remarks on the 'simultaneous birth of scientific cognition and the modern artistic-prosaic novel form', a comparison made more specific when he claims they are linked by the notion of an 'experimental' approach to reality: the secularisation of knowledge through laughter 'delivers the object, so to speak, into the fearless hands of investigative experiment – both scientific and artistic – and of a free experimental fantasy serving the aims of this experimentation'.[43] The comparison is significant in two respects. It alerts us, firstly, to an inevitably scientific moment in the pursuit of self-knowledge through discourse, which I will discuss below. Secondly, the comparison with science indicates the more exact sense in which we can describe a historical narrative as relativised. The dialogised narrative Bakhtin theorises is 'hypothetical' in a rather old-fashioned scientific sense, as a possible explanation the truth of which is established or challenged through a series of trials. There is thus all the difference in the world between this claim and the proposition that languages, narrative paradigms or generic structures are necessarily subjective or partial, an idea which prejudges the truth of particular works before they are ever submitted to 'dialogue'.

We can now fully appreciate the consequences of Bakhtin's decision to conduct an ethico-political argument by means of a meditation on the relation of author to hero in literary works. The relation of these two figures is reinterpreted many times in Bakhtin's career, and we may well feel that the recasting of it as a conflict between different languages constitutes some kind of break with the earlier formulations. Yet even in his theory of the novel there remains a tension between the actually different functions of author and hero, and the implication that as two 'people' or two 'voices' they are somehow equivalent, an implication which feeds off Bakhtin's relentlessly anthropomorphic vocabulary. The latter leads to the absurd hope that aesthetic objectivity or socio-historical concreteness – two terms for the consciousness of value Bakhtin prizes – will result from any old meeting of minds, a hope which, in fact, takes no account of the very specific aesthetic tasks Bakhtin sets the author. Providing the right kind of frame for one's hero is not so simple as it might appear.

But although it is misleading to describe the novel as a simple dialogue, the theme of testing, so prominent in Bakhtin's analyses, suggests a sense in which it is worth speaking of works as potentially dialogical. Granted, the confrontations we discover in the historical forms of dialogism are not between 'voices' but between a narratively expressed 'history' and 'images of languages'; it is still worth speaking of a conflict, even of a political conflict, between the values embodied in these different levels of a work. What is crucial is that the conflict – which appears in the form of 'double-voicing', 'stylisation' or 'internal dialogism' – can run both ways, either level providing the context through which the other is challenged. As Bakhtin shows with Dostoevsky and Williams with Brecht, it is as likely that the 'subjunctive' or 'novelistic' work will result in a critique of history as it is that it will reveal social forces at work behind the backs of unsuspecting characters. For Williams this was the most significant lesson of Brecht, who demonstrated how the 'reasonable' responses of individuals to their historical circumstances led only to defeat, a narrative movement which compels us to ask what is wrong with the circumstances, rather than what is wrong with Galileo or Mother Courage.[44]

The undeniable difference between the 'language' of narration and that of styles and voices does not, therefore, entail the dominance of one or the other, and in fact the distance between them is the historical precondition for novelistic dialogism. For the crux of the historical problem that the novel exists to correct is that neither the 'language' of historical description nor that of personal dialogue is 'truthful' in conditions where the events of public life have been cut off from private voices and languages. If the description of social forces appears as something incommensurable with the 'voices' of individuals, this fact is a consequence of the particular historical makeup of our 'heteroglossia', which, after all, is the material any writer must work from. The original goal of a 'participatory description' of the world thus takes a sociological turn in the late 1920s, as Bakhtin turns to narrative to provide the sense of concreteness which he first thought might come from phenomenological philosophy. The places and times which define the concrete moment of an utterance are now social places and historical moments, a shift which, I would argue, takes us from the abstraction of 'individuals' to the concrete. To know one's place one has to have some idea of how places and times are organised in the world, and it is to the credit of the Bakhtin school that they recognised that sociology and historical analysis are a necessary part of that knowledge.

Even the most astute theorising, however, has its limits. The Bakhtin school described the way in which a political problem, relating to the design of institutions of economic and social control, worked itself out in cultural forms. The distance between the available narratives of history and the languages of civil society continued to enforce itself, and was reflected in Bakhtin's oxymoronic description of his theory of the novel as a 'stylistics of genre' (DN, p. 259). That the predicament was not merely methodological is evident from the fact that, despite forty years of trying, Bakhtin could never quite reconcile the idea of genre with the idea of style. Instead, genre remained the term for describing 'finished and resolved whole[s]', while style clearly designated the syntactic and lexical patterns of identifiable social voices.[45] One more time, it seemed impossible to describe the intentional content of social forms and conventions – in this case, genres – without reducing them to the obviously individualistic category of voices. A dialogue among existing kinds of speech is not hard to envisage; to imagine a dialogue among genres, or works within a genre – that is only possible if one uses 'dialogue' as a metaphor for any cultural conflict, in which case the term doesn't mean very much. Bakhtin himself

couldn't imagine such a dialogue: it is notable, for instance, that he
never attempts to describe a dialogue between different chronotopes.
Instead, he tends to reduce genre distinctions to an opposition between works with recognisable generic structures – the epic or poetic
genres – and novelistic works which are, in essence, anti-generic.

That generic structure *per se* could appear oppressive testifies to
the depth of the problem Bakhtin was facing; perhaps the progressiv-
ist narratives of the 'actually existing socialism' of his time were
enough to put anyone off the idea. With no framework for analysing the
socio-ideological force of generic and narrative forms, one can easily
fall into the trap of supposing that 'forms', 'structures' and 'narratives'
only inhibit the expressive force of 'socio-ideological languages'. But
this tendency coexists in Bakhtin's work with a drive to overcome the
opposition, by identifying and theorising a form of realism, whether
this is the realism of the novel, the chronotope or the grotesque.
Whatever the specific technique, the intention is to discover a way to
connect the localised, 'semi-public' languages of the public square to
the larger, seemingly external, structure of world-historical events. In
his study of Rabelais this 'modernised' realism consists of the reconstruction of history in the shape of 'earthly' events, natural cycles
which set the terms both for the immediate labour process and for the
shape of a society as a whole. In the earlier and undoubtedly prepara-
tory study, 'Forms of time and of the chronotope in the novel', Bakhtin
describes the gradual emergence of a realistic chronotope, one in
which the events of everyday life and those of a larger history can be
mediated by a single set of historical markers.[46] Throughout these
formulations, the split, and the political consequences stemming from
it, remains a problem, but we can hardly blame Bakhtin for the lack of
a solution. If attempts to connect the languages of 'everyday life' with
sociological analysis lead to the reification of the former by the latter,
either in Bakhtin's theory or the actual practice of novelistic writing,
they tell us something very important about the state of our heteroglossia. The gap between them marks the place of a necessary but
absent intermediary between the texture of life in civil society and the
scientific aspirations of social theory.

There is, however, a dangerous temptation to reject the scientific
aspirations altogether in favour of an unqualified celebration of the
'everyday life' seemingly conjured up by heteroglossia – a gesture
often made in the name of democracy. Such celebrations have only a
tangential relation to Bakhtin's theory of the novel, and arguably none
at all to democracy. 'Experience, cognition and practice (the future)

determine the novel', claims Bakhtin, which indicates that novels are meant to do more – much more – than reproduce the intentions and images already available in everyday life.[47] To take the latter as given, and simply assign the novel the task of expressing them, is to relieve it, and ourselves, of the task of cognition altogether. Such a perspective reduces democracy to a matter of expression, disconnecting it from the need for accurate knowledge of social forms. The emphasis on novelistic experimentation leads in a very different direction, towards a conception of democracy as a collective learning process, dependent on cognition as much as open expression.

If the social analysis necessary to that process appears in the guise of an authoritative language, this is actually a political problem, not an excuse for dismissing social analysis as such. When systematic knowledge of social and economic processes is vested in the official institutions of the state and of the economy, democracy necessarily entails a certain amount of ideology-critique, a sort of mutual reconstruction of both the 'everyday experience' and the systematic knowledge. To some degree, Bakhtin envisages the novel as a form engaged in precisely this process of reconstruction. No doubt novelistic writing, in the broad sense Bakhtin intends, is part of this process. But the actual achievement of such a reconstruction is dependent on conditions of a different order as well: on the creation of new political institutions, programmes of popular education, democratic forms of the mass media, and so on. Lacking these, knowledge of one's 'place' in a society remains dependent on the suspect products of 'official' (to use Bakhtin's term) institutions. With this in mind, it is interesting to note that psychology and linguistics, i.e. social sciences, were not the only forms of ideology the Bakhtin school attacked: in later essays like 'Epic and novel' pathos rather than scientificity is singled out as the defining property of authoritative language. Indeed, this emphasis is more than apposite today, when the 'official' strata of liberal capitalist nations have made pathos-ridden appeals to 'everyday' language the cornerstone of their ideological strategy. In this situation worshipping at the altar of the everyday hardly recommends itself as a progressive approach. The comprehension of complex modern societies requires knowledge of a sophisticated, alas, even scientific kind. If the abstract narratives of public life appear impersonal, the prerequisite of democracy and the task of the novel is to find some way to connect these processes to the kind of choice and decision already present in the narratives of private and civil life.

Accompanying uncritical celebrations of the everyday we often find celebrations of history, celebrations which in their way are well supported in the texts of the Bakhtin school. I have already spoken of how Bakhtin's work strives to combine philosophy and social theory. Those with an interest in the former will probably have noticed that Bakhtin's description of dialogical phenomena can be interpreted as a sketch of what is known in the tradition of German idealism as self-reflection. But it is self-reflection with a twist, for it depends on the coexistence of two moments – voices or contexts – in a single utterance, as if a transcendental perspective arose from the conflict of two empirical ones. By what process is this self-reflection possible? The answer is cast in the terms of reifying social explanation: the mere passage of historical time is what makes the distance necessary for reflection possible. According to Bakhtin, new socio-historical contexts enable the framing and citing of previous discourse. But what makes possible new contexts? Not, as far as one can tell, anything connected to the act of reflection itself. Not, for example, any conscious social action. The concomitant of Bakhtin's belief in the uniqueness of every utterance is a conception of history as an anonymous process of change or becoming (*stanovlenie*), the movement of which guarantees a steady production of 'new' contexts.

Thus the distance necessary for self-reflection is something one can only wait for, because it arrives as a gift of history. Bakhtin portrays this predicament in a rather optimistic light, as a liberating form of contact with the force of historical 'becoming', but it has a frightening side as well, which we cannot afford to ignore. The valorisation of becoming or historical change as such not only invokes a metaphysics of history; on a more practical level, it disregards the need for the stability and security which many think is part of the good and desirable life. Franco Moretti has described how the ideology of modernity has always needed to strike a compromise between restless change and the idea of an achieved end.[48] It is a compromise no less necessary today, and Bakhtin's vision of perpetual non-coincidence and endless becoming, however useful rhetorically, does not recommend itself as a desirable historical situation, let alone a realisable one.

Whether such confidence in the productive power of anonymous history entails a corresponding lack of faith in the possibility of conscious collective change is thus the final question to be faced. If history is described as the random production of the new, then clearly certain cherished ideals of collective self-determination, including the ideal of popular power, are going to receive a rough ride. From this perspective, Bakhtin's shift to an emphasis on 'the people' as the privileged bearers of socially concrete and dialogical language may seem puzzling. In 1934 they take centre stage away from the great novelists, and while they retreat from the scene occasionally, they never yield their pivotal position. In 1961-62 Bakhtin revised the study of Dostoevsky, and the new central chapter he inserted displaced the novelist from the role of inventor of dialogism; hereafter, he is described as the culmination of a tradition with ultimately popular roots. It may at first appear that these revisions mark a regression to a relatively unspecific notion of dialogism, in which the simple interactions of popular life produce a dialogical consciousness more or less automatically. 'The people', that is, can sometimes appear as the incarnation of this homogeneous becoming, their historical sense being a natural attribute which can only be repressed by 'official' institutions. At its limit, this conception leaves us with an unending struggle between a 'serious' and fear-inspiring ruling stratum, clearly modelled on feudal forms of authority, and an ever sceptical populace, prepared, if necessary, to challenge the very concept of discursive truth.

Hence we are told that, in Rabelais, the parodic relation to language 'is deepened to the point of parodying linguistic thought as such'; truth has become 'afraid of entangling itself in discourse' (DN, p. 309). Such ironising is supposed to demystify and reduce the power of intimidating ruling-class language, but there is another way of interpreting it, which casts this distrust of language in less optimistic terms. In Lukács's *Theory of the Novel*, a work Bakhtin had translated, irony is also the dominant characteristic of a realist discourse. As in Bakhtin, it expresses that which cannot be put in words without betraying itself. But for Lukács the fact that the truth can only be expressed ironically is a sign of the fallen state of the world. Irony is an emblem of the frustration of human impulses in a world which is alien to them.[49] Why should we believe that Bakhtin's or Rabelais's popular sceptical tradition indicates a happier state of affairs?

There is certainly a sense in which the state of affairs Bakhtin describes is every bit as discouraging as that outlined by Lukács. The pure scepticism sometimes implied in Bakhtin's discussions of popular discourse is a strictly negative knowledge of history, summed up in the conviction that things will change, whether for better or worse. But if we look beyond those passages in which the people appear as one more metaphysical construct, we find more nuanced positions. Thus, in 'Discourse in the novel' the public square is, in some respects, the image of a counter-state, which has for its preconditions both the existence of variable 'private' interests and a public space in which these are artistically combined in the 'low genres'. There is, as it were, a popular version of 'aesthetic objectivity', with its own techniques and forms. More striking, however, is the treatment of popular culture in *Rabelais and his World*, which attempts to rediscover a utopian impulse in popular scepticism, and so turn it into but one pole of a positive, philosophical project. One cannot help noticing that this new conception is found in the only work of the Bakhtin circle which describes not a history in general, but a specific kind of history: the form of life shaped by the process of agricultural labour.

So while the principle of ambivalence, expressed in the images and language of carnival culture, is clearly a descendant of the principle of dialogism, it is no longer, strictly speaking, an axiom in a philosophy of language. Dialogism can enliven the deadening narratives of literary culture by drawing on the languages of a vibrant civil society; ambivalence recontextualises intimidating images of death and squalor by reintegrating them into the cycles of agricultural life. Its historical basis is not the materiality of language but the inextricable intertwining of birth and death; production, consumption and excretion; labour and the fruits thereof. Once again Bakhtin's appeal is to a crudely material or physical context, but with the difference that it is an already historicised material, a material, so to speak, in motion. So central is the natural cycle and the agricultural labour corresponding to it, that Bakhtin confidently assumes that it can be used as a model for all forms of history, personal, civil and political. Encompassing both the private dramas of domesticity and labour, and the rise and fall of states and kings, ambivalence is presented to us as the principle through which severed histories may be linked. *Rabelais* has been described as constellating the moment of Stalinism with that of absolutism,[50] but it could also be described as imposing the figure of modernity on an image of medieval culture. The change and ceaseless rush of the modern reappears, but with the added claim that the relativity of history is a 'joyful relativity', because historical change itself appears in the tangible form of agricultural labour. It is, Bakhtin assures us, productive change.

Productive, we might respond, only with the wisdom of hindsight. The history portrayed in *Rabelais* is, in a sense, just as purposeless as the intentionless logical necessity Bakhtin faced in the early 1920s. But whereas the phenomenological project was premised upon the isolation of the individual, the celebration of carnival assumes that access to the concrete depends upon entry into a communal existence. The former sought to reinsert values of a fairly abstract kind into public discourse; the values embodied in the latter verge on the naturalistic. In a sense, the democracy of carnival is too close to productive and reproductive processes, drawing its ideological weapons directly from them. What is lacking is an account of some figure comparable to the novelist, whose job it is to rework the local materials of everyday life into a 'participatory description' of the world, one capable of reconnecting the obligations and commitments of the everyday world to the necessarily more abstract processes of public historical life.

It remains only to emphasise how little this historical vision has in common with the purely formal democracy on offer from the liberal state. The democracy of carnival is indeed a collective democracy, grounded in civil society, in which the abstract identity of the citizen or subject is replaced by that of one who eats, drinks, procreates and labours. Utopian in the extreme, it describes a condition in which history is directly experienced in the texture of public social life. The pleasures of carnival are not the pleasures of mere talk but those of a discourse which has rediscovered its connection to the concrete. It is, of course, a vision rather than a programme, but one which draws a remarkable contrast with the public life we have come to accept as the norm. Perhaps when aesthetics cannot find its way into social theory, it does the best it can, ceasing to ensnare itself in words, but finding a way to speak.[51]

Notes

1 Mikhail Bakhtin, 'From the prehistory of novelistic discourse', in *The Dialogic Imagination,* ed. Michael Holquist, trans. Caryl Emerson and Michael Holquist, Austin, 1981, p. 71. Here and in the case of other standard English versions of Bakhtin's texts I have amended the translation.

2 The argument for Bakhtin as a 'materialist' version of Derrida is pushed hardest by Terry Eagleton in 'Wittgenstein's friends', *New Left Review,* 135, 1982, pp. 64-90, and Allon White in 'Bakhtin, sociolinguistics and deconstruction', in Frank Gloversmith, ed., *The Theory of Reading,* Brighton and Totowa, N.J., 1984, pp. 123-46. Robert Young thinks it doesn't work: see his 'Back to Bakhtin', *Cultural Critique,* 2, 1985-86, pp. 71-92, and Allon White's reply 'The struggle over Bakhtin: fraternal reply to Robert Young', *Cultural Critique,* 8, 1987-88, pp. 217-41.

3 This aspect of the circle's work is discussed by Katerina Clark and Michael Holquist in *Mikhail Bakhtin,* Cambridge, Mass. and London, 1984, pp. 3-6, 62-3 and by Tzvetan Todorov in *Mikhail Bakhtin: The Dialogical Principle,* trans. Wlad Godzich, Manchester and Minneapolis, 1984, pp. 12-13.

4 See Clark and Holquist, *Mikhail Bakhtin,* p. 64; Todorov, *Mikhail Bakhtin,* p. 94; I. R. Titunik, 'The formal method and the sociological method (M. M. Baxtin, P. N. Medvedev, V. N. Voloshinov)', in V. N. Voloshinov, *Marxism and the Philosophy of Language,* trans. Ladislav Matejka and I. R. Titunik, Cambridge, Mass., 1973, p. 177 (where Titunik argues that the concerns of Formalism and the Bakhtin school are

ultimately the same); Gary Saul Morson, 'The heresiarch of META', *PTL*, III, 1978, p. 408 (the work of the Bakhtin group is 'a logical development of formalist thinking'); White, 'Bakhtin'.

5 To put it a different way, philosophy and sociology take up the task of articulating and describing a context for the positive facts of linguistic forms, whether this is described in terms of the transcendental or the pragmatic conditions which make the act of discourse both possible and necessary. Since Saussure, this has meant ‐ exiling the forces responsible for linguistic change from the province of linguistics proper. It is for this reason that the critique of current linguistic practice must be based in part on principles derived from either philosophy or sociology. To some degree one could look on this as one example of what Jürgen Habermas describes as the need for a transcendental-pragmatic critique of the positivistic self-understanding of the sciences, in this case linguistics; see his *Knowledge and Human Interests*, 2nd ed., London, 1978, chapter 4 and Appendix.

6 Mikhail Bakhtin, 'Arkhitektonika postupka', ed. S. G. Bocharov, in *Sotsiologicheskie issledovaniya*, 2, 1987, p. 157; subsequent references are given in the text as AP, followed by page number.

7 This is the beginning of Bakhtin's polemical, almost ritual emphasis on the 'concrete', which is maintained throughout the later work (as the concrete meaning of utterances, the 'material' lower bodily stratum, and so on). Its verve derives from Bakhtin's opposition to the abstract ethics of neo-Kantianism.

8 Bakhtin, 'Avtor i geroi v esteticheskoi deyatel'nosti', in *Estetika slovesnogo tvorchestva*, 2nd ed., Moscow, 1986, pp. 9- 191, and 'Problema soderzhaniya, materiala i formy v slovesnom khudozhestvennom tvorchestve', in *Voprosy literatury i estetiki*, Moscow, 1975, pp. 6-71; subsequent references to the former essay are given in the text as AH, followed by page number.

9 Ferdinand de Saussure, *Course in General Linguistics,* ed. Charles Bally and Albert Sechehaye, trans. Wade Baskin, New York, 1974, p. 71.

10 Voloshinov, *Marxism*, p. 70.

11 Bakhtin, 'The problem of the text in linguistics, philology, and the human sciences: an experiment in philosophical analysis', in *Speech Genres and Other Late Essays*, ed. Caryl Emerson and Michael Holquist, trans. Vern W. McGee, Austin, 1986, pp. 119-20.

12 Bakhtin, 'Discourse in the novel', in *The Dialogic Imagination*, pp. 325-6; subsequent references are given in the text as DN, followed by page number.

13 Cesare Segre, 'What Bakhtin left unsaid: the case of the medieval romance', in Kevin Brownlee and Marina Scordiles Brownlee, eds., *Romance: Generic Transformations from Chrétien de Troyes to Cervantes,* Hanover, N.H. and London, 1985, p. 26.

14 See, for example the discussion of the 'fiction effect' in Michel Pêcheux, *Language, Semantics and Ideology* , London, 1982, pp. 118-20; and Pierre Macherey and Etienne Balibar, 'On literature as an ideological form', in Robert Young, ed., *Untying the Text,* London, 1981, pp. 79-99.

15 Bakhtin, 'Zametki' ('Notes'), in *Literaturno-kriticheskie stat'i,* Moscow, 1986, pp. 513-14.

16 But a very differently situated thinker, Gramsci, finds something of a connection. In his defence of the factory councils, Gramsci argued that they were based on the inescapable facts of a worker's situation, 'the industrial process in its immediacy', unlike political parties, which were voluntary bodies depending on the participation of people as 'abstract' citizens. See 'Unions and councils' and 'The party and the revolution', in *Selections from Political Writings, 1910–1920,* ed. Quintin Hoare, trans. John Mathews, London, 1977, pp. 98-102 and 142-6.

17 See the discussion of the significance of 'medium' and 'material' for modernist art practice in T. J. Clark, 'Clement Greenberg's theory of art', in W. J. T. Mitchell, ed., *The Politics of Interpretation,* Chicago, 1983, pp. 215-18.

18 Bakhtin, *Problemy tvorchestva Dostoevskogo* (*Problems of Dostoevsky's Art*), Lenin-

grad, 1929, p. 241. This is the first edition of the text revised in 1961-62 and retitled *Problemy poetiki Dostoevskogo (Problems of Dostoevsky's Poetics)*. The translation of the latter by Caryl Emerson (Manchester and Minneapolis, 1984) includes some extracts from materials excised in the revised edition (Appendix I, pp. 275-82). The citation here can be found on p. 280; subsequent references to the translation are given in the text as *PDP*, followed by page number.

19 See J. L. Austin, *How to Do Things With Words*, 2nd ed., Oxford, 1980, especially pp. 14-15.

20 Jacques Derrida, 'Signature event context', in *Margins of Philosophy*, trans. Alan Bass, Chicago, 1982, p. 326.

21 Voloshinov, 'Discourse in life and discourse in poetry: questions of sociological poetics', in *Bakhtin School Papers*, ed. Ann Shukman, Russian Poetics in Translation, vol. 10, Oxford, 1983, pp. 5-30.

22 So Medvedev's theory of genre describes the context of a genre as its place 'in real space and in real time': 'It presupposes some kind of "auditorium" full of listeners or readers, their particular kind of reaction, some kind of relation between them and the author' (P. N. Medvedev, *The Formal Method in Literary Scholarship: A Critical Introduction to Sociological Poetics*, trans. Albert J. Wehrle, Baltimore and London, 1978, p. 177). As for Voloshinov, the utterance is for him determined 'above all, by its immediate social situation' and this consists in the first place of the expected 'social audience': the utterance 'is precisely *the product of the reciprocal relationship between speaker and listener, addresser and addressee*' (*Marxism*, p. 86).

23 The contrast, presumably taken from Kant, of possibility and actuality, is another which looms large not only in Bakhtin's phenomenological writings, but also in works such as Medvedev's, so that he can say 'Only through social evaluation do the possibilities of language become actuality' (*The Formal Method*, p. 167).

24 The argument that Bakhtin has delivered a 'materialist' version of deconstruction typically avoids this dilemma. It assumes that the model of discourse implicit in the idea of heteroglossia is more or less the same as that implied by Derrida, but that it implies that social situations of a 'material' kind generate its various constituents. Perhaps a real choice isn't made, but then maybe it's a choice one shouldn't have to make.

25 See Benedict Anderson, *Imagined Communities*, London, 1983, Introduction.

26 Francis Mulhern, 'Towards 2000, or news from you-know-where', *New Left Review*, 148, 1984, p. 24.

27 Bakhtin, 'From the prehistory', especially pp. 61-83.

28 See also Bakhtin's 'Predislovie (*Voskresenie* L. Tolstogo)' ('Preface to Tolstoy's *Resurrection*), in *Literaturno-kriticheskie stat'i*, pp. 102-3.

29 See Habermas, *Legitimation Crisis*, London, 1976, pp. 111-30.

30 This argument is set out in Georg Lukács, 'Reification and the consciousness of the proletariat', in *History and Class Consciousness*, trans. Rodney Livingstone, Cambridge, Mass., 1971, pp. 83-222.

31 This section of *Problems of Dostoevsky's Poetics* repeats material from the 1929 version, *Problems of Dostoevsky's Art*.

32 See Habermas, *Knowledge and Human Interests*, chapter 9.

33 Thus Franco Moretti is justified when he claims the highest virtue propounded by dialogism is the liberal one of tolerance; see his *The Way of the World*, trans. Albert Sbragia, London, 1987, p. 151.

34 The classical argument against this reduction, which leads rather quickly to a kind of linguistic relativism, a night of 'discourses' in which all cows are black, is Jacques Derrida, 'The supplement of copula: philosophy before linguistics', in *Margins of Philosophy*, pp. 175-205.

35 The importance of this problem has been impressed upon me, in different ways, by my colleagues Peter Middleton and Robert Young.

36 See Bakhtin, DN, p. 300. I emphasise this because it is often claimed that Bakhtin was

the philosopher, Medvedev and Voloshinov the sociologists. But I. R. Titunik's point that Bakhtin shifts from descriptions of his project as sociological to descriptions of it as metalinguistic is fair enough, although I think this implies a weakening, not an improvement, in Bakhtin's theory; see Titunik, 'Bakhtin &/or Voloshinov &/or Medvedev: dialogue &/or doubletalk', in Benjamin A. Stolz, Lubomir Doležel and I. R. Titunik, eds., *Language and Literary Theory*, Ann Arbor, 1984, pp. 544-6.

37 Laurent Jenny, 'The strategy of form', in Tzvetan Todorov, ed., *French Literary Theory Today: A Reader*, trans. R. Carter, Cambridge &c, 1982,pp. 34-63.

38 See Bakhtin, DN, pp. 302-8 and 315-20 (on Dickens and Turgenev respectively), and 'From the prehistory', pp. 43-9 (on Pushkin).

39 Bakhtin also speaks of self-consciousness as the 'dominant' of Dostoevsky's works, thereby using a Formalist term to describe a decidedly un-Formalist device (*PDP*, p. 50).

40 To some extent Bakhtin's insistence on the value direction of all discourse prefigures Habermas's universal pragmatics, which similarly holds that built into discourse as such is the aim to reach an agreement regarding matters of right, truth and expression; see Habermas, 'What is universal pragmatics?', in *Communication and the Evolution of Society*, London, 1979, pp. 1- 68.

41 See Habermas, *Legitimation Crisis*, pp. 107-8.

42 See Raymond Williams, *Politics and Letters*, London, 1979, pp. 214-26.

43 Bakhtin, 'Epic and novel', in *The Dialogic Imagination*, pp. 24, 23.

44 See Williams, *Drama from Ibsen to Brecht*, London, 1968, pp. 277-90.

45 Medvedev, *The Formal Method*, p. 129.

46 Bakhtin, 'Forms of time and of the chronotope in the novel: notes toward a historical poetics' (Section VIII, 'The folkloric bases of the Rabelaisian chronotope'), in *The Dialogic Imagination*, pp. 206-24, especially pp. 206-16.

47 Bakhtin, 'Epic and novel', p. 15.

48 See Moretti, *The Way of the World*, chapter 1.

49 Lukács, *The Theory of the Novel*, trans. Anna Bostock, London, 1971, pp. 70-84.

50 Terry Eagleton, *Walter Benjamin, or Towards a Revolutionary Criticism*, London 1981, pp. 144-5.

51 My sincere thanks to David Shepherd, Robin Gable and Tony Pinkney for their very thoughtful comments on earlier drafts of this Introduction.

Graham Pechey

On the borders of Bakhtin: dialogisation, decolonisation

The unity of the emerging (developing) idea. Hence a certain *internal* open-endedness of many of my ideas. . . My love for variations and for a diversity of terms for a single phenomenon. The multiplicity of focuses. Bringing distant things closer without indicating the intermediate links.

Mikhail Bakhtin, 'From notes made in 1970-71'

I

The battle over Mikhail Bakhtin's theoretical and political legacy may now be said to have been joined in earnest. It is a battle which is strikingly analogous to the contention over Walter Benjamin that raged some years ago and now seems to have run out of steam; there are good reasons why the present contention won't go away so easily. In both cases, motifs of the most thoroughgoing secularism in history are held to compete with motifs deriving from highly traditionalist religious discourses, and accounts of the two writers then diverge on the question of which of the two sets of motifs is to have priority. The recent biography by Katerina Clark and Michael Holquist effectively identifies Bakhtin's known affiliation to the Russian Orthodox Church as the secret of all his writing, the ultimate signified of its diverse signifiers. Clark and Holquist also insist on the proleptic status of his early work, reducing the whole range of his thinking on discourse to a series of variations on the neo-Kantian ethical and epistemological themes which it elaborates. Bakhtin becomes in their hands a topic in the 'history of ideas'; a shamefaced theologian who adopts the opportunistic guise of a Philosopher of Freedom; yet another apostle of sociality as intersubjectivity.

Bakhtin's work is frozen in gestures that are far from novel and closed off from that forever-unresolved dialogue with the present which is its own most persistent thematic preoccupation.[1] This essay seeks to begin the process of rescuing Bakhtin from the cold storage of intellectual history and from the politically compromised liberal academy which presides over this immobilising exposition. At the most elementary pedagogic or popularising level this means putting his ideas *into circulation* among those best placed to use them: not only in the academy but also in the wider cultural politics of the left; and not only in Europe and North America but also in those cultures of the 'developing' world that are finding a path out of the structures of neo-colonial dependence and whose practice of popular deconstruction under the sign of 'decolonisation' might benefit from the most advanced theory of that practice to date.

To propose the 'circulation' of Bakhtinian concepts is not to propose anything that is foreign to their mode of being: movement or *migration* is inherent in them from the beginning; it is their normal condition. To find a resting place for any of these concepts is by the same token to lose it for ever. All of those well-known oppositions or couples are deeply metaphorical in the root sense of being always 'carried over', always in 'translation' from one context to another. (Contrast the even better-known oppositions of Saussure: would-be heuristic scientific terms which plainly replicate the oldest of metaphysical dichotomies, themselves epitomising the linguistic stasis which they offer to theorise). There is, we might say, a primary migration of concepts taking place in the work as left to us by Bakhtin himself – a migration which any account of his 'thought' must acknowledge at every stage. It is the failure to make this acknowledgement that speaks in the contradiction between Todorov's assertion, on the one hand, that the 'key' to Bakhtin lies in his 'philosophical anthropology' and, on the other, a single qualifying sentence in which we are told that each work 'contains the whole of his thought' while at the same time holding 'a slippage or displacement . . . at times barely perceptible yet ultimately most deserving of attention'.[2]

We can avoid the Casaubon-like *hubris* of Todorov's study – we can, that is to say, give full weight to the displacement that he otherwise ignores – by borrowing a motif from Bakhtin's biography and saying that his concepts are always in internal exile, paradoxically situated both within and beyond the borders of disciplines as traditionally defined and institutionally policed. This goes for the newer sectoral divisions of the 'human sciences' (linguistics, psychology, sociology) as well as for the older demarcations of 'philosophy' (ontology, ethics, epistemology). The notion of concepts as constitutively migratory allows us to break with the whole problematic of 'application', whereby concepts elaborated in a master-discipline are 'applied' (as in classical structuralism) to the object of another discipline. Equally inappropriate to Bakhtin is the priority of a stable 'metalanguage' hierarchically elevated over an 'object language': there is no priority among concepts that live on the borders which define them internally.

Besides this primary or internal migration of concepts there is also a secondary or external migration which takes place when concepts are transplanted geopolitically from 'East' to 'West' (or indeed from 'North' to 'South'), and in particular to cultures which have a long history of bourgeois development, such as England's; or when concepts are re-invented in a move to new territories of the sign untheorised by Bakhtin. If it is true that the condition of his greatest insights into the working of discourse is his decisive privileging of a genre that is bound up with the long dominance of print in European culture, it must also be conceded that the subordination of printed forms in our own time forces upon us a crucial readjustment – one that is itself wholly in the spirit of Bakhtin's enterprise.

Neither the centrality Bakhtin gives to the novel in theory nor the transformative activity he ascribes to it in history need be binding upon even the most devoted Bakhtinian in his or her analysis of contemporary cultural production. On the theory of film, which so fascinated the Russian Formalists and other elements of the Soviet avant-garde in the 1920s, Bakhtin is silent. At the same time, the pressure exerted by film and the newer mass media of (in Raymond Williams's phrase) our 'dramatised society' upon printed forms is clearly ripe for theorisation on the lines of Bakhtin's own well-argued claims for the influence of the novel on the older forms of writing.[3] Fidelity to Bakhtinism may well demand of us a reversal of the procedure whereby he took his stand in the novel and contemplated the other forms from that defamiliarising vantage-point; it may now be necessary to occupy the similar vantage-point offered by 'drama' in its manifold contemporary incarnations. Such re-inventions and shifts of focus – far from being inimical to Bakhtin's concepts – will actually guarantee their survival in as much as they carry forward the self-deconstruction which was the natural mode of these concepts while still in his hands.

II

Bakhtin's own term for his theory of discourse contains the notion of a boundary transgressed: *trans*linguistics. In this case a traditional boundary is refused – that separating linguistics from its parasitic complement stylistics – and a new one set up by bringing Saussurean linguistics and Formalist poetics into mutual critique. Saussure theorises language as a domain of norms; Formalism theorises literature as a domain of deviations: out of these theories of the synchronic regularity of the linguistic and the diachronic productivity of the literary Bakhtin develops a theory of the productivity of the sign in general and in both dimensions, a theory of language as social sign-production. This translinguistics occupies what Voloshinov calls, in the title of a text of 1930 cited by Todorov (p. 122) 'the borders between poetics and linguistics'. Or again: it is the effect of re-establishing poetics within rhetoric, in a move which re-articulates the ancient disciplines of discourse upon whose severance (once productive, but now disabling) Romantic aesthetics had been founded. Bakhtin completes the incomplete break made by Formalism with Romanticism by turning inside-out its re-invention of rhetoric within poetics: a theoretical revolution of no little historical significance which is nowhere explicitly spelt out but can be seen going on between the lines of the fierce polemics of the 1920s.[4] It is easy for this move to be overshadowed by the no less critical move to the novel which it so plainly prepares and which is both condition and result of the reversal of yet another Formalist hierarchical opposition – that which privileges 'discourse in poetry [art]' over 'discourse in life'.[5]

The move to the novel (what I've called its 'decisive privileging') is critical because it enables Bakhtin progressively to complexify the still somewhat undifferentiated notion of 'discourse in life', which might otherwise replicate the false homogeneity of 'practical language' or the generative inertia of *parole*. His revolutionary conception of 'literary' discourse as a field of struggle between a relatively productive new genre and relatively regular old (or 'poetic') genres – this conception follows from (and implies) the distinction between 'polyphony' and 'homophony' in prose fiction. This distinction of novel types is in its turn founded upon another: between double-voiced (or dialogical) and single-voiced (or monological) types of discourse in prose. In polyphony the former are dominant and the latter subordinated, while in homophony that hierarchy in the text's discursive economy is reversed. Dialogism of some kind and to some degree is a defining characteristic of the novel, as is its openness to that 'social diversity of speech types' which Bakhtin's English translators render as *heteroglossia*.[6] Indeed dialogism and heteroglossia are terms for (respectively) the 'formal' and 'social' modalities of the same phenomenon, and the novel might then be defined as the form of writing whose inside and outside are of the same order: intertextuality constitutively internalised. The novel for Bakhtin stands to the other (older) genres in the same relation as heteroglossia to the homogenising and unifying forces of language – forces among which these 'poetic' genres may themselves be included. Returning us as it does ineluctably to 'discourse in life' (now internally differentiated, radically heterogeneous), this moment of Bakhtinian theory might seem 'final' if it weren't, like all such moments, dialectically re-initiating.

It is at this point that Bakhtin raises, though perhaps never satisfactorily resolves, the key issue of the relationship between discourse and *power*. Any sociopolitical project of centralisation or hegemony has always and everywhere to *posit itself against* the ubiquitously decentralising (centrifugal) forces within ideology. 'Carnival' is the name Bakhtin gives to these forces in so far as they find expression in consciously parodic representations across a range of signifying practices; 'the novel' is the name he gives to their entry into the forms of *writing* at any time in history, but most influentially in the case of Rabelais and the line of comic fiction descending from him. Parallel to this opposition of 'carnival' to 'official' within cultures is another between whole national cultures which are 'self-sufficient' (in the sense of not knowing their otherness to others) and those which are no longer sealed-off and deaf to their polyglot ambience: Bakhtin understands the Renaissance as just such a moment of passage from closed to open across the cultures of Europe. Now all of these moments of Bakhtinian theory could of course be laid out in a diachronic series, identified with particular texts, seen (in short) as a 'development'. The biographical schema of Clark and Holquist commits them to this linear procedure, a narrative interweaving 'life' and 'ideas' and in that sense dominated by a 'chronotope' that would be identified by Bakhtin himself with the antitype of his hero Dostoevsky. Todorov's 'thematic division' in a 'systematic perspective' all but renounces chronology altogether for a synchrony of mutually entailing and presupposing theoretical concerns (p. 13). This might seem closer to the spirit of Bakhtin if it weren't very evidently predicated upon a dichotomy of 'narrative' and 'system' of the kind that Bakhtin has taught us to move beyond in the exemplary case of his critique of Saussure. With the notion of an *always reversible* migration of concepts we can begin to dispense with these equally inimical alternatives.

Where we begin our narrative of Bakhtin's thinking is a matter of indifference: if, however, we start (as I have done) with the field that announces its 'threshold' character in its very name, we could say that the concepts of translinguistics have migrated through literary history and the sociology of discourse to found a cultural theory (or theory of ideologies) of global pretensions. The next stage would be to rephrase 'have migrated' to 'are migrating' and to run the series in the opposite direction. Bakhtin's thought moves from oppositions 'within' to oppositions 'between' and back again, endlessly: an opposition within the novel parallels and at the same time occupies another opposition between the novel and other forms of writing; both of these in turn parallel and occupy an opposition within culture which is reproduced again between cultures themselves. A structuralist reading of these phases of Bakhtinian thought might see them as instances of the generation of meaning by metaphor and metonymy, in which relations of similarity and contiguity coincide and interpenetrate. Such a reading would surely falsify the resolutely paratactic 'syntax' of Bakhtin's thinking, with its eschewal of subordination or qualification, or indeed any merely logical relations whatsoever. The complex dialectic of 'within' and 'between' which powers the internal exile of its concepts resembles nothing so much as the process of *dialogue* in the strong sense that is so insistently invoked by the thought itself. In the simultaneous echoing and embedding of oppositions – their speaking to and through each other – we glimpse (long before deconstruction) the novelty of a theoretical discourse articulated by *dialogical* relations (see figure 1).

'discourse in life'	:	'discourse in art'
novel	:	poetry
dialogism	:	monologism
polyphony	:	homophony
heteroglossia	:	monoglossia
carnival	:	official
centrifugal forces	:	centripetal forces
'open' cultures	:	'closed' cultures
	'discourse in life' ...	

FIGURE 1

Radical readings of Bakhtin will not, then, refuse *any* narrative of his concepts; they will refuse only those narratives that seek to pull these concepts back to a primary instance or origin. When (for example) Clark and Holquist tell us that 'the act of authorship ... is the master trope of all of Bakhtin's work' or that 'Dostoevsky's polyphony illustrates the concept of authorship that Bakhtin had proposed at a more abstract level in 1919 in *The Architectonics*', we are in the presence of an impoverishment of Bakhtin's thought that beggars description.[7] The author-character relationship in Dostoevsky is reduced to a mere repetition in the realm of poetics of Bakhtin's early ethical argument about the relationship of self and other; a concrete instance is asked to recognise itself as an 'illustration' of the 'abstract' master-instance by which it has been fathered. As a preliminary and polemical answer to this we might want to argue that the polyphony/homophony opposition should be read in the light of the sociopolitical opposition of 'carnival' and 'official' generated in another moment of Bakhtinian theory, and indeed elaborated in an addition to the 1963 edition of the book on Dostoevsky. To avoid the danger of merely substituting a destination for an origin (with the same upshot of centring and closure) we would then need to insist on the opposition's mobility in either direction, its protean gaze: the polyphony of 'polyphony' itself.

Ken Hirschkop has recently thrown some light on this episode in the non-linear narrative of Bakhtin's thought by pointing to a general politicisation in the 1930s of concepts first elaborated in the 1920s. If in the earlier decade it had been a matter of the 'truth' of dialogism and polyphony versus the 'error' of monologism and homophony, in the later it is a matter rather of contending social forces – carnival and official, centrifugal and centripetal, heteroglot and monoglot.[8] This observation has two major implications for us. First, it suggests that our care to skirt the pitfall of a reductive narrative of Bakhtin's thinking shouldn't lead us into an asceticism so absolute that all shifts of emphasis over time must be denied. Secondly, on a different level, it reminds us that our own theoretical options in writing this narrative are themselves nothing if not political: that we have a choice as to which direction of migration we emphasise, and that the particular (re-)accentuation we give to a concept is always of an interested kind. A poetics or a politics? an ethics or a rhetoric? a phenomenology of consciousness or a nascent theory of social hegemony? – all of these are different accentuations, not the original homes of meaning.

In Bakhtin's later writing the politicisation of translinguistics has been replaced by the more 'philosophical' orientation described by Todorov (in the brief periodisation he offers) as a 'return to the great theoretical and methodological themes of the beginning' (p. 12). Certain gnomic formulations – '*To be* means *to communicate*', 'Life by its very nature is dialogical', 'A human act is a potential text'[9] – do indeed give a strong ethical and even ontological inflection to the concept of dialogism, but to speak of them as signalling a 'return to the beginning' (no doubt on a 'higher' level) is to forget that the contexts this concept has occupied in its always potentially recursive migration are ineradicable, internal to its constitution, and in the end resistant to any Hegelian sublation. In these very texts of the 1960s we find Bakhtin reiterating his long-standing opposition to the reach-me-down idealist dialectics of those who would impose an inverse teleology upon his writing career. 'Dialectics is the abstract product of dialogue': thus reads another gnomic utterance a few lines from the second of the three formulations cited above (*PDP*, p. 293). These 'philosophical' formulations can take their place in our narrative without our using the categories of a 'philosophical monologism' to immobilise them in a synthesising 'return' to the beginning. Taken in isolation they undoubtedly do give a self-identical cast to the concept of dialogism: to predicate anything of life (even Difference) is to succumb to metaphysics, against the sincerest of anti-metaphysical intentions. If, however, we remember in reading them that the concept is itself inherently dialogical – in the sense of being internally occupied by all the other contexts it has occupied in Bakhtin's work – there is no need for us as his radical readers to feel betrayed by the 'finalised' image of Bakhtin the philosopher that they seem to project: the image becomes yet another mask adopted by the thinker in the carnival of his writing. In seizing upon this image as the quintessential Bakhtin, his liberal readers effectively read his work as a homophonic *Bildungsroman*, where the image of the hero finally emerges as that of an apolitical philosophical populist practising a quietist ontology that was implicit in his thinking all along.

III

We can best bring to a focus our discussion of the dialogism of the concept in Bakhtin by taking a close look at the concept of dialogism. In particular we need to look at its own dialogical relation to 'dialogue', the commonsense and stylistic category whose sense it extends. Dialogue in the 'narrow' sense is merely 'a compositional form in the structuring of speech' (DN, p. 279); for stylistics this 'external' or 'open' manifestation of the phenomenon is all there is of dialogue in discourse: verbal turn-taking rather than verbal monopoly, monologue's technical opposite. Dialogue is, however, only the epiphenomenon of a generalised *inner* dialogism of all discourse, including that which is technically (in its 'outward form') monological.[10] 'The alternating lines of dialogue' attributed to individual speakers are 'grammatically disconnected', and linguistics can therefore have no terms for their real relations. Still less can it be expected to describe or discover the dialogue that inhabits every crevice of signification, animates every 'level' of language. Dialogism might be defined as the process of dialogue which is installed within the very semantics of discourse, organising the word's meaning and performing its 'creative work on its referent'.[11] Reference itself is a function of the word's dialogical orientation towards the 'alien word' – towards both the 'already uttered' which it answers and the 'answer-word' which it anticipates (DN, pp. 282, 280).

Now in all of Bakhtin's uses of the concept (sketchily summarised here) it is plain that 'dialogism' as it were *needs* 'dialogue' and necessarily alludes to its derivation from that more commonplace word. Between 'dialogism' and 'dialogue' there is the nexus which links the defamiliarising with the defamiliarised; from the perspective of dialogism dialogue is inseparably both the (theoretical) truth of discourse and its (practical) mystification. 'Dialogue' sustains the myth of monologue as pure non-interruption even as it contains the potential to deconstruct that besetting opposition. Bakhtin realises this potential by reversing the hierarchical opposition of dialogue and monologue, giving primacy to the former rather than the latter in a move that parallels Derrida's refunctioning of 'writing': dialogism is his term for dialogue's primacy and ubiquity in discourse. Or: provisionally borrowing the terms of Barthesian semiology, we could say that the new sign dialogism is constructed by conferring a new signified (roughly, 'language *as* verbal interaction') upon the old signifier *dialogue* which none the less brings its old signified (roughly, 'formalised verbal interaction') into the combination.[12] The new signifier *dialogue* is the old sign recycled and in transit to the new sign whose novelty is signalled by a neologism; in the heteronym dialogism the memory of two homonyms is continually exploited (see figure 2). This

Signifier: dialogue	signified: formalised verbal interaction	
Signifier: DIALOGUE		Signified: language *as* verbal interaction
DIALOGISM (new sign)		

FIGURE 2

generation and sustenance of the concept in a play of the strange and the familiar ensures that the 'object' or 'reality' to which it refers is neither an empirical immediacy nor some metaphysical attribute of Being. It remains in Marx's sense a *critical* concept only as long as we recognise that it has the same status as its object; it exposes the fetishisation of language by linguistics only as long as it is itself never fetishised. Against the notion of language as iterable signs defined by an abstract equivalence, dialogism says that nothing in discourse is exempt from a complex intertextuality. Words have the inner complexity of texts; texts have the outer relationality of signs: in this reconceptualisation which dialogism asks us to carry out, all three terms are transformed, and 'sign' in particular is neutralised as an operator of the commodification of language. Bakhtin's term for word-as-text/text-as-sign is the *utterance*: that phenomenon in which a speech-act of answering and a speech-act of anticipation-provocation historically coincide. The utterance functions in translinguistics as the sign does in linguistics: as the minimal signifying unit of discourse, or (better) that between which dialogical relations obtain. The concept of the utterance results from a strategic borrowing and reworking of its namesake in the German philological tradition and the Romantic theory of language from which that tradition springs.[13] It is as 'new' and 'critical' a concept as dialogism itself. If at first glance it seems ominously phonocentric and too direct a borrowing – if it seems not to share in the analogy I have suggested between 'dialogue' in the strong sense and *écriture* or between dialogism and *différance* – then we will have to direct the doubter to the way it *works* in Bakhtin's thinking. It is the means by which he 'thinks' the intrinsic non-identity of the discursive against the mere exchange-value of the sign (commodity), while at the same time distinguishing the *historical* uniqueness of its units from the *natural* uniqueness of 'things' (see figure 3).

discourse

SIGN   UTTERANCE

iterable _____ unique

COMMODITY   THING

the extra-discursive

FIGURE 3

IV

In this account of the primary migration of Bakhtinian concepts I have thus far played down the problems they pose for his radical readers, the inadequately theorised areas and dimensions which open the space for those liberal readings that are now coming through. By postponing the confrontation of these problems until we reach (as we now do) the discussion of the onward migration of concepts into new contexts, we are able to see them under the aspect of their possible resolution. Of the questions recently asked, the most pressing are probably these: How can dialogism be both the natural state of language and the liberating practice that Bakhtin often claims it to be? If it is in this sense 'natural', how then does 'monologism' ever get a foothold in discourse? Can any text ever be monological? These questions may be answered by looking closely and critically at the detour Bakhtin makes in order to return to 'discourse in life' and rethink it as a field of the articulations of discourse and power characterised by the inscription of social in linguistic hegemony.

Everything hinges on the claims Bakhtin makes for the novel, and how we are to take them. Risking yet another summary definition, we might say that the novel is the self-consciousness and (at least partial) thematisation of dialogism; it is the form of writing in which what is signified is discourse itself. The novel foregrounds not the technical materiality of language but the social materiality of discourse: the irreducibly plural material of social relations – of contradiction and historical becoming – is at once the irreducible material of the novel and its object of representation. Dialogism becomes 'an event of discourse itself, animating from within and dramatising discourse in all its aspects' (DN, p. 284). The *an sich* of sociolinguistic diversity becomes the *für sich* of a relativised and relativising 'linguistic consciousness', and the novel in Bakhtin's view is nothing more or less than the (written) site of this modulation.

Now this case for the novel is made in the context of that 'politicisation' of translinguistics noted earlier: it is in this phase that the novel is decisively set up as the *Leitmotiv* of his cultural theory and the hero of his literary historiography. The tendency towards an *essentialist* polarisation of double- and single-voiced discourse 'types' (and by extension of dialogism and monologism) has been overcome, and in its place we have an opposition which takes the active and historical form of a contention of 'forces'. The opposition is not only more nuanced – with the 'rhetorical genres' occupying a half-way position between the novel and the 'poetic genres' – it is also wholly rethought as a matter of the determinate historical perspective offered by the novel and the determinate historical agency it exerts. The monologism of the canonical genres is not an essence inhering in them; it is rather an effect that becomes evident when the demystifying perspective of novelistic discourse has done its work. This exposure then in turn results in a kind of hindsight whereby the traditional disciplines of discourse (poetics, rhetoric, and later stylistics) can be seen as accomplices in the monologism of writing. But even before this retrospective insight became possible (thanks to Bakhtin himself), the novel's own agency in history had effected – over two centuries – a 'novelisation' of the older genres, dissolving their always 'conditional' monologism with a certain provisional and limited dialogism. Monologism is, then, never an absolute: as the 'false consciousness' of discourse it is both practically modified and theoretically exposed by the dialogism it vainly seeks to occlude. It is only *known* when the novel's militant dialogism (its '*auto-criticism of discourse*') finds its theorist in Bakhtin (DN, p. 412).

Two other modifications wrought by Bakhtin's 'politicised' translinguistics need to be emphasised. First, the residual formalism of his discourse typology is superseded by a more 'sociological' account of the 'double voice': its variants only properly belong within the novel when both intersecting 'voices' approach the condition of actual or possible 'social languages', ideologically-charged idioms in which the sharp semantic difference and clear-cut physiognomy of their models in 'social heteroglossia' are preserved intact. Secondly, polyphony drops from Bakhtin's vocabulary as this limit case of dialogism in dominance takes its place at the end of a continuum of novelistic possibilities – possibilities which *all* novels are now seen as variously realising. Dialogism as the very principle of structuring, dissolving the unities of 'character' and 'plot'; dialogism as the *action* of the novel; plot as mere 'motivation' or a dimension of monological paraphrase circumstantiating and 'dramatically' resolving a 'great dialogue' of authorial and other voices which inwardly resists all resolution: when at least some of these features of polyphony become predicable of any novel, it becomes difficult to sustain the notion of homophony except as a conceptual shorthand for a relatively weak dialogism. It is around this 'strong' case for the novel in general that Bakhtin develops a wider case about cultural hegemony.

Schematically this moment in theory might be represented as one in which the 'negative' poles of four of his key oppositions are played down as their 'positive' poles are foregrounded and enter into complex analogical relations. Of these 'positives', *carnival* is the most deserving of attention, in as much as it is in this practice of inverting social hierarchies that the alternative and unofficial practice of heteroglossia becomes anti-official and at least potentially oppositional. It also becomes more inclusive in a semiotic sense; carnival covers the whole nexus linking discourse with spectacle and gesture and with the signifying possibilities of bodies in space; carnival is (in short) the theatre of history: broadly popular in its content, if exceptional in its occasions. Carnival stands to heteroglossia as novelistic polyphony stands to the novel in general: the first of these relations is the reflex in 'life' of 'discourse in art'. At the same time, carnival stands to polyphony as heteroglossia stands to the novel in general: a relation between discourse and writing in their more ongoing modes finds its reflex in a relation between performance and writing at their most assertive.

Now these analogical relations are less important than the continuous interrelation that their schematism throws into sharp relief, the common implication of all their terms as social 'forces' in semiotic (ideological) reality. Beyond this, the neat symmetry of the scheme has itself been destroyed by the virtual bracketing-out of polyphony. Squeezed on one side by the novel as such (whose dialogism is now universal), polyphony is no less under pressure from carnival, which now virtually usurps its place as the type of anti-hierarchical semiotic practice. While still firmly distinct, novel and heteroglossia and carnival are assimilated to one another in a kind of mutual contagion; and, while nowhere denied their force, the 'negatives' of these 'positives' – the canon, monoglossia, and 'official' culture – are presented as embattled even in their domination, secondary to the unruly reality over which they claim priority (see figure 4). The whole tone of Bakhtin's case is almost programmatically hyperbolic in a way which would remind us of Theodor Adorno ('the dialectic advances by way of extremes') if the Russian weren't as optimistic and populist in his

oppositional

CARNIVAL	POLYPHONIC NOVEL
'discourse in life'	'discourse in art'
HETEROGLOSSIA	NOVEL IN GENERAL

alternative

FIGURE 4

orientation as the German is pessimistic and elitist.[14] His theory of social hegemony is written almost exclusively from the standpoint of a perennial counter-hegemony always in the making – always having the last laugh as it were on the monoglot powers-that-be but never *winning* in any properly political sense. In other words, the true priority of heteroglossia is never realised as decisive victory: the forms of its militant self-assertion constantly imply that priority which the monoglot and centralising forces have constantly to posit themselves against; they never secure for it the reward of power.

V

There is no doubt whatever that this case amounts to a politicisation of Bakhtinian theory in a critical conjuncture of Soviet history. The populist cast of its politics may be read as explicitly conformist in the international context of the rise of fascism and the post-1934 line of a popular front; equally it may be read as implicitly subversive in the national context of Stalinism. It is also 'political' in a more general sense, however we may specify (or speculate over) the ambiguities of its intervention in a particular historical moment. Any argument which so insistently implicates traditional poetics in the drive towards an authoritarian monoglossia in the nation state cannot have any illusions about its own transcendence of politics. Radical readings of Bakhtin might, however, register some uneasiness with the utopianism of this politicised theory and with the (so to speak) 'undertheorisation' of areas that are critical to any fully explanatory and politically helpful hegemonic theory.

Bakhtin might be said to undertheorise the ways in which a monoglot hegemony is historically organised and to overestimate the political effectivity of the disunifying and carnivalising forces to which it is opposed. The contending forces seem to be starkly polarised and to operate in abstraction from the institutional sites in which the complex relations of discourse and power are actually negotiated: Bakhtin stands (we might say) in the opposite corner to Foucault, and we need a Gramsci to hold the ring between them. The onward geopolitical migration of Bakhtin's concepts brings these *lacunae* to light, and it also helps to explain them as functions not only of a particular national-historical experience but also of the philosophical tradition he inherited. Russia had leapfrogged a whole epoch of social development in Bakhtin's own lifetime; a living museum of Europe's feudal past became that continent's concrete future. Besides his society's historical exemption from a long period of bourgeois hegemony, there is the peculiarity of the (German) philosophical tradition he starts from: a body of theory which nourishes itself on a vicarious experience of other peoples' (England's and France's) bourgeois revolutions and whose totalising elaboration is in inverse proportion to the failure or non-occurrence of that revolution in practice. German idealism is the text of a cultural revolution which *stands in for* its political counterpart instead of carrying forward and consolidating it, as in the English and French cases. Categories for the detailed historical understanding of bourgeois hegemony are clearly not to be found in this grand theoretical hypostasis of Romantic writing. The roll-call of Bakhtin's literary heroes – Dante, Rabelais, Goethe, Dostoevsky – follows the same pattern: all spring from social formations which are either pre-bourgeois or 'world-historically' retarded in being quasi-feudal absolutisms.

The English novel provides a crucial test: Bakhtin's readings of (in particular) Sterne and Dickens are as sophisticated stylistically as they are historically dubious. Eighteenth-century comic fiction is conceived in the light of its own Rabelaisian or Cervantic self-image – that is to say, in a supra-historical 'European' perspective, out of the context of the complex cultural-hegemonic process in which even this non-canonical form of writing plays its part. Dickens is little more than a continuation of this 'second stylistic line': Fielding or Smollett in nineteenth-century guise. A satisfactory reading of late Dickens (say *Little Dorrit*, which Bakhtin discusses) would need to understand the subtle adjustment of power relations that is at stake when this 'aristocratic' line of comic fiction is plebeianised and not only fused with sentimental writing, but sharpened in its social criticism by the Jacobin novel – that other 'bourgeois' mode, with its vision of individuals not as moral types (knaves or fools) but as the bearers of structures who are locked into the complicities of a system which eludes their will or consciousness. Bakhtin acknowledges the fusion of 'lines' in general terms as a phenomenon of 'the beginning of the nineteenth century', but is unable to specify in national-cultural or national-linguistic terms its hegemonic bearings and effects (DN, p. 414). To do so is to see the radicalism of Dickens's vigorously dialogised heteroglossia as an ambiguous affair: not politically compromised in a culpable sense, but none the less objectively implicated with other quasi-private initiatives in projecting hypothetically a more acceptable hegemony. Bakhtin's conception of social hegemony is more or less confined within the idea of an 'official' culture and exemplified by feudalism and Stalinism. This model of a static monolith which somehow escapes social and historical determination is inadequate even for those versions of social power, let alone the bourgeois order in its maturer manifestations.

At the same time there is nothing in the concept of dialogism that prevents us from using it to explain the organisation of hegemony itself. The complex of ideological themes brought under the head of 'bourgeois individualism' is not (need we say) the work of 'individuals'; the liberal-humanist subject is constructed in a subjectless process of history by forms of writing and speech that are effective only to the extent that they are powerfully (if only provisionally) dialogised. In the English development it is Renaissance tragedy that first fills this historical role, as Catherine Belsey's recent work has shown.[15] The novel is a relatively late arrival in the same development. Coming as it does in the aftermath of the revolutionary crisis variously mimed in advance by Renaissance tragedy, the novel reminds the 'Augustan' public sphere of its outer and lower limits – confronting that communion of disembodied gentlemanly minds either with the grotesque body or with the feminine 'other' which it excludes. The dialogised languages of fiction in these comic and sentimental 'stylistic lines' only constitute a liberating practice in the sense that they hypothesise new subject positions within relations of gentry and patriarchal power that remain unchallenged. When this twin hegemony faces more or less open resistance in the radical and early-feminist fiction of the late eighteenth century, there is a loss: these novels' ability to project the ubiquity of the political is bought at the cost of a certain narrowing of that broad heteroglot base which (as we have seen) Dickens was to restore to fiction in the next century.

Dialogism makes possible incorporation, then, as well as resistance: witness the liberal 'social problem' novel (Gaskell, Eliot *et al.*) in which social- and regional-dialectal speech and subaltern ideological discourses enter into colloquy with a sympathetic authorial voice, just as subaltern classes and class fractions were then being incorporated in the wider process of social hegemony – a process which is itself dialogical.[16] Dialogism only ends where repression or rule by decree begins; and in a liberalising metropolis that mode of social power was only to be found in its imperial relationship with the subject peoples of the Empire, those external 'racial' others who were exploited not only economically but also ideologically, in as much as they helped to elevate even the domestic 'class' other (the worker) to the status of master. The liberal novel's mutual accommodation of languages is carried on within a notable national introspection, relegating the

Empire to the margins of the plot as a source of legacies or place of emigration. When the colonial other *is* represented in fiction it is in the genres of adventure romance and travel writing, and then only as an 'objectivised' image in a world without historical becoming; as a third person who can never be the second person of dialogue; as an ontological other who is exhausted in a 'mass' (ethnic) characterisation and only contingently an *individual*. A liberal and problematising fiction colludes with its imperial and romanticising counterpart in implying 'white' metropolitan subjects who *are* individuals, free agents of history.

But just as the dialogism of one is provisional, so is the monologism of the other always subject to dialogical leakage which can be exploited for the ends of resistance both within fiction and beyond. The rise of nationalism among the Empire's subject peoples is such a phenomenon of leakage, ironically aided by the Empire's own educational apparatus. Within English fiction one of its results is the deft parodic inversion of imperial romance in Schreiner and Conrad whereby at least one side of the imperial relationship is dialogised – that of the colonising subject himself. Kipling's work uses the voices of subordinates on both sides of that relationship to confront the imperium with the poly- and heteroglossia under its sway; Forster's India is produced by the more classically liberal and realist means of writing a 'social-problem' novel about the imperial dimension that its Victorian prototypes had so regularly marginalised.

VI

This complex interrelation of novelistic and social dialogism in the history of the organisation of bourgeois hegemony in England does not so much invalidate Bakhtin's concepts as put them to a stringent and in the end strengthening test. It would in any case be wrong to see Bakhtin as a passive victim of Russia's historical experience and a passive conduit of a philosophical tradition which prevented the exceptionalism of that experience from knowing itself as exceptional. From this distance in space and time we can see that the exaggerated claims made for the novel and for dialogism are an understandable emphasis, given the kind of political intervention he is making. In the work of the 1930s on the novel there is a strong element of what Bakhtin himself would call 'hidden polemic', and the antagonist who remains unnamed, though often plainly implied, is Georg Lukács.[17] Bakhtin signals his dissent from their common Kantian and Hegelian tradition in so far as he poses against a conception of the novel that is wholly *epistemological* and *aesthetic* in its terms a conception that is just as resolutely *political* and *semiotic*. Encoded within this (though not as its transcendent 'truth') is a whole view of the relationship between the bourgeois and proletarian revolutions and of the meanings these political practices give to democracy. Which is only to say that the antithetical valorisations Bakhtin and Lukács give to the distinction between novel and epic are more than just an academic issue, a difference between scholars. Lukács's early version of this distinction would have been (some common ground notwithstanding) too Hegelian for Bakhtin's liking, but it is when Lukács maps it on to a distinction *within* the novel between 'realism' and the various modernist pathologies of representation – when epic 'narration' is dogmatically elevated over mere 'description' – that the gap between them opens up.

The fall from the motivated signification of epic to the arbitrary signification of the novel, from the comfortable bonding of the signified to the fearful freedom of the signifier – this world-historical lapse is reproduced from 1848 on in the European novel and only redeemed later in the unexplained isolated instances of Tolstoy and Thomas Mann. The fall from the noumenal to the phenomenal which the novel ambiguously reflects is reversed only when the immediate transparency of history overcomes the signifier's intrusive materiality. In other words, Lukács praises a bourgeois genre to the extent that it looks back to a classical genre and practises that genre's backward-looking (preterite) narrative mode, and he does so at a moment when the novel has effectively usurped the role of 'identical subject-object of history' which had been filled by the proletariat in an intermediate phase of his thinking.[18] In Bakhtin the break with epic is decisive and it is specified in terms of the novel's commitment to the 'unresolved contemporaneity' of the present (DN, p. 346).[19] Lukács raises the novel to canonical status; it becomes in his hands a genre in the classical sense – effectively the literary equivalent of those pseudo-classicising political forms with which (as Marx observes in the *Eighteenth Brumaire*) the bourgeoisie clothes itself in its phase of consolidation. Bakhtin insists on the novel's resistance to any canonisation; instead he displaces on to it not only that inherent capacity for self-criticism and self-interruption that Marx (in the same text) ascribes to the proletarian revolution, but also that heteroglot struggle of languages which is a feature of the bourgeois revolution in its early stages of ideological preparation and active insurgency.

Now if neither Bakhtin nor Lukács adverts directly to the actual present of Stalinist repression, it must be said that their common silence has very different effects. Bakhtin's argument on the novel reminds the Soviet system (as it were) of the bourgeois revolution it never really had *and* the proletarian revolution it was then betraying and reversing, in favour of a neo-absolutism. Lukács's argument licenses a convenient renunciation of politics in as much as it reduces the proletariat to an agent of the historical realisation of that lost unity and 'given' totality that is adumbrated in the epic and ironically echoed in the novel. Bakhtin's claims for the novel and dialogism are of no use practically or theoretically either to Stalinism or to liberal versions of democracy. Even if his concepts in their formulation seem to display a residual Romantic tendency to conceive of all *institution* as somehow inauthentic, this is a small price to pay for what the hidden polemic against Lukács brings to light. Posed as it is against Lukács's contemplative non-intervention, Bakhtin's case could never misrecognise its own discursive status, and neither should we. It could never be made to square with that agnostic attitude towards power so characteristic of liberalism in its high-minded shadow-boxing with Stalinist and other authoritarianisms.

VII

I have been arguing that the migration of Bakhtin's concepts into 'our' context exposes and explains their inadequacies; this wandering and transplantation is also the condition of their self-correction. The urgent task of Bakhtin's radical readers is, then, to push his concepts still further on in their journey, putting them to still more demanding tests. One such test is the theorisation of drama.

Bakhtin says little about drama, and some of what he does say is dismissive: 'drama' is set up as one of the novel's great antitypes, 'poetry' (lyric poetry, one presumes) being the other. It sometimes seems that drama (even more perhaps than poetry) is accorded a place in his theory only in order to show what the novel triumphantly *isn't*. The drama is for Bakhtin hostile to any dialogism: dramatic discourse is made up only of objectivised speech – 'represented positions' – organised in relationships that are themselves thoroughly objectivised, utterly subordinate to an 'ultimate semantic authority' (*PDP*, p. 188). Neither the compositional absence of this authorial authority nor the compositional presence of characters' dialogue does anything to qualify this inherent homophony of the genre; these technicalities are on the contrary the pliant means of its implementation; any weakening of the drama's monolithic unity 'leads to a weakening of the dramatic effect' (*PDP*, p. 17). The only exceptions are the medieval mysteries ('formally' polyphonic in having a plurality of voices though without their 'interaction') and Shakespeare (whose dramatic practice contains the 'germs' of polyphony but only across the whole *oeuvre*) (*PDP*, pp. 33-4). This absolute theoretical distinction with its accompanying (unexplained) historical exceptions was made in the original 1929 version of the Dostoevsky book. Later we find it poised on the brink of its own dissolution in a footnote where Bakhtin explains that by 'drama' he means 'pure classical drama', 'the ideal extreme of the genre. Contemporary realistic social drama may, of course, be heteroglot and multilingual' (DN, p. 405). No names are named, and the small print ensures that the distinction is not frontally challenged. What is more, Bakhtin does not say that 'realistic social drama' *dialogises* the heteroglossia it incorporates. Still, the concession together with the new exception are surely lethal to the distinction in its original form. It is in any case incompatible with the concept of 'novelisation' which effectively denounces the hermetically sealed divisions of traditional poetics by insisting that all genres since the late eighteenth century have been transformed by the novel's activity in history. To imply even by omission that drama escaped this process is to reflect unfavourably on that powerfully destabilising force that Bakhtin's more general case claims for the novel.

Two questions then: is there a novelised drama, and does novelisation entail dialogisation? Lukács – from whom Bakhtin seems to have borrowed the term if not the concept itself – cites naturalist drama as an instance of the leavening of drama's 'totality of movement' by the novel's (quasi-epic) 'totality of objects'. Such plays 'always include a number of characters who serve only to illustrate the social *milieu* for the spectator'.[20] Bakhtin would no doubt agree with the characterisation of naturalism as novelised, even if on different (certainly non-Hegelian) grounds. For him the novelisation of naturalist drama would amount to little more than a taking over of certain secondary features of nineteenth-century realist fiction; it is unlikely that he would have seen it as bringing any dialogisation in its train. One name that *we* would associate with a radically novelised drama – dialogised indeed to the point of polyphony – is that of Bertolt Brecht. Brecht gains Bakhtin's notice only in passing as a representative of the 'realist grotesque' which 'reflects at times the direct influence of carnival forms';[21] Brecht is also almost certainly one of the unnamed names in the qualifying footnote quoted earlier.

Rescuing Brecht from these containing margins and parentheses of

Bakhtin's writing is one way of promoting the self-deconstruction which his concepts need in order to survive. The example of epic theatre would be provocative even without these fleeting references to its inventor, simply by virtue of its claim to be a dramaturgy perversely geared to the production of non-dramatic effects. Even as texts for reading, Brecht's plays mobilise devices of deliberate interruption and commentary, with singers and narrators and scene-headings presenting the action under the sign not of the necessary but of the exemplary-which-is-also-reversible. Epic theatre seeks to strip the speech of characters of what Bakhtin would call 'objectivisation' and free it for entry into dialogical relations with the discourses of interruption. This dialogism of its spoken signification extends in production into whatever else may be made to signify on the stage, including (and above all) gesture.

The close analogy between epic theatre and novelistic polyphony is made plain in the (itself quasi-theatrical) metaphor Bakhtin uses when he says that objectivised speech in a homophonic context behaves 'like the person who goes about his business unaware that he is being watched' (*PDP*, p. 189): Brecht himself might have used these terms in a characterisation of 'illusionist' theatre. If gestures (like words) can be objectivised – as Bakhtin's metaphor, turned back on itself, can be made to suggest – then gestures (like words) can be dialogised. This is presumably what Benjamin means when he describes the gestures of epic theatre as 'quotable'.[22] The agents of this double-voiced quotation of speech and gesture are best described as 'actor-narrators', those displaced and dispersed author-functions that supplant the singular and imperiously absent authorial subject. These actor-narrators can no more be described as 'characters' than the hero-ideologues who are their precise counterparts in the polyphonic novel. The typical roles of Brechtian theatre are those that Bakhtin claims the drama cannot put to consistent use: the rogue, the clown, and the fool; 'images' of infinite non-communication and *irresolution* in as much as everything they do or say is fraught with dialogical ambiguity (DN, p. 405).

Now the case of Brecht is not presented here as an exercise in his heroisation; neither is it presented as a simple 'refutation' of Bakhtin on drama. On the contrary: with Bakhtin's help we can see that what Brecht projects and seeks to realise in epic theatre is nothing less than a (non-)dramatic dialogism; that it is called 'epic' precisely because its every word and movement is not only 'shown' but *told*, inwardly divided between 'dramatic' actualisation and an 'epic' retrospection which both ironises them and hypothesises alternatives. Then, in a second move – one which deconstructs the absolute distinctions of both Brecht and Bakhtin – we can use the programmatic dialogism of epic theatre as an optic for a re-reading of the whole history of drama, or at least a qualification of that monolithic unity which Bakhtin opportunistically (and in the end uncertainly) attributes to its forms. Having named Bakhtin's anonymous modern exception, we can freely set about reducing the latter's exceptionalism. By 'thinking' epic theatre in Bakhtin's terms as a drama which is radically novelised and dialogised, our understanding of it can include the notion of its specificity along with the notion of its affinities among other and earlier forms of drama. Or, to put it another way, novelisation in Brecht so jogs the generic memory of drama as to bring about a return to the carnivalesque; it revives in fully enacted versions (and of course under particular historical conditions) those parodic practices whose translation into writing first produced the novel and which have haunted even the serious forms of drama throughout its history.

The authority for this last sweeping generalisation is none other than Bakhtin himself, in an area of his theory where he is not under a local theoretical imperative to set up drama as the novel's antitype. Classical tragedy 'did not fear laughter and parody and even demanded it as a corrective and complement', institutionalising it in the comic play that regularly followed the tragic trilogy, while Shakespearean tragedy incorporates the carnivalesque as an organising principle even of its central tragic meanings.[23] With these prototypes of European drama brought into a deep internal relationship to the carnivalesque (complementary in one case, constitutive in the other), it is difficult to see how any argument about drama's intrinsic monologism can be sustained. It also becomes clear that there is not much in the actual history of drama that can be made to serve the kind of 'apophatic' definition of the novel that Bakhtin elsewhere denounces on general methodological grounds in his polemic against the Formalists.[24] What might count as 'drama' for this purpose is at most those plays produced within a neo-classical aesthetic ideology that enforces a rigorous *Stiltrennung*, elevating the 'high' (or serious) over the 'low' (or comic) in the forms of writing. Alternatively – turning from certain historically-specific conditions of the production of drama to certain no less historically-specific conditions of its *re*production – 'drama' might mean that pale 'literary' shadow of the theatre of any period that is constructed in the academic study of play texts by themselves. It is within this institutional relocation that drama comes to be conceived in sub-Hegelian (Lukácsian?) terms as a unilinear dynamic of collision and ultimate resolution, losing its historicity along with its discursivity. 'Dramatic dialogue is determined by a collision between individuals who exist within the limits of a single world and a single unitary language' (DN, p. 405): notice how Bakhtin invokes just these terms in building his case for a dramatic homophony.

With Bakhtin's help, then, it is possible to move beyond Brecht's polemical counterposition of epic to illusionist theatre and to rediscover in any drama those dialogical relations whose 'abstract product' is the closed dialectic of a 'dramatic' resolution. Drama is perhaps not so much monological in essence as *monologised* by being read as 'literature' rather than theatre. Bakhtin might have recognised in drama a synchronic version of that diachronic distance which (as he claims) makes an ancient genre like the 'Sophistic novel' seem monological only because the heteroglossia against the background of which it emerges – and with which it dialogically interacts – cannot be reconstructed at this historical remove (DN, p. 373). Drama would then have a status in his theory rather like that of the 'first stylistic line' in European fiction, in as much as it approaches heteroglossia 'from above' yet can only be seen to be doing so if we restore to it its manifold semioticity – in short, its theatricality. The modes of this theatricality are of course historically variable, but one could perhaps argue that what Williams calls 'the raised place of the stage' continuously alludes to its antecedent in 'the raised place of power'.[25] The performative utterances and gestures of absolute power that Renaissance tragedy (for example) places in quotation marks are the elements of one such mode, a very influential one. Theatre casts over the forms of state ceremonial and juridical process a certain referential opacity and semantic ambiguity: the 'power' of theatre we might say lies in its *formal* parody of the 'theatre' of power. That 'deconsecration of sovereignty' which Franco Moretti identifies as drama's peculiar articulation of the late sixteenth-century social crisis is in this sense only a thematisation of this deep structure of early-bourgeois theatre in England, filled out by a borrowing of forms from that other (unraised) place: the 'public square' of carnival.[26]

Only by such a materialist understanding of theatre could Bakhtin have averted the fall into an idealist misrecognition of drama that his materialist understanding of the novel paradoxically forces upon him, in all the enthusiasm of its overstatement. We have only to look at the field of metaphor upon which the general Bakhtinian theory of discourse draws in its earlier formulations to see that a materialist semiotics of theatre is wholly compatible with that theory. The utterance is a 'speech performance'; discourse is the '"scenario" of the event'; it relies on the 'chorus support' of other voices: a semiotics of this kind is positively encouraged by these explicitly theatrical metaphors that Bakhtin's theory uses to establish its materialist credentials.[27] Bakhtin's uncharacteristically epistemological conception of drama finds the means of its undoing – and hence the means of its squaring with his anti-Lukácsian conception of the novel – in the tropology by which his conception of 'discourse in life' was first elaborated.

VIII

Our argument has effectively come full circle: a problem thrown up in the secondary migration of Bakhtin's concepts finds its solution anticipated in an early phase of their primary migration. The problem of drama cannot of course be left there – if only because the modes of its semioticity inhabit in our time a multitude of institutional sites besides theatre. It is beyond the scope of this essay – and my own competence – to follow through the qualitative cultural changes that this exponential growth of the dramatic has brought about. There is, however, one other territory (this time in the literal, geopolitical sense) by which those self-displacing concepts might be challenged, and it is hinted in the following questions: what can they offer to anyone theorising or intervening in the cultural politics of decolonisation? does the consistent European-ness of their reference amount to a Eurocentrism?

It might seem that Bakhtin lines up behind Hegel and Marx and Lukács in that easy elision whereby the epithet 'world-historical' can be made to suggest that history is in the gift of Europe.[28] Equally we could argue with a decisively countervailing force that his concepts are nothing if not precisely designed to theorise *otherness*, including their own: that they can theorise not only the metropolitan practice of 'othering' (already discussed) but also the answering practice of Europe's 'others' in which the 'otherers' are themselves othered. Counter-hegemonic revolutionary cultures are being actively fought for and organised throughout the Third World against difficult and even deadly odds, as the differing cases of (say) Kenya and Nicaragua attest. In these territories the articulation of discourse upon power is not susceptible to the genteel mystifications of the metropolis; dialogue cannot be misrecognised as 'communication'; cultural struggle therefore has a life-or-death ferocity for which the only European parallel is the religious struggles of three centuries ago. The problems encountered in this struggle need for their solution a theory which neither submits politics to a cultural sublimation nor reduces culture to a mere expression of the political or economic. To take one example from the most aggressively 'othered' of the 'other' continents: progressive writers in Africa are divided between and also within themselves on the question of whether to decolonise writing in the coloniser's language or in a territorial vernacular which is itself (thanks to the arbitrary geography of imperialism) only problematically a 'national' language.[29] A Bakhtinian understanding would break beyond this polarisation of monoglot options to the notion of a multilingual field where the languages of coloniser and colonised are indelibly inscribed within each other and which oppositional initiatives should seek to exploit rather than escape.

This 'interinscription' of unequally empowered languages is to be found in its most advanced and ineradicable development in the least likely of (African) places: the apartheid state itself. What has guaranteed this is that territory's long history of very close colonial encounter and the peculiar vertical coextension of 'colony' and 'metropolis' within its borders. Any Bakhtinian looking for a clear case of monologism would none the less seem to have found in apartheid an unassailable empirical instance: here after all is a stridently racist discourse inimical to any dialogism, incapable of being legitimated 'downwards' among those it is expressly designed to exclude. How, then, does this brutally material 'fiction' relate to South Africa's heteroglot reality? Is apartheid exhausted in an enumeration of its modalities of repression? The system which combines apartheid and capitalist relations is a coloniser's dream: on the one hand an oligarchy with an internal structure of consent whose members enjoy a seemingly infinite social mobility because of their access to capital; on the other a majority with neither of these advantages ruled by decree from the oligarchy installed above it. If liberal outrage at this system is as morally vehement as it is practically impotent, that is because it lets the (bourgeois) side down by applying *extra*-economic coercion in the context of a mode of production where the purely *economic* coercion by which the surplus is 'normally' extracted can be mystified as 'freedom'. This impeccably Marxist account of the system is accurate as far as it goes; but it is only with Bakhtin's concept of dialogism and Gramsci's concept of hegemony that we can understand how its power is at once held and resisted.

Military conquest, capital accumulation, class formation: these deeply determining processes in the prehistory of apartheid will not explain either its stamina or its weakness unless a complex history of successive and coexisting hegemonies is allowed to be at least equally determining and at the same time understood as having a discursive (dialogical, multilingual) dimension which is inescapable. Apartheid is not a triumph of repression; it is a politics of permanent crisis whose curiously apologetic postures take their character from a primal failure which can never be acknowledged. Its direct coercion can silence discourse only piecemeal and contingently, in a killing or gaoling. It is a proof that that seemingly purest of monologisms – a discourse of purely unilateral instrumentality subserving naked repression – is always unrealisable this side of a genocidal final solution, a sociopolitical *reductio ad absurdum* which will be suicidal for its practitioners.

If the system's own self-description is (as Derrida suggests) 'untranslatable', exemplifying the *exclusion* it signifies, it is also true that the word apartheid cannot be deployed in a single sentence of the language from which it springs without recalling a linguistic miscegenation which accompanied its sexual counterpart in the early days of slave-ownership.[30] Afrikaans masks with its aggressively 'Dutch' lexis a syntax and intonation and idiom which are creolised through and through. The word apartheid is one such lexical item: slogan of the Afrikaner 'victory' of 1948, it would be free from contamination only if always intoned in isolation, predicated of nothing and having nothing predicated of itself. Like the word, the system that it signifies was only inaugurated when the elements of its political deconstruction were already in place. The Afrikaner cultural struggle which 1948 translated into political power had been patiently waged over decades and through a range of initiatives whose unifying theme was the national language. The ironies which haunted it from the past were only compounded by others it encountered in the very moment of its political success, both of them determining from within Afrikanerdom's characteristic strain of verbose apology before the world. Using cultural struggle as a means to political and then economic power, a temporarily stable class alliance engaged an economically dominant rival whose hegemonic trajectory was exactly the reverse of its own.

This other white tribe – the 'English' – had not only inherited an automatic dominance from the structure of the Empire; it also had a special pedagogic and linguistic relationship with the African majority which was founded and expressed in the schools and missions and in journalism. In its drive to win hegemony and scale the heights of capital, Afrikanerdom sought to break this long-established dialogue by legitimating among the majority a displaced mirror-image of its own monoglot ethnicity in a clutch of anachronistic tribalisms based territorially in the 'homelands'. It is rather as if the liberal novel that 'English' hegemony was in the course of writing had been rudely interrupted by a neo-imperial romance that needed for its composition the imposed silence of a police state. The very success of this rewriting was its undoing: to the extent that it has replaced the selective dialogisation of South Africa's heteroglot reality by its own sealed-off utopia of mutually deafened 'minorities', it has created a new generation of the oppressed and exploited whose scenario is predicated upon an alienation from *both* 'white' hegemonies. *Their* cultural struggle is now more than the holding operation it was through the long political quiescence of the 1960s; it is now a full-blown and politically combative counter-hegemony. The passage from forms of alternative writing and performance to forms of directly oppositional practice has produced a dialogisation without limits, a polyphony that cuts across all ethnic and linguistic lines. No single sociopolitical genre can encompass this multifarious popular deconstruction in which the skills of revolutionary counter-violence and of a parody in its own way just as deadly are never far apart.

IX

'Sociopolitical genre'? This concept – licensed if not 'authorised' by the texts of Mikhail Bakhtin – makes explicit a strong implication running through this essay, and it is not offered as a mere manner of speaking, an expressive 'as it were' of argument. Genres for Bakhtin are the 'relatively stable typical *forms of construction of the whole*' in discourse; they organise and finalise not only the 'literary' or 'rhetorical' utterance but also the most spontaneous and ephemeral of 'everyday' utterances.[31] There is every encouragement in Bakhtin for extending the concept of genre in the other direction to include the hegemonic projects of classes and class alliances in history, so long as we remember that it has already been transformed precisely by being predicated over the whole of discourse without exception. This generalisation of generic regularities is Bakhtin's answer to the (absolute) grammatical regularities of 'language' in linguistics which find their summation and upper limit in the pseudo-totality of the sentence. What ensures that 'genre' is already at least potentially a sociopolitical category in Bakhtin is his use of the novel to think the unthinkable: a genre which is 'essentially not a genre' but which exists only in so far as it 'imitates' and 'rehearses' other (non-'literary') genres; a whole constituted only in the 'playing' and alienation of other kinds of whole.[32] The notion of a unity formed in the 'combination' of 'subordinated, yet still relatively autonomous, unities' – of 'style' as an 'internal politics' determined always by its 'external politics (its relationship to alien discourse)' – such a notion might just as well have been derived from a study of social hegemony (DN, pp. 262, 284). The canonical genres in their 'ideal extreme' would then be not so much analogues of the absolutist state as accomplices in that state's belief in the absoluteness of its rule. Conversely, the novel is not the bearer of a particular political content ('popular', 'democratic', 'progressive'); it is a means of imagining the truth that no rule is absolute. Its only politics is the insistence on the necessity of politics, of dialogical struggle, of power *as* struggle. To understand the radicalism of Bakhtin's thinking is to have seen that in his concepts the border of the sociopolitical has always already been crossed.

Notes

1 Katerina Clark and Michael Holquist, *Mikhail Bakhtin,* Cambridge, Mass. and London, 1984.
2 Tzvetan Todorov, *Mikhail Bakhtin: The Dialogical Principle,* trans. Wlad Godzich, Manchester and Minneapolis, 1984, pp. 94, 12; subsequent page references are given in the text.
3 See Raymond Williams, *Writing in Society,* London, 1984, pp. 11-21.
4 This case is argued at greater length in my 'Bakhtin, Marxism and post-structuralism', in Francis Barker *et al.,* eds., *Literature, Politics and Theory: Papers from the Essex Conference, 1976-1984,* London and New York, 1986, pp. 104-25.
5 See V. N. Voloshinov, 'Discourse in life and discourse in poetry: questions of sociological poetics', in *Bakhtin School Papers,* ed. Ann Shukman, Russian Poetics in Translation, vol. 10, Oxford, 1983, pp. 5-30.
6 Mikhail Bakhtin, 'Discourse in the novel', in *The Dialogic Imagination,* ed. Michael Holquist, trans. Caryl Emerson and Michael Holquist, Austin, 1981, p. 263; subsequent references are given in the text as DN, followed by page number.
7 Clark and Holquist, *Mikhail Bakhtin,* pp. 80, 242.
8 See Ken Hirschkop, 'Bakhtin, discourse and democracy', *New Left Review,* 160, 1986, pp. 92-113.
9 Bakhtin, 'Toward a reworking of the Dostoevsky book', Appendix II to *Problems of Dostoevsky's Poetics,* ed. and trans. Caryl Emerson, Manchester and Minneapolis, 1984, pp. 287, 293 (subsequent references are given in the text as *PDP,* followed by page number), and 'The problem of the text in linguistics, philology, and the human sciences: an experiment in philosophical analysis', in *Speech Genres and Other Late Essays,* ed. Caryl Emerson and Michael Holquist, trans. Vern W. McGee, Austin, 1986, p. 107. See also Todorov, *Mikhail Bakhtin,* p. 18. These texts date from the period 1959-61.
10 Voloshinov, 'Literary stylistics', in *Bakhtin School Papers,* p. 118.
11 Voloshinov, *Marxism and the Philosophy of Language,* trans. L. Matejka and I. R. Titunik, New York, 1973, p. 116.
12 See Roland Barthes, *Mythologies,* trans. Annette Lavers, London, 1972, pp. 114-15.
13 See Voloshinov, *Marxism,* p. 83.
14 Martin Jay, *Adorno,* London, 1984, p. 15.
15 See Catherine Belsey, *The Subject of Tragedy,* London, 1985.

16 See Robert Gray, 'Bourgeois hegemony in Victorian Britain', in Jon Bloomfield, ed., *Class, Hegemony and Party,* London, 1977, pp. 73-94.

17 In 1924 Bakhtin began, but soon abandoned, a translation of *The Theory of the Novel:* see Clark and Holquist, *Mikhail Bakhtin,* p. 99. The Bakhtin/Lukács relationship is discussed by Clark and Holquist on p. 288, and more fully by Eva Corredor in 'Lukács and Bakhtin: a dialogue on fiction', *The University of Ottawa Quarterly,* LIII: 1, 1983, pp. 97-107.

18 See Fredric Jameson, *Marxism and Form,* Princeton, 1971, pp. 189-90; see also the excellent discussion of Lukács by John Frow in *Marxism and Literary History,* Oxford, 1986, pp. 9-17.

19 See also 'Epic and novel', in *The Dialogic Imagination,* pp. 3-40.

20 Georg Lukács, *The Historical Novel,* London, 1962, p. 96. The first edition of this book was in Russian, and was published in Moscow in September 1937. Ken Hirschkop informs me that 'Lukács did not even know of Bakhtin until fairly late in his life, so if there was borrowing involved there is only one direction it could have travelled. "Epic and novel" was originally a lecture given at the Gorky Institute in 1941, so the dates certainly allow for that possibility' (letter of 11 June 1983). See Bakhtin, 'Epic and novel', p. 39, and the Conclusion to the 1963 edition of the Dostoevsky book (*PDP,* p. 271). There is no reference to novelisation in the 1929 edition.

21 Bakhtin, *Rabelais and his World,* trans. Hélène Iswolsky, Cambridge, Mass. and London, 1968, p. 46.

22 Walter Benjamin, *Understanding Brecht,* trans. Anna Bostock, London, 1973, pp. 19-20.

23 Bakhtin, *Rabelais,* pp. 121, 275. See also 'From the prehistory of novelistic discourse', in *The Dialogic Imagination,* pp. 53-6.

24 P. N. Medvedev, *The Formal Method in Literary Scholarship: A Critical Introduction to Sociological Poetics,* trans. Albert J. Wehrle, Baltimore and London, 1978, pp. 86-8.

25 Williams, *Writing in Society,* p. 15.

26 Franco Moretti, 'Tragic form as the deconsecration of sovereignty', in *Signs Taken for Wonders,* London, 1983, pp. 42-82. See also Michael D. Bristol, 'Carnival and the institutions of theater in Elizabethan England', *ELH,* L, 1983, pp. 637-54.

27 Voloshinov, 'Discourse in life' pp. 21, 15.

28 See Edward Said, *Orientalism,* Harmondsworth, 1985, pp. 153-6, and David Fernbach's Introduction to Karl Marx, *Surveys from Exile,* Harmondsworth, 1973, pp. 24-8.

29 See Ngugi wa Thiong'o, *Decolonizing the Mind: The Politics of Language in African Literature,* London, 1986.

30 Jacques Derrida, 'Racism's last word', *Critical Inquiry,* XII, 1985, pp. 290-9. A 'Critical response' to Derrida by Anne McClintock and Rob Nixon is to be found in *Critical Inquiry,* XIII, 1986, followed in turn by an answer from Derrida himself (pp. 140-70).

31 Bakhtin, 'The problem of speech genres', in *Speech Genres,* p. 78.

32 Bakhtin, 'From notes made in 1970-71', in *Speech Genres,* p. 132.

Tony Crowley

Bakhtin and the history of the language

Historians have constantly impressed upon us that speech is no mere
verbalisation of conflicts and systems of domination, but that it is the very
object of man's conflicts. (Foucault)

One of the most remarkable facts about the history of the language as
a field of academic research in recent years has been its tenacious
resistance to modern theoretical work. This is surprising given the
centrality of questions of language and history in modern theory. It is
all the more surprising given the enormous theoretical and speculative foundations of the discipline of historical linguistics in the nineteenth century – ranging from anthropological to geological concerns
– of which the history of the language was a sub-branch. Yet it is none
the less true that the sort of debates which have dominated literary
studies have had no place in the history of the language. One pertinent,
if historically odd reason for such an omission is that the field has been
characterised by a rigorous adherence to the Saussurean division
between what is properly internal and external to the study of language. According to this division internal linguistics was to concen-
trate on the formal relations between units within a system; external
linguistics on the relations between language and race, languages and
political history, language and institutions and so on.[1] The result of the
division was a field of study largely devoted to formal linguistic inquiry
with only minor, and certainly untheorised, attention paid to questions of what was termed 'style'.

However, with the shifts which have taken place within modern
theory itself a new situation has developed. The theoretical drift away
from the more arid types of formalism to what can be described as
more discursive and, both implicitly and explicitly, political forms of
critique has had deep effects. Across fields such as linguistics, literary

criticism, philosophy and historiography, there has been a significant appreciation of the social constitution of their objects and the political implications of the methods of treatment of such objects. A key set of texts in this shift has been those of Bakhtin, whose influence, it seems, continues to grow apace. Yet if such influence in these fields has been significant, not least in the production of an historical self-consciousness, it is ironic that these texts have had almost no influence in the field in which their importance seems obvious. For like that of the other major theorists, Bakhtin's work has been resolutely ignored in the history of the language, despite the fact that his work seems to offer a number of crucial insights which open up new directions in the field. His theoretical and historical treatment of forms of discourse appears to provide the foundations for bridging the gap between the internal and external approaches – or if not bridging the gap, then exposing the division as theoretically untenable and regressive. The importance of this is that if the gap were to be bridged, or exposed as a false division, the field would be radically altered in terms of both its methodology and its aims. Therefore the aim of this essay will be to explore precisely such a possibility by considering the relevance of Bakhtin to the field of study entitled the history of the language.

The key concepts

It is possible, and indeed his translators frequently do it, to draw up a glossary of the key Bakhtinian terms. If such a glossary were to be compiled with particular reference to those terms relevant to the study of the history of the language then it would necessarily include the coupling of dialogism and monologism along with monoglossia (*odnoyazychie*), polyglossia (*mnogoyazychie*), and heteroglossia (*raznorechie*). Therefore in considering the utility of these terms to the field under consideration it will be necessary first to ascertain the ways in which Bakhtin uses them in his own analyses. The two terms dialogism and monologism are evidently central to his work and yet, as Ken Hirschkop has noted, they are terms whose function alters across his texts.[2] The change can be characterised as the politicisation of philosophical concepts, and takes place between the early and later texts. In the early use these terms refer to opposed 'world-views', one of which (monologism) is superseded by the other in an ethical and teleological progression. In their later use, however, the terms are employed in at least three distinct ways. First, to refer to the historical forces which are in conflict in discourse: dialogical versus monological forces. Second, to the effects brought about by the conflict: monological or dialogical forms of discourse. Third, to the nature of the conflict itself: given that the forces are always in conflict, the form which dominates at any one time has to engage in constant dialogical re-negotiation with the other in order to retain its position. This development from a static view of opposition to the perception of active historical conflict is crucial, since its stress on dialogical struggle as the foundation of all forms of discourse allows for the relation between particular dialogical and monological forms to be theorised from an historical perspective. They can thus be viewed as the results of precise social struggles in which their status and position are always at stake. This in turn means that, rather than an ethical and teleological viewpoint, these terms now embody a political mode of analysis which facilitates not simply readings of past formations of discourse, but the possibilities of interpreting and changing those discursive forms which dominate our present.

The general principle to be abstracted from this theoretical politicisation is that all forms of discourse – from the smallest units to the national language and beyond – are shot through with social and historical conflict. With regard to the history of the language this is a revolutionary principle, since it threatens to deconstruct the rigid polarisation of interests which had been its fundamental tenet. For rather than privileging internal over external concerns, Bakhtin's premiss means that such a hierarchy would be reversed; but more than this, it would also mean that those forces which had been thought of as not properly belonging to the field would now be viewed as constituting it. The complex relations between, for example, languages and political history are taken in the Bakhtinian perspective to embody the conflict of social forces which will produce particular discursive forms, effects and representations. For the history of the language, if this view were taken seriously, this would mean that its static conception of language, in which any particular language moves through evolutionary stages of being, would have to be replaced by the view which saw the very concept of a language as already the result of particular social conflicts. The field would then have to be more concerned not only with questions of history and struggle but with a self-conscious reflection of the role of the field in such struggles. It is this which has been so markedly absent from the field as yet, and this which is necessary for the field to give an adequate account of its object.

If dialogism–monologism are key themes in Bakhtin's work in general, then monoglossia, polyglossia, and heteroglossia would seem to have particular importance for the history of the language. Yet these terms also shift their signification in his texts, and it is likewise important to distinguish their differing uses. In one set of uses, mirroring the static conception of opposed forces set out in the early dialogic–monologic pairing, these terms referred to stages in the historical being of language. Monoglossia therefore would be the primary state of being of a language which reflected directly the self-enclosed 'world-view' of its speakers. Homeric Greek might be cited as such a monoglossic form, since it signalled its blindness to difference and desire for purity in its division of the world into Hellenes and Barbaroi (Greek speakers and the rest). Such a form is represented as self-sufficient and self-originating and approaches a theological status which is typified in Socrates's claim in *Cratylus* when he refers to the language 'in which the Gods must clearly be supposed to call things by their right and natural names'.[3] Another example of the monoglossic language might be Anglo-Saxon, since it too was often represented as the purest form of a particular language. In this representation it was the 'true English' before it was bastardised in its miscegenation with the Norman French.

According to the same teleological and ethical order presented earlier, monoglossia is superseded by polyglossia when the self-sufficient language becomes conscious for the first time of otherness. In *Cratylus* such otherness is already perceptible in Socrates's references to geographic, historical, social and gender-related variation which needs to be suppressed, by way of the *etumos logos*, in order to recover the divine language of truth. However, once the perception of differences has entered then the self-enclosed Ptolemaic language becomes irreversibly transformed into the open Galilean set of languages in a variety of relations with one another. Latin would play the role of polyglossia to the Greek monoglossia since Latin came into existence aware of itself as precisely not self-sufficient but derived at least in part from its Greek forebear. In such a shift the absolute confidence of self-origination is relativised by the acute awareness of historical roots and therefore dependence.

The final stage in the schema occurs when polyglossia is supplanted by heteroglossia and both internal and external differences are uncovered. In this stage of being a language drops the absolute and relative unity characteristic of its former stages and thus reveals the full dialogic and heteroglot reality of its pluralistic character:

> . . . the internal stratification of any single language into social dialects, characteristic group behaviour, professional jargons, generic languages,

languages of generations and age groups, tendentious languages, languages
of the authorities, of various circles and of passing fashions, languages that
serve the specific socio-political purposes of the day, even of the hour. . .[4]

At this stage any positing of unity becomes a transparent fiction by
which the complex inter-relational differences of all these languages is
suppressed.

The teleological and ethical tone which accompanies this schema is
one which Bakhtin never quite manages to lose. For it is always and
everywhere the case that dialogism is preferable to monologism and
heteroglossia to monoglossia. The validity of this view will be challenged later, but first it is necessary to demonstrate the limitations of
such a view and the attempts made by Bakhtin to overcome them. For
Bakhtin it is clearly the case that polyglossia and heteroglossia are
ethically superior to monoglossia, since in the transformation from
the earlier to the later stages, 'Language is transformed from the
absolute dogma it had been within the narrow framework of a sealed-
off and impermeable monoglossia into a working hypothesis for com-
prehending and expressing reality . . . Only polyglossia fully frees consciousness from the tyranny of its own language and its own myth of
language.'[5] In this transformation the forces of liberation are victorious
in their conflict with those of narrow dogmatism, and yet if such a view
is followed to its (teleo-)logical conclusion then it can only follow that
we live today in a world in which the forces of linguistic liberation have
triumphed. It is an argument made by Bakhtin when he argues that we
too live in a world which is beyond monoglossia:

> We live, write, and speak today in a world of free and democratised
> language; the complex and multi-leveled hierarchy of discourses, forms,
> images, styles and linguistic consciousnesses was swept away by the
> linguistic revolutions of the Renaissance. European *literary* languages –
> French, German, English – came into being while this hierarchy was in
> process of being destroyed . . . For this reason these new languages
> provided only very modest space for parody: these languages hardly knew,
> and now do not know at all, sacred words . . . (PND, p. 71)

Such optimism could only be brought about by rigid adherence to a
teleological schema whose accuracy would be disproved by one quick
glance at the historical conditions which actually prevail in our world.
However, it is at this point that the shift which took place in the use of
the dialogism–monologism pairing has further relevance. For under
the influence of the politicised conception of those terms, the relations
between monoglossia, polyglossia and heteroglossia appear very
differently. Rather than seeing these terms as referring to opposed

stages of linguistic being in an irreversible teleology, the politicised view sees them as forms and representations of language brought about by social and historical conflicts. Monoglossia, in such a view, would be the product of the dialogical struggle between opposing tendencies, and although it achieves a certain stability its status could never be absolute: 'It must not be forgotten that monoglossia is always in essence relative. After all, one's own language is never a single language: in it there are always survivals of the past and a potential for other-languagedness . . .' (PND, p. 66). Monoglossia is now a result of historical circumstances which can be altered rather than a primary, pure stage of language. Its representation as a version of the pure Adamic language in which world and word meet is the result of the desire for purity rather than historical accuracy.

Once this shift had been made, the impossibility of monoglossia (and in consequence polyglossia and heteroglossia) as actual stages of linguistic being led to the crucial, axiomatic statement on the processes of historical becoming in language: 'At any given moment of its historical existence, language is heteroglot from top to bottom: it represents the co-existence of socio-ideological contradictions between the present and the past, between differing socio-ideological groups in the present, between tendencies, schools, circles and so forth . . .' (DN, p. 291). In the same sense in which dialogism can refer to both a form of discourse and the founding principle of all such forms, heteroglossia is also one of the historical representations of a language as well as its grounding characteristic. From this the importance of the historical, conflictual nature of all discourse is apparent, and it is this which is of greatest significance for the historian of language.

The conflict of opposing tendencies is characterised by Bakhtin as the perpetual dialogic struggle between centripetal forces whose aim is to centralise and unify, and centrifugal forces whose purpose is to decentralise. The crucial point is that in their struggle the relations between such forces will differ in their forms and effects at different historical periods. At one time, and under specific historical conditions, centripetal forces will organise a certain form of discourse as the centralised, unified, authoritative form, and thus monoglossia and monologism will be effected. At another the centrifugal forces will be victorious and any such attempts at unity will become impossible. All forms of discourse and representations of language become dialogised in this process as effects whose forms are created by the particular historical arrangements of the opposed forces at any one time.

An example of such a discursive representation, and one with particular relevance for the history of the language, is the 'unitary language'. This is not, as it is represented in the title 'the history of the language', a historical fact waiting to be discovered, but a discursive form which has to be fought for: 'Unitary language constitutes the theoretical expression of the historical processes of linguistic unification and centralisation, an expression of the centripetal forces of language. A unitary language is not something given (*dan*) but is always in essence posited (*zadan*)' (DN, p. 270). Both the formal unity which it has, and the cultural unity whose purpose it serves, are the effects of massive centralising forces overcoming heteroglot differences. The sites of such struggles, ranging in Bakhtin's account from Aristotelian poetics to Indo-European philology, are the fields in which such significant discursive effects are achieved.

This brief account of Bakhtin's work has concentrated upon the important transformation of the central concepts and their consequent relevance for historians of the language. The shift is crucial in that it focuses attention on the various institutionalised sites of struggle in which the competing forces meet, and so enables historians to trace the battle lines of the conflict and the complex relations by which discursive effects and power are inter-related. There are, however, problems with such an account which specifically involve the level of abstraction at which such concepts are deployed, the lack of historical specificity, and a consequent failure to lose entirely the ethical and teleological tone which was attached to the early use of these concepts. These problems in turn mean that the specific questions of the relations between discourse and power are not fully answered. In the rest of this essay, therefore, the aim will be to give a sketch of one period of historical struggle between centripetal and centrifugal forces in order to develop the possibilities of their use and to tackle the problem of historical specificity. The site of conflict will be the history of the language in late nineteenth-century Britain and its desired object, the 'standard language'.

The formation of the unitary language
The history of the language as a distinct field of study with major cultural significance first appeared institutionally in mid to late nineteenth-century Britain. Taking as its object a concept already inscribed in the politics of centripetalisation, *the* language, this field was at the heart of a number of important cultural debates. In their work on

language the linguistic historians produced texts and readings whose effects across a whole range of discourses were a necessary part of the process of establishing cultural hegemony. In particular the concept of the 'standard language', and the uses to which it was put, was one of the central factors in this hegemony, and its role will be examined later. First it will be necessary to point to the discursive and political effects of the new field of study.

Bakhtin's argument claimed that linguistics, stylistics and the philosophy of language had been major centralising forces in the history of cultural formations whose method had consisted of seeking for unity in the face of diversity. Such methodology focused upon both formal unity, by means of the identification and stabilisation of common linguistic features and their uses, and cultural unity, by means of an ordering of certain cultural functions of discourse and language. The attempt to forge unity took many forms: 'The victory of one reigning language (dialect) over the others, the supplanting of languages, their enslavement, the process of illuminating them with the True Word, the incorporation of barbarians and lower social strata into a unitary language of culture and truth . . .' (DN, p. 271). The double-edged nature of unifying processes is significant in the task of achieving hegemonic rule in that it not only seeks the centralisation and solidification of grammatical or cultural forms but also insists at the same time that the cultural significance of such forms be centralised and solidified. Without the successful fulfilment of both tasks hegemonic rule in this area cannot be assured.

If the politicised version of Bakhtin's scheme is followed then it becomes clear that the nineteenth-century linguistic historians were engaged in a major way in the dialogic struggle between centripetal and centrifugal forces. However, as will be demonstrated, it is apparent that their work was not simply a form of centralisation which excluded diversity, since it is something of an oversimplification in Bakhtin's account to suggest that a form of discourse is simply either monologic or dialogic, or a language only monoglossic, polyglossic, or heteroglossic. What is striking about the work of the linguistic historians and its role in this respect is that, as in any effective hegemony, the forms with which they worked, and the representations which they effected, are protean. They change to meet the historical requirements of hegemonic rule, which are in turn dictated by the levels of resistance, necessities of inclusion, patterns of exclusion and so on. It is for this reason that the language is figured sometimes as a monoglossia, at others a polyglossia, and yet others a heteroglossia. The particular situation in which a representation is to be deployed dictates the form of the representation.

The social aims revealed in the texts produced within this field, to whose end representations were formulated, were principally three: national unity, social unity, and unity of political purpose in the imperialist project. Taking the first of these aims, one of the most overt demands of any group making a claim for itself as a nation in the nineteenth century was to claim a monoglot language and history as its own. The monoglot language had the function of marking off the nation's citizens from all others and binding them together in a fictional national equality, since it appeared not to recognise either internal or external otherness – though in fact it will be argued later that it did precisely this. According to one linguistic historian language was the perfect instrument to reflect deep structural unity: 'It is evident therefore that unity of speech is essential to the unity of a people. Community of language is a stronger bond than identity of religion or government, and contemporaneous nations of one speech, however formally separated by differences of creed or of political organisation, are essentially one in culture, one in tendency, one in influence.'[6] In such a reading the unity of the monoglot language can operate as a guarantor of the depth of true cultural unification in the face of superstructural division. Against opposed political forces, however, such unity might well have been shattered if it had not been posited upon the basis of a seamless continuity of the present and past which seemed to offer further evidence of the durability of the nation. Writing of the education of the English schoolboy, one linguist made this representation of the language:

> Perhaps the next important step, is that his eyes should be opened to the Unity of English, that in English literature there is an unbroken succession of authors from the reign of Alfred to that of Victoria, and that the language which we speak *now* is absolutely *one* in its essence, with the language that was spoken in the days when the English first invaded the island and defeated and overwhelmed its British inhabitants.[7]

The eradication of linguistic difference in this example takes the form of a banishment of historical alterity in favour of a unified and radically synchronic system. Its effect is to suppress questions of change by pitting them against the posited depth of cultural unity enshrined in the language.

If the unity of the nation was seen as a question of ensuring the stable security of its self-definition, then the question of social unity took a distinct but related form. For once national unity had been posited there then remained the task of erecting a mythical form of equality in the area of citizenship. Here too the representations of language were important, since in such depictions the language became the cipher for those qualities of liberality, decency and freedom which were also held to be characteristic features of British society. Moreover precisely the same qualities were attributed to the language and its speakers, and thus on the question of word-borrowing one linguist was able to comment that 'the English language, like the English people, is always ready to offer hospitality to all peaceful foreigners – words or human beings – that will land and settle within her coasts.'[8] The language was to be revered sacramentally, 'worthy of our holiest and never-ceasing devotion', on the grounds that 'it will bear to future ages the sentiments of a free, generous, and singularly energetic race of men.'[9] This absolute symmetry of values shared by English speakers, their language, and the society in which they lived, was a common representation in a number of different discourses. Perhaps one of the most interesting and durable was that which saw this symmetry as stemming precisely from the fact that all three members of this holy trinity were held to be free from fixed rules which would constrict them. All three are gloriously irregular and unconstitutional in any precise sense of the term, and so the English language '. . . is like the English constitution, and perhaps also the English church, full of inconsistencies and anomalies, yet flourishing in defiance of theory. It is like the English nation, the most oddly governed in the world, but withal the most loyal, orderly and free.'[10]

These discursive representations had a specific role in the achievement of cultural hegemony in this period in its predication of a nation at one with its past, present and future, and which had arranged for itself the best of all possible social orders. It was a united, organic order in which liberality, consensus and freedom were the guiding principles. The forces of centripetalisation, however, were not confined to a united language internal to the British state, since the historical situation demanded rather more. The consolidation of Britain as the imperial state required the extension of the monoglot language beyond the national boundaries until English became that frequently desired object, 'the world language'. The imperial language sought to extend its domain over the whole world: 'That language too is rapidly becoming the great medium of civilisation, the language of law and literature to the Hindoo, of commerce to the African, of religion to the scattered islanders of the Pacific. The range of its influence, even at the present day, is greater than ever was that of the Greek, the Latin,

or the Arabic, and the circle widens daily.'[11] Outstripping other em-
pires in the reach of its ambition, the imperial language was represented as carrying its liberal and decent qualities on to the world stage
in order to take its rightful place: 'English is emphatically the language
of commerce, of civilisation, of social and religious freedom, of progressive intelligence, and of an active catholic philanthropy; and
beyond any tongue ever used by man, it is of right the cosmopolite
speech.'[12] Such properly ordained linguistic domination meant of
course that the 'cherished and sanctified institutions of its native soil'
which were borne along with the language would be transmitted to
those regions which fell under its sway. One linguist felt that this would
eventually bring about a linguistic and cultural order in which the
world would be 'circled by the accents of Milton and Shakespeare'. He
concluded that this argued for 'a splendid and novel experiment in
modern society', in which English would be the monoglossic language
'so predominant over all others as to reduce them in comparison to the
proportion of provincial dialects.'[13]

The importance of such representations of the language is the
historical confirmation of Bakhtin's assertions about the study of
language. Such representations indicate the force of centripetalising
tendencies in the formation of cultural unity as they are set against the
historical differences of the past (in stressing national continuity), the
present (in praising the liberality of the social order), and the future (in
the promise of world domination).They are crucial in the processes of
hegemonic dissemination in working towards a suspension of major
differences in favour of minimal but durable unity and commonality.

Such are the general characteristics of the discursive and political
effects of the new field of study in its early period. For a more specific
analysis of such effects it will be necessary to turn to the actual
material engagements of the field in the cultural debates of the period.
The major project undertaken within the field of the history of the
language was the recording of the unitary 'standard language', a term
recorded as having been coined in the 1858 *Proposal* for the *New/
Oxford English Dictionary.* The context for the coinage was the debate
about what was to be included within the dictionary, a debate which
in the very fact that it took place at all ruled out the possibility of the
'standard language' pre-existing its appearance in the dictionary. The
lexicographers argued that the language did exist as a fact to be
recorded by asserting that 'as soon as a standard language has been
formed, which in England was the case after the Reformation, the lexi-
cographer is bound to deal with that alone.'[14] In fact the arguments

about whether there was such a standard form had raged for well over a century and a half, its *locus classicus* being Locke's extension of his arguments in favour of social stability to language, particularly in his warnings of the dangers of formal and semantic instability which so preoccupied the eighteenth century. For the nineteenth-century British historians, however, the 'standard language' was not a pre-existing fact – despite their theoretical protestations – but a unifying concept which gathered the materials upon which they had to work into an organised and delimited object. It was to become an object fully determined and centripetalised in the *Proposal* for the dictionary, the guidelines for its editors (the 'Canones Lexicographici'), and the eventual text itself. Moreover, it was to be not simply an object possessed of internal unity but one which also carried significant external centripetalising force.

The formulation of 'standard English' as a set of determinate linguistic forms and meanings can be traced in the texts of the history of the language and can be characterised as a form of monoglossia. The *Proposal* itself set out the monoglossic intentions of the lexicographers which were indicated by five principal delimitations: to ascertain the vocabulary by recording 'every word in the literature of the language'; to privilege writing over speech by professing to 'admit as authorities all English books'; to set the limits of English by marking off the historical point at which the language originated; to illustrate the meaning of the terms of the language; and finally, to settle their etymological history.[15] The purpose of these delimitations was to enable the recording of the 'standard language', which in this early use clearly refers to the literary language. In this task the monoglossia which is constructed is only relative since the historians were well aware of both the arbitrariness of their delimitations and the historical other-languagedness of English. However, in its centralising and authoritative influence even this relative monoglossia was highly important.

That such a monoglossia was theorised and constructed at this time is a problem if the early Bakhtinian use of the term is followed, since he had claimed that with the Renaissance and its consequences the national European languages had become polyglossic. If the later use of the term is followed, however, the problem disappears and the formation of such a monoglossia is explicable in terms of the conflict of opposing forces. In fact its appearance is related to those many other practices of centralisation and unification which occurred in nineteenth-century Britain. The processes of urbanisation and the consequent erection of national yet centralised forms of authority in institutions such as the police force, bureaucratic government and elementary education are parallel to the task of the linguistic historians in their own field. For the monoglossic standard literary language had a quite specific role to play in the formation of hegemony, since it offered a means of disciplining citizens with the purpose of ensuring that they took up only certain positions within the social order. The standard literary language, to be learnt in the novel forms of elementary education which appeared contemporaneously with it, was related to the requirements of an advanced technological form of capitalism, and in particular the need for a literate workforce. The linguistic historians, as with their professional counterparts in government, education and the police, to name a few of the organising agencies, were engaged in centralising and unifying work which had a clear relation to certain forms of power, since they provided the theoretical justification and the material exemplification of a certain form of 'standardised' literacy. This is not to attack such an effect, but to indicate its cultural significance and its implication with a number of other discursive practices.[16]

However, the relations between a monoglossic form and its discursive effects are perhaps most evident when considering a later development of the use of the term 'standard English'. In the later use it referred not to the literary language but to the language of the literate; if in the first use of the term it had referred to a linguistic 'fact', then in its later use a social fact became the basis of its definition: 'Standard English, like Standard French, is now a class dialect more than a local dialect: it is the language of the educated all over Great Britain.'[17] Its later *Oxford English Dictionary* definition gave it to mean 'a variety of the English language which is spoken (with modifications, individual or local), by the generality of the cultured people in Great Britain'. In this sense of the term the relations of the monoglossic 'standard language' to forms of discursive power are explicit: the monoglossic form is simply that of the powerful, the best, the educated, the cultured, of Great Britain. All other usage is relegated to the dialectal, provincial, rustic, and poor forms of the language.

The consolidation of 'standard English' as the monoglossic form spoken by the great and the good is a process which continues throughout the nineteenth and early twentieth centuries. Its effects on non-standard speakers were evident, since, as one observer of the urban proletariat argued when speaking in terms of liberal identification: 'always noisy, we rarely speak, always resonant with the din of many voiced existence, we never reach that level of ordered articulate utterance: never attain a language that the world beyond can hear'.[18] It is a silencing which appears to lend weight to Bakhtin's claims for the powerful blindness and exclusion brought about by monoglossia and its monologic forms. And yet, as the politicised version of these concepts indicates, it never can be the case that such forms triumph absolutely to bring about the silencing of the excluded other. Instead it is necessary to recall that such a victory is relative and determined by the historical situation. Rather than a total exclusion, the monoglossic 'standard language' and the processes by which it was disseminated brought about a precise pattern of inclusion which placed its subjects in certain positions and hierarchical relationships. The monoglossic form did not exclude differences but hierarchised them: posited as the central form, it then had ranged around it dialectal, class, gender and race-related differences in an inferior relation to its own powerful status. It was not blind to, but in a keen dialogical relation with, the heteroglot reality of the languages of a modernised society. It did not refuse difference but marked itself off as the form which could not be used by certain speakers, whilst at the same time damning their own speech as inferior. This is exemplified in the evidence provided by a non-standard speaker:

> This will be understood by a case of which I was told in a parish in Dorset, where the lady of the house had taken a little boy into day-service, though he went home to sleep . . . the lady began to correct his bad English, as she thought his Dorset was; and, at last, he said to her weeping 'There now. If you do meake me talk so fine as that, they'll laef at me at hwome zoo that I can't bide there'.[19]

The silencing which certain observers perceive does not in fact take place; what occurs rather is the production of hesitancy, a faltering with words felt to be alien and difficult, and a sense of shame and inferiority when meeting with social and linguistic 'superiors'.

The task embodied in the erection of a monoglossic form in such circumstances, characterised by both formal and cultural unity, is the legitimation of a particular system of power relations. This takes place by the formation of an appearance of equality which in fact masks a hierarchy and which brings about the sacramentalisation of the authoritative words of which monoglossia is composed. These words, and the genres to which they belong, are forms whose authority attends them and which brook no argument. Or at least they strive for that end; for the important historical lesson is that such authority is not absolute but merely gathers to itself the appearance of finality and incontestability. For the spring of dialogism never runs dry, heteroglossia is always ranged against monoglossia, and carnival lies just beneath the surface. The observer who had previously noted the silence of the working class elsewhere notes their noisy entry into the forbidden territory:

> We gazed at them in startled amazement. Whence did they all come, these creatures with strange antics and manners, these denizens of another universe of being? . . . They drifted through the streets hoarsely cheering, breaking into irritating laughter, singing quaint militant melodies . . . As the darkness drew on they relapsed more and more into bizarre and barbaric revelry. Where they whispered, now they shouted, where they had pushed apologetically, now they shoved and collisioned and charged. They blew trumpets, hit each other with bladders; they tickled passers-by with feathers; they embraced ladies in the streets, laughing generally and boisterously. Later the drink got into them, and they reeled and struck, and swore; walking and leaping and blaspheming God.[20]

It is not silencing which has taken place, as this observer had previously claimed, but a denial of forms of discourse and power which would permit anything other than carnivalesque mayhem.

This short account of the way in which a monoglossic form of the language can be constructed to a particular end supports Bakhtin's claim for the constant struggle which takes place in discourse. Yet there are problems with his argument. For if the conflict which characterises social life is resolved in one way then monoglossic and monologic forms dominate, the word of the father is the last word, and authoritative discourse appears to be the only form permitted. If the conflict is resolved in another way, however . . . then what? At this point there is a genuine problem in Bakhtin's work which centres on the difficulty of what it is which is to oppose monoglossia and monologism. For surely in modernised and differentiated societies certain forms of unity and organisation are necessary? Without them it is impossible to see how social life could be conducted. But if this is so then it must mean that there will be a necessary suspension of absolute heteroglossia in favour of unifying tendencies at particular levels. In Bakhtin's work, however, such a suspension does not seem conceivable, and instead an authoritarian form of monoglossia faces an ineffectively pluralist heteroglossia in a sterile binary opposition. Such an opposition clearly needs to be avoided, and the means of getting around it lies in taking the later politicised concepts which Bakhtin had articulated to their logical conclusions by stressing the importance of the historical context of the relations between the differing forms of discourse. Only then can they be evaluated politically, and it is this which needs to be explored by a consideration of specific historical examples.

Political contexts

It is clear that forms and representations of discourse and language play crucial roles in the operations of hegemony briefly considered above. Yet what is most significant from the perspective of those who are attempting to understand and change hegemonic rule as currently constituted is that such roles are not fixed but plastic. This is to argue that Bakhtin's stress on the differing relations between the concepts articulated in the politicised version of his histories of discourse is correct. Yet it is also clear that his preference for heteroglossia and dialogism, typified in his extravagant claims for novelistic discourse, needs to be challenged. This challenge has to read his work against itself by arguing that if the forms of discourse and language, and the roles they play, *are* dependent upon their historical and political contexts, then it is possible that in certain contexts a preference for heteroglossia and dialogism would be politically regressive. If monoglossia and monologism are not essentially absolute static forms then it is possible that they could play an important role in the struggle against certain authoritarian forms rather than reinforcing them. The question is this: if the ruling forces can adapt monoglossic, polyglossic, and heteroglossic forms and representations to their own purposes, then why cannot the forces which oppose them do likewise?

In order to answer this question both theoretically and with regard to empirical evidence, it is necessary to turn to another historical philologist whose work was also concerned with the connections between discourse and power. Gramsci commented in one of his *Prison Notebooks*: 'Every time the question of language surfaces, in one way or another, it means that a series of other problems are coming to the fore: the formation and enlargement of the governing class, the need to establish more intimate and secure relationships between the governing groups and the national-popular mass, in other words to reorganise the cultural hegemony.'[21] Gramsci's stress on the importance of language in the formation of cultural hegemony is essentially a political theorisation of Bakhtin's more elliptical assertions. For Gramsci, however, the importance of language lay not merely in this area but in the fact that at a more abstract level it functioned as a paradigm for the operations of social change and the achievement of hegemony. Thus it was at one and the same time involved in political practice and a blueprint for it. As Franco Lo Piparo has argued in

Lingua Intellettuali Egemonia in Gramsci, the concept of hegemony was derived at least in part from the work of the 'spatial linguists' at Turin, and in particular from the work of Gramsci's supervisor for his thesis in historical linguistics, Matteo Giulio Bartoli.[22] Essentially the argument of the 'spatial linguists' was that linguistic change was brought about by the effect of the prestigious speech community's language in its contact with the languages of non-dominant neighbouring speech groups. Rather than by means of direct imposition, the 'spatial linguists' saw change as being effected by the operation of prestige on the one hand, and active consent to change on the other. Thus the spread of any particular linguistic feature, as it passed from the dominant community through to its subordinates, would be brought about by consent rather than coercion and would eventually become universal. If this argument as to the formation of Gramsci's concept of hegemony is correct then the importance of language to his work is central, for not only does it operate as the marker of social conflict, it also functions as the model for the means by which such conflicts are broached and resolved.

Given the central role ascribed to language, it is no surprise to find that Gramsci asserts implicitly the necessity of a language programme for any group which aspires to cultural hegemony. However, and it is at this point that his work takes a theoretical and practical line distinct from that of Bakhtin, Gramsci's argument is that in the historical and political conjuncture in which he was located, rather than arguing for heteroglossia, what was required was precisely the organising force of a monoglossia. If Bakhtin, faced with the increasing centralisation and brutal forms of unity engendered by Stalinism, had argued for the importance of diversity and pluralism, Gramsci, faced with a divided and multi-factional national-popular mass, stressed the need for unity. His argument in favour of a unitary language was based on the difficulties of organising an illiterate mass in a society in which literacy was largely the prerogative of the governing class. The argument is a useful reminder of the need to historicise theoretical debates:

> If one starts from the assumption of centralising what already exists in a diffused, scattered but inorganic and incoherent state, it seems obvious that an opposition on principle is not rational. On the contrary it is rational to collaborate practically and willingly to welcome everything that may serve to create a common national language, the non-existence of which creates friction particularly in the popular masses among whom local particularisms and phenomena of a narrow and provincial mentality are more tenacious than is believed. (p. 182)

In this historical situation a preference for heteroglossia over monoglossia would be a reactionary stance, given that it would serve only to heighten the differences which exist to prevent necessary forms of unity. In a situation in which a linguistic hierarchy exists, a refusal to work for common and unified forms is tantamount to support for an unjust distribution of power. If that refusal to intervene institutionally is based on an abstract rather than historical evaluation of monoglossia and heteroglossia, then what in effect is brought about is a denial of access to the forms by which organisation can take place: 'In practice the national-popular mass is excluded from learning the educated language, since the highest level of the ruling class, which traditionally speaks standard Italian, passes it from generation to generation, through a slow progress that ... continues for the rest of one's life' (p. 187). Gramsci's assertion that 'the "question of the language" has always been an aspect of the political struggle' can be seen to be analogous to many of the arguments proposed by Bakhtin. The difference, however, is that Gramsci pushes Bakhtin's arguments to the limits by refusing to attach any ethical overtones to them. For Gramsci, unlike Bakhtin, it is the historical situation which will enable the cultural activist to evaluate which are to be the required forms of discourse and language. Thus, although Bakhtin's preference for heteroglossia is correct when analysing the formation of the 'standard language' and its role in the cultural hegemony of Britain, it is correct only in regard to this particular historical conjuncture. The repressive and centralising forms of unity demanded by the imperialist state offer an example of a monoglossic language, and monoglossic forms of discourse, which need to be resisted by the privileging of heteroglossia and dialogism. But the diffuse and politically disorganised situation of Italy, in which lack of forms of unity amongst the national-popular mass served the interests of the governing class, requires a quite different analysis.

The fate of nations which have managed to escape from colonial rule and the historical complexities involved in such processes serve as further counter-examples to Bakhtin's preferences and again stress the need for historical specificity in the analysis of such situations. The preference for pluralism and difference may well be a laudable one: but history demonstrates that forms of unity and organisation may be a prerequisite before such an achievement can be attained. One example of a nation which defeated its colonial masters in a revolutionary struggle, and for which the question of the language was important, was America. After the War of Independence an important cultural task for the newly liberated people was the necessity of constructing a monoglossic 'federal English' by which they would at once mark themselves off as distinct from their former masters and posit themselves as a united federal nation. As one of the most famous of the linguists involved in this task, Noah Webster, argued in 1789,

> We have therefore the fairest opportunity of establishing a national language, and of giving it uniformity and perspicacity, in North America, that ever presented itself to mankind. Now is the time to begin the plan. The minds of the Americans are roused by the events of a revolution; the necessity of organising the political body and of forming constitutions that shall secure freedom and property, has called all the faculties of the mind into exertion; and the danger of losing the benefits of independence has disposed every man to embrace any scheme that shall tend, in its future operation, to reconcile the people of America to one another, and weaken the prejudices which oppose a cordial union.[23]

In this role the language was to act precisely as an abnegator of the differences which prevented union; in such a role, at such a time, its monoglossic function was radical rather than conservative. (In the altered historical circumstances of the present, of course, the relations between, and the political nature of, the centripetal and centrifugal forces has changed.)

Perhaps the most interesting example of the way in which the cultural functions of monoglossia and heteroglossia change historically is provided by Britain's oldest and last colony: Ireland. In early twentieth-century Ireland the English language served as a monoglossic language which, blind to the political differences which beset it in its use in Ireland, attempted to silence Irish aspirations for an independent national identity while at the same time ramming home the triumphalist position of the imperialists. This was the historical situation within which Joyce's texts were written and against which they were set. The familiar scene in *A Portrait of the Artist as a Young Man* in which the English Dean of Studies and Stephen discuss the propriety of the word 'tundish' is a good illustration of the social conflict embodied in discourse as it entails questions of political, literary and cultural identity. It is a debate which ends in silence for Stephen as he feels himself to be beyond the pale of the monologic tradition embodied in the Dean's 'best English': 'The language which we are speaking is his before it is mine. How different are the words *home, Christ, ale, master,* on his lips and on mine! I cannot speak or write these words without unrest of spirit. His language, so familiar and so foreign, will always be for me an acquired speech. I have not made or accepted its words. My voice holds them at bay. My soul frets in the shadow of his language.'[24] The monoglot language, at once familiar and foreign, necessary but felt to be alien, carries with it the force and violence of colonial oppression. It does not produce absolute silence but presents the colonial subject with a problem to which there appears to be no answer: how to engage in discourse without, in using the oppressor's language, reinforcing one's own dispossession.

The answer Joyce provided in this war with monoglossia and monologism was to pit against these forces absolute heteroglossia and dialogism. At the end of the 'Oxen of the Sun' chapter of *Ulysses* Joyce terminates what appears to be an account of the seamless development of the unitary language posited by linguistic historians with this:

> Waiting guvnor? Most deciduously. Bet your boots on. Stunned like seeing as how no shiners is acoming. Underconstumble? He's got the chink *ad lib.* Seed near free poun on un a spell ago a said war hisn. Us come right in on your invite, see? Up to you, matey. Out with the rof. Two bar and a wing. You larn that off of they there Frenchy bilks? Won't wash here for nuts nohow. Like chile velly solly. Ise de cutest colour coon down our side. Gawds teruth, Chawley. We are nae fou. We're nae tha fou. Au resevoir, Moosoo. Tanks you.[25]

Against seamless unity Joyce posits various forms of poly- and heteroglossic difference. Against the teleological arrogance of a literary tradition sure of its beginning and end Joyce undertakes an act of massive usurpation by placing himself as its culminating, triumphant master. Already in this extract from *Ulysses* we can read the language of *Finnegans Wake*. It is the language of absolute heteroglossia which explodes the very possibility of *a* (determinate) language by insisting on the intertextuality of all linguistic forms. It is likewise the language of absolute dialogism since, as even its title demonstrates, it is the language in which no form has only one meaning and all questions have at least two answers. Against the striving for purity characteristic of monoglossia and monologism and typified by that desperate search for the *etumos logos*, Joyce sets *Finnegans Wake* and the 'abnihilisation of the etym'.[26]

In this sense then Joyce enacted a form of political and cultural national self-assertion by attacking and resisting the colonial monoglossic language and its monologic traditions. The radical tools which he employed in this task were the heteroglot differences which had been suppressed or ranked as inferior. However, in what may be termed, optimistically, post-colonial Ireland (semi-post-colonial Ireland might be more apt), a new historical situation has arisen which requires a different cultural analysis. Again this is relevant to the development and use of Bakhtin's concepts, since it reveals how a distinct historical conjuncture, and one which has been formed within fifty years of Joyce's act of rebellion, will dictate what attitude is to be taken to forms of language and discourse. The linguistic situation in contemporary Ireland is complex: in the Republic of Ireland the official language of the state is Gaelic, though most people use a form of English (Hiberno-English) in their everyday interaction. In Northern Ireland, a separate state still under direct British rule, the dominant form is Ulster English (also known as Ulster Scots), while there are also small but growing numbers of Irish republicans who attempt to use only Gaelic for their everyday purposes. The linguistic complexities of the situation are perhaps mirrored only by its political difficulties, in particular the sustained urban guerrilla war which provides the back-drop for intricate and apparently intractable political viewpoints. Given the difficulties of the linguistic and political situation, it is not surprising that cultural activists have sought for forms which might engender unity at the expense of differences seen to be destructive and harmful. Thus the poet and cultural critic Tom Paulin has recently appealed for a 'federal concept of Irish English' modelled on Webster's 'federal English'. Such a monoglossic form would be a major radical step in Irish politics and culture since it would be tantamount to ignoring the border which currently divides Northern Ireland from Eire. It would lead, it is claimed, to an ideal cultural unity:

> Thus in Ireland there would exist three fully-fledged languages – Irish, Ulster Scots and Irish English. Irish and Ulster Scots would be preserved and nourished, while Irish English would be a form of modern English which draws on Irish, the Yola and Fingallian dialects, Ulster Scots, Elizabethan English, Hiberno-English, British-English and American-English. A confident concept of Irish English would substantially increase the vocabulary and this would invigorate the written language. A language that lives lithely on the tongue ought to be capable of becoming the flexible written instrument of a complete cultural idea.[27]

The role of language in the formation of cultural unity such as that aspired to here can only be undertaken by a language which has a certain level of stability and confident unity. It would necessarily be a monoglossic language which, though aware of its historical indebtedness to other languages, would be sure of a central place in a unified culture. In such an historical development the role of the monoglossic language would again be radical and progressive rather than narrow and dogmatic.

The force of these examples is not to discredit the validity of Bakhtin's theoretical distinctions but to demonstrate the necessity of developing them further in order to increase their utility for theories of discourse. The examples serve to show how the highly abstract and ethical evaluation which attaches to these concepts in Bakhtin's work is an impediment which can only be eradicated by specific historical analyses which take into account the relative state of the different forces. This has significant implications for the history of the language since it means that the field, while necessarily employing these concepts, will have to do so in a way which demonstrates a clear view of the historical and political contexts to which they are related. In turn this reveals the central significance of the question of power and its distribution. For although Bakhtin is correct in arguing that there is a constant conflict of centralising and decentralising forces in discourse, it sometimes appears as though this conflict takes place without historical cause and to little historical effect, save that of producing fresh discursive conflict. However, as the examples above demonstrate, the struggle between dialogism and monologism, and that between monoglossia, polyglossia and heteroglossia, is not simply a conflict of discursive tendencies and effects but a conflict in which what is at stake are precisely forms of power and their distribution. The political status of any particular form of discourse or representation of language cannot be decided in advance, since they depend on the historically specific forms of power which they engender. It is this which both historians of language and Bakhtin scholars will need to recall.

Notes

1 The Saussurean division is formulated in the *Course in General Linguistics,* Introduction, chapter 5.
2 See Ken Hirschkop, 'Bakhtin, discourse and democracy', *New Left Review,* 160, 1986, pp. 93-5.
3 *Cratylus* 391e, in *The Dialogues of Plato, vol. 3: Timaeus and other Dialogues,* trans. B. Jowett, London, 1970, p. 138.
4 Mikhail Bakhtin, 'Discourse in the novel', in *The Dialogic Imagination,* ed. Michael Holquist, trans. Caryl Emerson and Michael Holquist, Austin, 1981, pp. 262-3; subsequent references are given in the text as DN, followed by page number.
5 Bakhtin, 'From the prehistory of novelistic discourse', in *The Dialogic Imagination,* p. 61; subsequent references are given in the text as PND, followed by page number.
6 G. P. Marsh, *Lectures on the English Language,* New York, 1860, p. 221.
7 W. W. Skeat, *Questions for Examination in English Literature,* Cambridge, 1873, p. xii.
8 J. Meiklejohn, *The English Language: Its Grammar, History and Literature,* London, 1886, p. 279.
9 Rev. M. Harrison, *The Rise, Progress and Present Structure of the English Language,* London, 1848, p. 378.

10 G. C. Swayne, 'Characteristics of language', *Blackwoods Edinburgh Magazine*, March 1862, p. 368.

11 E. Guest, *A History of English Rhythms*, 2nd ed., London, 1882, p. 703.

12 Marsh, *Lectures*, p. 23.

13 T. Watts, 'On the probable future position of the English language', *Proceedings of the Philological Society*, IV, 1850, p. 214.

14 *Proposal for the Publication of A New English Dictionary*, London, 1858, p. 3.

15 The principal aims are set out on pp. 2-8 of the *Proposal*.

16 For a historical account of processes of centralisation in this period, see Gareth Stedman Jones's *Languages of Class*, Cambridge, 1983. For work which concentrates on the deployment of particular forms of language and literacy and their relation to the prevailing political contexts in French history, see R. Balibar, *Les français fictifs: le rapport des styles littéraires au français national*, Paris, 1974, and R. Balibar and D. Laporte, *Le français national: constitution de la langue nationale commune à l'époque de la révolution démocratique bourgeoise*, Paris, 1974.

17 H. Sweet, *Sounds English*, Oxford, 1908, p. 7.

18 C. F. G. Masterman, *From the Abyss*, London, 1908, p. 25.

19 W. Barnes, *A Glossary of the Dorset Dialect*, Dorchester, 1885, pp. 34-5.

20 Masterman, *From the Abyss*, p. 3.

21 Antonio Gramsci, *Selections from Cultural Writings*, London, 1985, pp. 183-4; subsequent page references are given in the text.

22 See Franco Lo Piparo, *Lingua Intellettuali Egemonia in Gramsci*, Bari, 1979.

23 Noah Webster, *Dissertations on the English Language*, Boston, 1789, p. 36.

24 James Joyce, *A Portrait of the Artist as a Young Man*, Harmondsworth, 1960, p. 189.

25 Joyce, *Ulysses*, Harmondsworth, 1986, p. 347.

26 Joyce, *Finnegans Wake*, London, 1971, p. 353.

27 Tom Paulin, 'A new look at the language question', in *Ireland and the English Crisis*, Newcastle upon Tyne, 1984, p. 191.

David Shepherd

Bakhtin and the reader

What a recent book calls 'the return of the reader' is hardly a sensational event – the reader has been back with us for long enough now to make further welcoming receptions unnecessary. Indeed, it would seem that this familiar figure never really left, but lingered even in the unlikeliest of places: Elizabeth Freund has argued that, although the reader was 'banished by doctrinal fiat' from the most notorious of Anglo-American critical schools this century, 'a suppressed and unacknowledged reader-oriented criticism' was crucially constitutive of the whole project of New Criticism.[1] However, despite the sheer volume of reader-oriented work, the bewildering multiplicity of guises assumed in it by the reader means that questions about how best to theorise the concept are still being asked and still worth asking. And, as is clear from some of the other contributions to this volume, the issue of how the reader might best take advantage of her/his widely acknowledged importance has lost none of its urgency.

To bring Bakhtin to bear is to risk seeming to rehearse the tired gesture by which the Soviet theorist is burdened with the credit for having, either singlehandedly or with a little help from his friends, always already anticipated and surpassed the most significant theoretical trends of recent decades. But in fact there is no theory of reading or the reader to be plucked ready-formed from the diverse Bakhtinian legacy. Bakhtin does, it is true, make numerous references to readers and their importance. But their systematic cataloguing would be of little value: neither in isolation nor taken together will such references yield worthwhile insights unless they are approached critically from the standpoint of Bakhtin's broader theories of discourse. The purpose of this essay is thus a two-fold and modest one: to pinpoint those aspects of Bakhtin's work which seem most relevant and useful to a reader-oriented project, and to place these aspects alongside and against some of the best known reader-oriented theories, illuminating their aporias and indicating possible new directions.

It is that most frequently exegetised of Bakhtin's texts, 'Discourse in the novel', which provides our starting point. In this elaboration of the concept of dialogism, Bakhtin continually refers, with characteristic terminological largesse, to reader, listener, understander, and varying combinations of the three which suggest that, for the purposes of this particular essay, they are essentially interchangeable. And if the definition of dialogism itself begs numerous questions, the same is even truer of this shady reader. What he is *not* is clear enough – he is opposed to the 'passive listener' assumed, from the standpoint of traditional stylistics, to lie beyond the self-sufficient, 'closed authorial monologue' which is the literary work.[2] His role is one of 'active understanding' enabling the dialogic encounter of historically determinate utterances, each of which not only takes account of what has already been said about its object, but is also always oriented towards and shaped by an anticipated response. Although Bakhtin here describes the process in terms of spoken rather than written language, he does go on to contend that such an orientation towards their reader is characteristic of Tolstoy's works:

> Active understanding . . . , by bringing what is being understood within the new horizon of the understander, establishes a number of complex interrelations, consonances and dissonances with what is being understood, enriches it with new moments. It is precisely this kind of understanding that the speaker takes account of. Therefore his orientation towards the listener is an orientation towards the particular horizon, the particular world of the listener, it introduces completely new moments into his discourse: what takes place here is an interaction of different contexts, different points of view, different horizons, different expressively accented systems, different social 'languages'. The speaker seeks to orient his discourse with its own determining horizon within the alien horizon of the understander and enters into dialogic relations with moments of that horizon. The speaker penetrates the alien horizon of the listener, constructs his utterance on alien territory, against his, the listener's, apperceptive background. (DN, p. 95/282)

The similarities between this and other theoretical readers are striking – the terms 'horizon' and 'apperceptive background', for example, recall the familiar categories of 'horizon of expectations' (Jauss) or 'literary competence' (Culler). Indeed, Allon White has characterised dialogism as 'a kind of reader-oriented self-consciousness' which 'can be compared to the effect created in discourse by the "implicit reader" spoken of by Wolfgang Iser', so that 'Bakhtin thus anticipated much of the current German thinking about reception'.[3] But this evaluation of the possible relationship between Bakhtin and German reception theorists does not lie easily with White's overall emphasis on the sociolinguistic import of Bakhtin's theory. At first sight, Iser's 'implied reader' does have much in common with the Bakhtinian listener: his contribution to the meaning of literary texts is apparently one of 'active understanding' without which textual signification is impossible. Iser informs us that the term 'incorporates both the prestructuring of the potential meaning by the text, and the reader's actualisation of this potential through the reading process'.[4] But this formulation of the implied reader's constitutive powers begins the ineluctable process by which he is made to relinquish them. Even as he encounters and fills the various 'blanks' and 'vacancies' in the text – an activity without which the text cannot possess wholly determinate meanings – Iser's reader must remain constantly mindful of what at one stage is referred to as the 'ultimate meaning' of the text.[5] The traditional dominance of the 'prestructuring of the potential meaning', despite all appearances to the contrary, goes essentially unchallenged, and the text's apparent indeterminacies emerge as just another aspect of its comforting, all-embracing determinacy. The problem is, as Robert Holub has pointed out in his often devastatingly incisive account of German reception theory, that 'Iser wants . . . a way to account for the reader's presence without having to deal with real or empirical readers.'[6] When he says 'the literary text enables its readers to transcend the limitations of their own real-life situation', Iser signals most clearly his profound discomfort with any notion of readership which might actually make a difference, might question the capacity of literature 'from Homer right through to the present day' to exercise its transcendent charm on successive generations of essentially unchanging readers. Hardly surprising, then, that when he does escape his ambivalent existence as both real being and textual function, the implied reader should come to represent 'a transcendental model which makes it possible for the structured effects of literary texts to be described'.[7] Ultimately it is difficult to understand why he should be called a reader at all.

Interestingly, in a piece written in the 1970s, Bakhtin is witheringly dismissive of such an approach:

> Contemporary literary scholars (the majority of them Structuralists) usu-
> ally define a listener who is immanent in the work as an all-understanding,
> ideal listener . . . This, of course, is neither an *empirical* listener nor a
> psychological idea, an image of the listener in the soul of the author. It is an

abstract ideological formulation . . . In this understanding the ideal listener is essentially a mirror image of the author, replicates him. He cannot introduce anything of his own, anything new, into the ideally understood work or into the ideally complete plan of the author. He is in the same time and space as the author or, rather, like the author he is outside time and space (as is any abstract ideal formulation), and therefore he cannot be *another* or other for the author, he cannot have any *surplus* that is determined by his otherness.[8]

It is possible to see the (implied) reader in 'Discourse in the novel' as trapped in this Iserian limbo between supposed activity and actual passivity only if, as is all too often the case, dialogism is uncritically accepted as a description of the immanent characteristics of a certain generically defined type of text (the novel). Bakhtin's opposition of novelistic language to poetic, his account of the history of the novel as the history of a genre, and his descriptions of the features of hybridisation, stylisation, parody, and so forth which mark discourse as novelistic – all may seem strongly to suggest that the dialogic character of language is something inherent in it, something fundamentally intratextual. The reader–listener–understander of 'Discourse in the novel' would thus be reduced to, at best, a metaphor for the productive playing out of stylistic tensions. However, the constant sliding throughout the essay between speaking and writing, listener and reader, although it leads to a certain theoretical fuzziness, actually goes hand in hand with an unremitting emphasis on the dependence of dialogism on a context which is crucially *not* intratextual, but external to the enclosure of the text: 'every word smells of the context or contexts in which it has lived its socially intense life, all words and forms are inhabited by intentions' (DN, p. 106/293). As Ken Hirschkop has written, 'the dependence of textual meaning on social situation is by now an accepted Bakhtinian axiom. But the full import of this relational definition of meaning is often evaded' . . . One of the most enabling insights of radical Bakhtin criticism is the recognition that dialogism and its antonym monologism are not inherent characteristics of particular types of (literary) discourse, that 'meaning lies neither in text nor context but in the relation between them . . . dialogism and monologism are not different kinds of texts, but different kinds of intertextual configuration'.[9] Bakhtin's account of the novel and dialogism, even as it seemingly accepts and bolsters the self-sufficiency of 'literature', insistently gestures to a world outside it; and as the intratextual gives way to the intertextual, it is possible to glimpse a reader no longer threatened by Iserian redundancy. 'Discourse in the novel' ends with a discussion of the 'reaccentuation' of novelistic characters and languages, their acquisition of different resonance and meaning in different contexts. This comes about because

> in the changed dialogue of languages of the age the language of the image begins to sound in a different way, for it is illuminated differently, is perceived against a different dialogising background. . .
>
> There is no gross infringement of the author's will in reaccentuations of this kind. The process can be said to take place *in the image itself*, and not only in the changed conditions of perception. These conditions have only actualised in the image a potential already present in it (at the same time, it is true, weakening others). It can be claimed with some justification that in one respect the image has been better understood and heard than before. In any case, a certain misunderstanding is here combined with a new, deepened understanding. (DN, p. 231/420)

In this passage we see Bakhtin struggling to negotiate the same difficulties which were to defeat Iser in his attempts to theorise the relationship between stable or determinate textual meaning and the variable or indeterminate supplement required to complete it. There is a strong attachment, evinced elsewhere in the essay, to the notion of authorial authority over textual meaning, and a concomitant reluctance to confront the implications for this authority of a fully theorised notion of reception. Hence, perhaps, the striking absence of any mention of a reader, and the predominant use of the passive voice to describe the process and effects of reaccentuation. At the very moment when it would seem most apt to reintroduce it, the notion of 'active understanding' as a constitutive moment of dialogism is nowhere to be seen. Instead we have the familiar Bakhtinian image of the 'dialogising background', with all its disturbing connotations of passivity and secondariness. However, the suggestion that reaccentuations subsequent to the text's production are somehow always already inscribed in the text, for all that it seems to go hand in hand with this apparent move away from the centrality of active understanding, in fact offers, as we shall shortly see, a way of going beyond the somewhat restrictive dichotomy of determinacy and indeterminacy.

The theorist whose work comes most readily to mind in relation to Bakhtin's notion of active understanding is Stanley Fish, scourge of the literary-critical profession and imperious adversary of Wolfgang Iser. Fish tackles the problem with panache, grandly dismissing the opposition of determinacy and indeterminacy, arguing instead that 'determinacy and decidability are always available not, however, because of the constraints imposed by language or the world – that is, by entities independent of context – but because of the constraints built into the context or contexts in which we find ourselves operating.'[10] The most important 'contexts' for Fish are his notorious 'interpretive communities', through which he can seemingly account for just about any eventuality:

> Interpretive communities are made up of those who share interpretive strategies not for reading (in the conventional sense) but for writing texts, for constituting their properties and assigning their intentions. In other words, these strategies exist prior to the act of reading and therefore determine the shape of what is read rather than, as is usually assumed, the other way round. . . [This] explains why there are disagreements and why they can be debated in a principled way: not because of a stability in texts, but because of a stability in the makeup of interpretive communities and therefore in the opposing positions they make possible. Of course this position is always temporary (unlike the longed for and timeless stability of the text). (p. 171).

The interpretive community seems to represent a space in which reading as 'active understanding' can proceed apace, and stand revealed as the only condition of possibility of textual meaning: texts mean anything at all only when they are read, and what they mean depends entirely on the shared values of those reading them. Variations in meaning are accounted for by processes of negotiation and attempts at persuasion carried out by members of interpretive communities with different shared ideas about what the meaning of a given text is. It is possible for one person to persuade another over to his way of thinking because people share enough common ideas about what does and does not make sense to allow decisions to be made about the acceptability or unacceptability of this or that interpretation. (Fish describes in detail how this process works in his final chapter, 'Demonstration vs. persuasion: two models of critical activity'.)

But there is something distinctly fishy about this model of dialogue between reader and text, and reader and reader. Its witty advocacy of communal interpretive strategies and values cannot mask the disabling absence of any convincing explanation of how exactly the interpretive community comes to be constituted. Although he does speak of 'the power of social and institutional circumstances to establish norms of behaviour' (p. 371), Fish's contexts are as a rule 'situational' rather than social or historical. It is enough that interpretive communities can be pointed to as existing: if Fish's logic is followed through, their workings and pervasiveness are such that they can neither not exist nor have ever not existed. Furthermore, the operations of inter-communal persuasion are such as to preclude any meaningful notion of crisis or conflict, or even of the most rudimentary kind of change. Hence the paradox by which, in taking issue with Iser's distinction between determinate and indeterminate textual meaning, Fish is able to argue that Iser is wrong precisely because it is possible for him to be right: 'It is just that the distinction itself is an assumption which, when it informs an act of literary description, will *produce* the phenomena it purports to describe.'[11] William Ray has characterised well just how Fish's reader is for ever doomed to move, like the Vatican, from one state of certainty to the next: 'Fish's reader knows no anguish, can provoke no change in himself. Theoretically capable of persuading others, he can never outflank the beliefs of the institutions that define him; he can trigger no revolutions: the discipline will always have already understood, assimilated, indeed produced, any arguments for its realignment he might generate.'[12] Thus when Fish himself poses the question of what implications his argument has for literary criticism as traditionally practised, he breezily answers 'none whatsoever' (p. 370). Everything must remain the same because, even when there is an apparently radical shift, the new circumstances and their underlying assumptions following from this shift will be based on the same type of consensus as informed the old.

So interpretive communities, despite their apparent promise of providing a framework for understanding the historical and institutional factors in the activity of reading, turn out to be little more than a mirror image of the very ahistorical textual determinacy they are supposed to supersede. But, rather than succumbing to the powerful temptation to dismiss Fish as too clever by half, it is worth returning to Bakhtin for possible ways of giving Fish's model some of the rigour it so perversely eschews. It is not difficult to understand why Bakhtin should have been more reluctant than Fish to abandon notions of textual meaning not wholly dependent on the shared predispositions of readers. If the text has a determining role in the way it is read, this is because the socially and historically inscribed meanings of its constitutive utterances are never forgotten:

> There is neither a first nor a last word and there are no limits to the dialogic context (it extends into the boundless past and the boundless future). Even *past* meanings, that is, meanings born in the dialogue of past ages, can never be stable (finalised, ended once and for all) – they will always change (be renewed) in the process of subsequent, future development of the dialogue. At any moment in the development of the dialogue there are immense, boundless masses of forgotten contextual meanings, but at certain moments of the dialogue's subsequent development along the way they are recalled and invigorated in renewed form (in a new context).[13]

The contrast between Bakhtin and Fish emerges particularly starkly in the light of Fish's rather slippery formulation of the same problem: '[Words] always and only mean one thing, although that one thing is not always the same. The one thing they mean will be a function of the shape language *already has* when we come upon it in a situation, and it is the knowledge that is the content of being in a situation that will have stabilised it' (p. 275). The constitutive tension, the historically conflictual dynamic of discourse insisted on by Bakhtin is reduced by Fish to the stasis of an ill-defined situationality. Bakhtin, it will be recalled, speaks in 'Discourse in the novel' of a process of 'reaccentuation' '*in the image itself*, and not only in the changed conditions of perception'. The later text provides a timely reminder that 'the image itself' is not an originary instance, free from the tensions of dialogism until its insertion into it during reading, but *already* contextual, *already* dialogic. We should not be misled by the word 'itself', so often used in criticism to signal the essential nature of something, stripped of extraneous accretions: for Bakhtin the image can be itself only because, as an utterance, it cannot exist without these 'accretions', without context, which cannot satisfactorily be described as either secondary or primary with regard to the textual 'image'. Thus Bakhtin's position is not, as might appear from the earlier quotation from 'Discourse in the novel', that all possible future meanings are always already inscribed in a text from the very moment of its production, but rather that a text continues to bear the marks of its past historical engagements which, as well as being open to recontextualisation, must also place some limit on the nature and degree of that recontextualisation. Determinate meaning exists to the extent that the production of meaning is contextual, and contexts are not freely interchangeable or, *pace* Fish, wholly encompassed by the historical moment of a given interpretive community. If the activity of reading is based on dialogic relations between reader and text, and text and context, then these are relations which have a past as well as a present. A simple opposition of determinacy and indeterminacy is ultimately inadequate as a means of theorising this immensely complex position.

As for the reader/critic who engages in this activity, for Bakhtin the most important thing is the concrete social and historical milieu in which s/he operates. The alternative to the reader-as-textual-function criticised by the late Bakhtin is to be found in one of the disputed texts of the 1920s. Although it refers specifically to Formalist theories of the nature of sound in poetry, the following passage from Medvedev/ Bakhtin's *The Formal Method* possesses much broader significance for the general problem of readership:

The work is a part of social reality, not of nature. . . The sound cannot be understood within the bounds of the individual organism or of nature.

Therefore, the problem of the signifying sound and its organisation is connected with the problem of the social audience, with the problem of the mutual orientation of the speaker and the listener, and the hierarchical distance between them. The resonance of the signifying sound is different, depending on the character of the social interaction of people, of which the given sound is an element. The social audience is constitutive to the signifying sound and its organisation.[14]

What all this would seem to suggest, then, is that the meaning of a text will change as it is read in new contexts by always historically and socially situated readers who will always bring to it (shared) presuppositions about, among other things, the nature of literature, literary meaning, aesthetic value and so on, and may in turn find these presuppositions being modified in the process of their dialogic encounter with the text. However, it is important never to lose sight of the fact that the character of the text-reader encounter is dialogic: if the meanings of the text are indissociable from the reader's active understanding, then that understanding in its turn must strictly speaking be equally indissociable from the encounter with the text, must be precisely context-specific. In other words, the dialogic act of reading is disruptive of the seemingly fixed positions of text and reader; these positions cannot come through the dialogic encounter unchanged because they do not pre-exist it. Difficult though this may be, it is important not to lapse into what John Frow calls an 'assumption of entities fully constituted prior to the textual process'.[15]

There are further consequential differences in the ways Fish and Bakhtin treat the *effects* of readers' positioning. Fish refers in the subtitle of his major work on the subject to 'the authority of interpretive communities'. The authority of a given community, and that of the interpretations it puts forward, is for Fish something essentially suasive, not coercive. Criticism is 'a matter (endlessly negotiated) of persuasion' in a world where 'political and persuasive means . . . are the same thing' (pp. 17, 16). Authority derives from powers of argument, and is therefore always open to challenge ('negotiation') by superior powers. This is all part and parcel of Fish's closed, crisis-free world of enduring consensus and certainties, and sounds reassuringly polite and gentlemanly. But, as Elizabeth Freund pertinently remarks in the conclusion to her chapter on Fish, 'Fish's position so far has refused to face up to the ways in which the authority of interpretive communities might become grimly coercive. The salutary curb on subjectivity, without a corresponding curb on the authority of consensual norms, remains troubling. The appeal to the imperialism of agreement can chill the spines of readers whose experience of the community is less happily benign than Fish assumes.'[16]

Authority in Bakhtin, by contrast, is something altogether 'less happily benign', has a more recognisable and often more sinister character. Against the dialogical production of meaning within a socially stratified and historically developing language there operate forces of centralisation which seek to restrict the range of intertextual relations, to curtail and constrain the subversive proliferation and dispersal of meaning, to assert the congruence of word and single meaning. As usual in Bakhtin, these forces have several names – monoglossia, monologism, authoritarian or authoritative discourse, the language of poetry and epic. But just as dialogism cannot be reduced to an essence of novelistic language, so monologism cannot be explained away as a property of non-novelistic or 'poetic' texts. Perhaps even more explicitly than for dialogism, Bakhtin insists on the social, historical and political contextuality of monologism: 'the authoritarian word demands our unconditional acknowledgement, and not at all a free mastering and assimilation ... It is indissociably fused with authority – political power, an institution, a personality – and stands or falls together with it. It is impossible to divide it, to agree with one thing, accept another, but not entirely, and to reject totally a third' (DN, p. 156/343). However unelaborated Bakhtin's evocation of authority, it profoundly unsettles any idea that Fish's endlessly negotiated persuasion is always and everywhere the order of the day.[17] Bakhtin's work demonstrates an acute understanding of just how naively idealistic it would be to assume that in any dialogue, literary-critical or otherwise, all contributions carry equal weight. Some voices are louder than others, even if they are not the ones articulating the most elegantly convincing arguments. That Bakhtin should have been so aware of the possible true meanings of discursive authority is hardly surprising. 'Discourse in the novel' was written in 1934, the year in which Socialist Realism was declared the officially sanctioned 'method' for Soviet literature and art in general; the monologic, restrictive understanding of the term as a simple synonym for 'Party-mindedness' was not long in following.[18] This was symptomatic of a more generalised process whereby the Stalinist state gathered to itself the right of first and last word on all matters of import. In the cultural sphere this meant not only an insistence on 'portrayal of reality in its revolutionary development', a goal whose posts were constantly changed to accompanying declarations of its immutability. It also set in train a project (one which continued well beyond the Stalin years) of establishing, often with peculiarly unsubtle authority, definitively monologic intertextual relations between past and present cultural artefacts and the context allotted to them. Thus Socialist Realism acquired precursors in the literature of the 1920s and earlier; Soviet literature in general became the organic continuation of the enduring literary 'heritage' of the nineteenth century, thanks in particular to the mediating and transitional role of key writers such as Gorky; Soviet culture, although 'multinational' to the extent that it contained elements of the cultures of all the constituent nations of the Soviet Union, was at the same time to be a unified whole; and the notion of 'popular' or 'mass culture' was to acquire an unremittingly negative resonance. The cost of the imposition of this rigid set of relations by a state for which politics was so often more than a matter of mere persuasion was, as is well enough known, a high one in terms of lives and of squandered cultural opportunities. What happened to culture in general and literature in particular under Stalin and afterwards is a grim and stark illustration of what critical authority can mean; there are many now silent witnesses of the consequences of trying to draw the monologic voice of the Stalinist state into dialogic interchange.

No doubt many would argue that this is all a grotesque anomaly, that the role of politics and ideology in matters literary and cultural in the West is negligible by comparison, that Stanley Fish is by no means wrong to associate authority in the production of stable, determinate textual meaning with the free give and take of mutual persuasion in a mercifully pluralist academy rather than with the brutal ukases of state centralism. But of course the conflation of the absence of 'Stalinist' politics with the absence of politics in general is in itself a profoundly political gesture which cannot conceal the discernible similarities between, for example, Soviet and Western notions of tradition and national cultural heritage and their importance to the practices of criticism: as well as on coercion, Stalinist politics relied on notions of tradition, 'Russianness' and so on whose appeal was enormously powerful, not to say persuasive. And arguments about the politics of literature and culture are by no means unknown even within our own more homely institutions. What is important at this point is that when Bakhtin is introduced into the specific area of reader-oriented theory, this brings us ineluctably to acknowledge those questions of politics and ideology which are bracketed out, consciously or otherwise, by theorists such as Iser and Fish. Iser's notion of readerly activity is never allowed to develop enough for its accompanying politics to be examined. Fish, for all that he recognises the political undisinterestedness of the activities of his interpretive communities, defines that quality within unacceptably narrow confines; the authority of his arguments rests upon a principled refusal to inquire what, outside the walls of the academy, might underpin them.[19]

An approach to the reader through Bakhtin thus leads irresistibly beyond the confines of a putative self-contained encounter between an individual person and an individual text – from the 'microcosm of response' to the 'macrocosm of reception', to borrow the terms of Robert Holub's contrast between the two doyens of German reception theory, Iser and Hans Robert Jauss (p. 83). Indeed, from a Bakhtinian viewpoint, Jauss's project of re-theorising literary history, discredited in Germany, in order to realise what he saw as its potential as a 'challenge to literary theory', seems the most promising of the most frequently anthologised reading theories of recent years. Jauss took as his starting point the idea that 'literature and art only obtain a history that has the character of a process when the succession of works is mediated not only through the producing subject but also through the consuming subject – through the interaction of author and public'.[20] His principal means of achieving this integration of aesthetic reception and history was to be his 'horizon of expectations'; but, just as Iser's implied reader was to prove disablingly nebulous, so Jauss's key concept fell prey to a debilitating lack of rigour. Robert Holub conveys well just how difficult it is to pin down: 'The trouble with Jauss's use of the term "horizon" is that it is so vaguely defined . . . "Horizon of expectations" would appear to refer to an intersubjective system or structure of expectations, a "system of references" or a mind-set that a hypothetical individual might bring to any text' (p. 59). Holub here suggests that the horizon of expectations is a property of a text's reader or readers, in line with Jauss's assertion that 'The coherence of literature as an event is primarily mediated in the horizon of expectations of the literary experience of contemporary and later readers, critics, and authors' (p. 22). However, at other times the horizon of expectations is referred to as a property of the text: 'the horizon of expectations of a work allows one to determine its artistic character by the kind and the degree of its influence on a presupposed audience' (p. 25). This ties in with what Jauss promisingly calls the 'dialogical character of the literary work' (p. 21) – a formulation emphasising an apparent similarity with the Bakhtinian approach to reception and its refusal to privilege either text or context. This double-edged conception of the horizon of expectations might actually be very productive, but its potential remains sadly unrealised. Jauss's orientation towards the extra-textual is short-lived as, in seeking to find a way of 'objectifying' the horizon of expectations for a given work, he looks for evidence in the first place to the very text whose reception he intends it to account for. This is an inevitable consequence of his strict hierarchisation of the horizons of expectation: 'the meaning of a work is always constituted anew, is a result of a coincidence of two factors: the horizon of expectations (or *primary code*) implied by the work and the horizon of experience (or *secondary code*) supplied by the receiver.' In thus reinstituting a traditional primacy of the text, Jauss puts himself in a position where he is unable to follow through the full implications of his notion of the dialogic character of texts. His description of the encounter of text and reader as 'a game of questions and answers', in which the text has most of the questions *and* the answers, is redolent of a notion of dialo*gue* stripped of the complexity and dynamic tension which make Bakhtinian dialog*ism* so productive and valuable – a dialogue between two pre-existent, stable entities.[21] So, although he says that 'the interpreter must bring his own experience into play, since the past horizon of old and new forms, problems and solutions, is only recognizable in its further mediation, within the present horizon of the received work' (p. 34), Jauss effectively disqualifies the 'experience' of the 'interpreter' as soon as he has recognised it and takes refuge in the very enclosure of purely literary history he set out to rupture. His characterisation of 'literary' texts takes on an inevitably familiar resonance: 'Literary works differ from purely historical documents precisely because they do more than simply document a particular time, and remain "speaking" to the extent that they attempt to solve problems of form or content, and so extend far beyond the silent relics of the past.'[22] Jauss fails to carry through the challenge, which he began by calling for, to the notion of literature as an autonomous entity independent and transcendent of history. Although he makes great play of 'that properly *socially formative* function that belongs to literature' (p. 45), he all too quickly loses sight of the fact that the concept of literature is also socially *formed*, that its social and historical reception is, as Bakhtin points out, one of its key constitutive moments.[23]

Thus, brought to bear on some of the best known reader-oriented theories, Bakhtin insistently requires the restoration of an often excluded history, and focuses attention on 'the relations of discourse and power' which Jane Tompkins, at the conclusion of her survey of reading as a historically specific activity, identifies as the proper concern of criticism.[24] The question immediately begged by this, however, is whether there is anything peculiarly Bakhtinian about such an emphasis, which can be said to subtend many of the best known 'alternative' critical projects of recent years. Within the narrower field of reading theory, a good deal of work has been done on 'institutional' factors, understood as more than just those at work within the literary-critical academy – factors such as the mechanisms and institutions of publication and distribution of books, including those producing and policing the division between 'high' and 'popular' literature, or the potential of feminism to transform entrenched notions of reception.[25] These are precisely the kind of factors to which, as we have already seen, Bakhtin more often than not refers only in passing, or whose relevance to his model of discourse he leaves largely implicit. Nevertheless, this does not automatically diminish Bakhtin's potential contribution to such approaches – a point confirmed if we look briefly at the place occupied by Bakhtin, whether explicitly or implicitly, in the work on questions of reception and reading done in recent years by Tony Bennett.

In *Formalism and Marxism* Bennett addresses the Jaussian theme of literary history, in particular the Russian Formalist model to which the German theorist is extensively and openly indebted. He focuses on the critique, in *The Formal Method*, of the Formalists' notion of a fundamentally closed literary system whose dynamic is independent of history in the broader sense, and elaborates on this by showing how the Rabelais book reveals the dependence of a text's 'literary' qualities on 'the different political and ideological conjunctures which the text enters into during the course of its historical existence'.[26] He thus arrives, through Bakhtin, at precisely the kind of formulation of the problem to which Jauss comes tantalisingly close before infuriatingly shying away from its full implications. Bennett's subsequent work on 'reading formations' represents an attempt to examine these questions of reception more closely, to specify more precisely the conditions under which texts enter such conjunctures; a reading formation ('a set of intersecting discourses which productively activate a given body of texts and the relations between them in a specific way') might well be described as an 'interpretive community' understood in proper relation to institutional and political factors not exhausted by the narrowly academic parameters to which Stanley Fish confines himself. It is striking that, although he refers at one point to Voloshinov's *Marxism and the Philosophy of Language*, Bennett makes no explicit mention of Bakhtin in his discussion of the relationship between texts and reading formations. Had he done so he might have avoided the lapse into a Fish-like nihilism which leads him, in quite properly questioning the auratic status of 'the text itself', to state bluntly that the text 'has no meanings which can be traduced'.[27] On the other hand, elsewhere Bennett, again without explicit reference to Bakhtin, defines the reading formation squarely in the spirit of the dialogic understanding of text-context relations: 'The concept of reading formation . . . is an attempt to think context as a set of discursive and intertextual determinations, operating on material and institutional supports, which bear in upon a text not just externally, from the outside in, but internally, shaping it – in the historically concrete forms in which it is available as a text-to-be-read – from the inside out.'[28] The difficulty of maintaining this purchase on the dialogic relation of text and context which Bakhtin so insistently requires is at no point underestimated by Bennett – hence, perhaps, the extensive refining of the concept of reading formations and the understandable scarcity of examples illustrating how they can be seen to operate. Hence, too, his refreshingly frank admission in the earlier article that he is not really very sure of what the practical consequences of his rethinking of text-context relations might be.[29]

And indeed, it is far from easy to know exactly where or how to begin to use a Bakhtinian theory of reading. More precisely, to return to the title of this chapter, it is perhaps not immediately obvious what a theorist as complex, contradictory or just plain difficult as Bakhtin can do for a 'reader' – a reader such as a student in a 'literature' (or perhaps 'cultural studies') course where there *is* a text in the class, a reader with a more or less vague sense of his/her own empirical pre-constitutedness, and a probably greater sense of the reality of a 'text-to-be-read' which stubbornly resists immediate interrogation of its ontological status. My contention (largely untried, and so tentative and speculative) would be that in such a situation the most immediately useful aspect of Bakhtin is precisely that close attention to the features of texts which has so often led to his being used in a markedly conservative way. Bakhtinian textual analysis, if predicated on a proper, thorough understanding of dialogism and the utterance, offers possibilities of working 'from the inside out' in such a way that the very difficulties of 'active understanding' can become a means of making explicit the conditions of possibility of that understanding and of past understandings of the text – that is, of grasping the untenability, celebrated time and again by Bakhtin, of a too stark opposition of 'inside' and 'outside', 'text' and 'context' so often initially challenged but ultimately reinstated by other theorists of reading.

106   David Shepherd

Notes

1 Elizabeth Freund, *The Return of the Reader: Reader-Response Criticism*, London and New York, 1987, p. 42.

2 Mikhail Bakhtin, 'Slovo v romane', in *Voprosy literatury i estetiki*, Moscow, 1975, p. 87; English translation in Bakhtin, 'Discourse in the novel', in *The Dialogic Imagination*, ed. Michael Holquist, trans. Caryl Emerson and Michael Holquist, Austin, 1981, p. 274. Since I find the Emerson and Holquist version of the passages from 'Discourse in the novel' cited in this essay somewhat wordy and imprecise, I have used my own, very substantially different, translations; subsequent references are given in the text as DN, followed firstly by the page number for the original Russian, then by that for the Emerson/Holquist translation.

3 Allon White, 'Bakhtin, sociolinguistics and deconstruction', in Frank Gloversmith, ed., *The Theory of Reading*, Brighton and Totowa, N.J., 1984, pp. 128, 129.

4 Wolfgang Iser, *The Implied Reader: Patterns of Communication in Prose Fiction from Bunyan to Beckett*, Baltimore and London, 1974, p. xii.

5 Iser, *The Act of Reading: A Theory of Aesthetic Response*, Baltimore and London, 1978, p. 98.

6 Robert Holub, *Reception Theory: A Critical Introduction*, London and New York, 1984, p. 84; subsequent page references are given in the text.

7 Iser, *The Act*, pp. 79, 227, 38.

8 Bakhtin, 'Toward a methodology for the human sciences', in *Speech Genres and Other Late Essays*, ed. Caryl Emerson and Michael Holquist, trans. Vern W. McGee, p. 165 (translation slightly modified).

9 Ken Hirschkop, 'The domestication of M. M. Bakhtin', *Essays in Poetics*, XI: 1, 1986, p. 80, 81. There is no room here to go into the full significance of this formulation. The potential it confers upon Bakhtin's texts as tools of cultural, as opposed to merely literary analysis, is explored in Hirschkop's 'Bakhtin, discourse and democracy', *New Left Review*, 160, 1986, pp. 92-113.

10 Stanley Fish, *Is There a Text in This Class? The Authority of Interpretive Communities*, Cambridge, Mass. and London, 1980, p. 268; subsequent page references given in the text for quotations from Fish are to this work.

11 Fish, 'Why no one's afraid of Wolfgang Iser', *Diacritics*, XI: 1, 1981, p.7, quoted in Holub, *Reception Theory*, p. 103. Holub gives a good critical account of the Fish-Iser debate (pp. 101-6); see also Freund, *The Return*, pp. 148-51.

12 William Ray, *Literary Meaning: From Phenomenology to Deconstruction*, Oxford, 1984, p. 169.

13 Bakhtin, 'Toward a methodology', p. 170.

14 P.N. Medvedev, *The Formal Method in Literary Scholarship: A Critical Introduction to Sociological Poetics*, trans. Albert J. Wehrle, Baltimore and London, 1978, p. 102 (translation modified).

15 John Frow, *Marxism and Literary History*, Oxford, 1986, p. 183.

16 Freund, *The Return*, pp. 110-11.

17 On the frequent paucity in Bakhtin of detailed discussion of institutional factors, and the difficulties this can cause, see Frow, *Marxism*, pp. 98-9, and Hirschkop, 'Dialogism as a challenge to literary criticism', in Catriona Kelly, Michael Makin and David Shepherd, eds., *Discontinuous Discourses in Modern Russian Literature*, London and New York, 1989, pp. 27-35.

18 The simplistic but widespread idea that Socialist Realism was from the very beginning imposed by force on a community of writers and artists almost universally hostile to it has been cogently challenged in a recent important study: Régine Robin's refreshingly subtle and discriminating *Le réalisme socialiste: une esthétique impossible*, Paris, 1986, offers a closely argued account of the complex beginnings and troubled development of the concept.

19 Richard Wortman presents a devastating analysis of Fish's failure to escape from

'a literary world, separate from society, that is an invention of the literary mind' in his attempt to account for changes in the accepted reading of Books XI and XII of *Paradise Lost*: see Fish, 'Transmuting the lump: *Paradise Lost*, 1942-1982', and Wortman, 'Epilogue: history and literature', in Gary Saul Morson, ed., *Literature and History: Theoretical Problems and Russian Case Studies*, Stanford, 1986, pp. 33-56 and 275-93 (p. 286).

20 Hans Robert Jauss, 'Literary history as a challenge to literary theory', in *Toward an Aesthetic of Reception*, trans. Timothy Bahti, Brighton, 1982, p. 15; subsequent page references given in the text for quotations from Jauss are to this article.

21 Jauss, 'Esthétique de la réception et communication littéraire',in Zoran Konstanti-nović, Manfred Naumann and Hans Robert Jauss, eds., *Literary Communication and Reception: (Proceedings of the IXth Congress of the International Comparative Literature Association)*, Innsbruck, 1980, pp. 15 (my italics), 16. The possible significance of Bakhtin's work for an aesthetic of reception was not lost on Jauss: see Andrei Corbea, 'L'esthétique de la réception comme théorie du dialogue', *Cahiers roumains d'études littéraires*, 3, 1986, pp. 21-30. Corbea's account of Jauss's description of aesthetic pleasure in terms of alterity and self-Other dialogue (pp. 25-6) suggests that Jauss's un-Bakhtinian understanding of dialogue may result in part from a failure to distinguish sufficiently between the position taken by Bakhtin in 'Author and hero in aesthetic activity' and that taken in 'Discourse in the novel' (on the differences between these positions, see Ann Jefferson's contribution to this volume, pp.162-4).

22 Jauss, 'History of art and pragmatic history', in *Toward an Aesthetic*, p. 69.

23 On Jauss's failure to break out of the enclosure of literary history, see also Holub, *Reception Theory*, pp. 53-82; Manon Brunet, 'Pour une esthétique de la production de la réception', *Études françaises*, XIX:3, 1983, pp. 65-82; and Rita Schober, 'Réception et historicité de la littérature', *Revue des sciences humaines*, LX: 189, 1983, pp. 7-20.

24 Jane P. Tompkins, 'The reader in history: the changing shape of literary response', in Tompkins, ed., *Reader-Response Criticism: From Formalism to Post-Structuralism*, Baltimore and London, 1980, p. 226.

25 For details of the kind of sociological approach called for by the East German Manfred Naumann (see his 'Remarques sur la réception littéraire en tant qu'événement historique et social', in Konstantinović, Naumann and Jauss, eds., *Literary Communication and Reception*, pp. 27-33) and attempted in the GDR, see Holub, *Reception Theory*, pp. 128-46. Peter Humm *et al.*, eds., *Popular Fictions: Essays in Literature and History*, London and New York, 1986, addresses the division between 'high' and 'popular', and contains several contributions which deal with the institutional factors affecting the reception of texts: see especially Graham Holderness, 'Agincourt 1944: readings in the Shakespeare myth', pp. 173-95, and Paul O'Flinn, 'Production and reproduction: the case of *Frankenstein*', pp. 196-221. Finally, a wide range of approaches to questions of reception from the standpoint of gender is to be found in Elizabeth A. Flynn and Patrocinio P. Schweikart, eds., *Gender and Reading: Essays on Readers, Texts, and Contexts*, Baltimore and London, 1986 (Schweikart's contribution, 'Reading ourselves: toward a feminist theory of reading', pp. 31-62, raises a number of important issues, including the need to overcome the common tendency to over-privilege one of text or context at the expense of the other).

26 Tony Bennett, *Formalism and Marxism*, London and New York, 1979, p. 92. It is perhaps worth noting here that Bakhtin's own versions of literary history are characteristically non-uniform, and emphasise the fruitlessness of any attempt to view Bakhtin's work in terms of over-arching coherence: as often, for Bakhtin to be of use here it is necessary to turn certain aspects of his thinking against others. Thus, as Joan DeJean has pointed out, whereas the Rabelais book denies literary history its traditional autonomy, the study of Dostoevsky seems to do the opposite

and validate a more 'purely literary history' ('Bakhtin and/in history', in Benjamin A. Stolz, Lubomir Doležel and I. R. Titunik, eds., *Language and Literary Theory,* Ann Arbor, 1984, p. 235). And elsewhere Bakhtin speaks of the qualitatively different, transcendent 'great time' ('bol'shoe vremya') inhabited by valuable cultural products – most notably, and perhaps most disarmingly, at the end of the passage quoted above (p. 97) about the limitlessness of dialogic context; see also his 'Response to a question from the *Novy Mir* editorial staff', in *Speech Genres,* pp. 1-7.

27 Bennett, 'Texts, readers, reading formations', *Literature and History,* XI, 1983, pp. 216, 224.

28 Bennett, 'Texts in history: the determinations of readings and their texts', in Derek Attridge, Geoff Bennington and Robert Young, eds., *Post-Structuralism and the Question of History,* Cambridge &c., 1987, p. 72. There is a more explicit indebtedness to Bakhtin in John Frow's elaboration of a politics of reading which is in many ways close to that of Bennett: see the final chapter of *Marxism and Literary History.*

29 See Bennett, 'Texts, readers', p. 223.

Nancy Glazener

Dialogic subversion: Bakhtin, the novel and Gertrude Stein

Feminists have readily enlisted Bakhtin's writings for the project of replacing the patriarchal account of individualistic literary creation with a politicised account of the social production of literature. Bakhtin's own work is not markedly feminist: he wrote mainly about canonical male authors, flirted with *auteur* theories of literary creation, and was conspicuously silent about feminism and the social effects of gender difference.[1] Nevertheless, his combination of linguistic theory, narratology and cultural analysis meshes appealingly with materialist and post-structuralist currents in contemporary literary studies, and it appears to be hospitable to the inclusion of gender as an additional, significant social and discursive category. Bakhtin derives the heteroglossia of literary discourses – their multiplicity and their tendentious interaction – ultimately from the stratification of social life, in which different social groups create distinctive discourses from their common language; as a result, the meaning of a word is always a function of its torque, of its being turned to incommensurate purposes by speakers who use it in different discourses. Likewise, these discourses, products of discrete but inextricable social formations, depend so much on their interrelationship for their intelligibility that they are ultimately significant only in relation to the entire complex of language use. Discourses cannot be tailored semantically to the expressive intentions of an individual without betraying the social fabric from which they have been cut.

Thus, from a feminist point of view, Bakhtin's project has at least two major attractions. First, his assertion that literature represents a struggle among socio-ideological languages unsettles the patriarchal myth that there could be a language of truth transcending relations of power and desire. Second, Bakhtin's insistence that words and discourses have socially differential significance implies that linguistic and literary forms are necessarily shaped by the gender relations that structure society. In Bakhtin's conception of the utterance, language always registers not only the subjectivities of its speaker and its intended addressee but also the historical traces of the repeated and varying appropriations of words by individuals who are socially constituted. The concept of the subjectively-defined utterance en-sures that for as long as gender has a share in the social constitution of subjectivity, part of every utterance's social intelligibility will derive from its orientation toward gender.

Fiction transforms social discourses in the course of representing them, so that they do not transparently reflect their social origins but are (at least) doubly ideologised. If one extrapolates from Bakhtin's theories, gender might be imagined to enter fictional texts in several ways: as an object of represented discourse (through discussions of maleness and femaleness, either in the abstract or as embodied in characters); as an actual or imaged subjectivity that inflects discourse (due to the genders of author, characters, and audience); or as a structuring discursive absence in the text. In any of these cases, the problematic of gender inhabits the texts with a polemical force that might be superficially downplayed or denied, but that has the poten-tial to be elaborated. 'Every age re-accentuates in its own way the works of its most immediate past', Bakhtin writes, thereby opening the way for feminists to sift the novels of patriarchy for evidence of the effects that women's oppression, suppression, exclusion, co-option and – more optimistically – successful cultural activity have had on literary production.[2]

In light of Bakhtin's convergence, at this general level, with feminist analysis, I would like to examine more carefully two of his theories that have been most eagerly adopted by feminists. I hope to convey that Bakhtin's interrelated ideas about the subversiveness of the dialogic novel and its carnivalesque origins, though valuable and provocative, cannot be appropriated for feminism without revision and re-contex-tualisation. Bakhtin's concept of the carnivalesque function of the novel closely resembles some feminist conceptions of the feminine as an anarchic, somehow inherently subversive force. I hope in the first half of my essay to consider the extent to which such a purely symbolic subversive force can be credited with effectively disrupting the official categories that confer and contain meaning, and to propose a way of mediating between what I will designate the essentialist and reflexive conceptions of such disruptive forces. I will also suggest that only a more complicated understanding of the revisions and accommodations that accompany any apparent subversion can enable relatively disempowered groups like women to appraise their political successes and defeats accurately.

Although, in Bakhtin's theories, no one controls language and meaning securely – since all are continually being reconstituted and resisted by the only media through which they can produce meaning – feminists assert that some subjects, including women, are more distorted and constrained than others by the languages available to them. To investigate the compatibility between Bakhtin's ideas about language and literature and some of the concerns of twentieth-century feminism, I will use some of Bakhtin's own methods of discursive analysis in the second half of this essay to examine Gertrude Stein's subversion of classic realism. Stein's version of realism reveals the particular estrangements from language and divisions of subjectivity suffered by women in a specific historical and ideological milieu, and it implies an understanding of the ideological status of novelistic discourses different from – and illuminating for – Bakhtin's.

Underlying both sections of this essay is my proposal that the concept of the anarchically disruptive, diffusely subversive Other, which parts of Bakhtin's work and certain strains of feminist theory have endorsed, is more mystifying than enlightening, and that it tends to overshadow the analysis of particular strategies for ideological contention and subversion. Strategies like Stein's, though meaningful and effective, are historically delimited, inextricable from their circumstances of production, and calculated rather than anarchic. Indeed, the historicist methods provided by Bakhtin himself in other parts of his theory and by other kinds of feminist analysis can lead to the discovery of these strategies. Subversion never accomplishes a clean break or an unambiguous negation, and cultural analysts, feminist and other, ought to avoid oversimplifying the process and effects of subversion without giving up substantive political critique.

Dialogic ideologies in the novel

Bakhtin defines the novel as an intermingling of discourses, unified by the author's significant orchestration but none the less preserving their ideological discreteness. The novel typically foregrounds the social differentiation of these discourses by embodying them in characters who occupy distinct social worlds; it stages their interaction through the confrontations of characters, and usually it sets them against a narrator's diverse and socially significant modes of description, explanation, and judgement as well.[3] Furthermore, these incommensurate discourses are not only represented, they are themselves the means for representing the world of the novel. Between the poles of complete objectification (a language portrayed as a dead thing, worthy of satire but in no way productive) and reverential transmission (the mode by which authoritative discourses are conveyed), novelistic discourses are dialogic, speaking to each other and to the author (conceived of as an intentional position, not an expressive subjectivity).[4]

In so far as Bakhtin historicises the novel and assigns a comparative value to it, however, the concept becomes unstable. Bakhtin sometimes describes the novel as a genre distinct from the epic, the drama, or poetry, emphasising the power of novels to open into ongoing history (in contrast with the bounded world of epic) and to subvert official or high discourses by relativising them (in contrast with the monoglossia he ascribes to drama and poetry). But at other times he suggests that only one kind of novel conforms to this definition – the heteroglossic, dialogic novel, exemplified by Dostoevsky – whereas other texts that he also identifies as novels are more monologic and epical, and not at all subversive. Bakhtin's conception of the novel uneasily promotes several claims: the roots of the novel in ancient serio-comic genres and in the carnivalesque modes of popular discourse in the Renaissance; the novel's early (pre-nineteenth-century) association with low genres (DN, p. 379); the novel's formal capacity to represent heteroglossia; and the potential within the novel form for differing degrees of ideological conformity or enforcement.

To some extent, these claims can be organised around two issues. The first concerns the historical intelligibility of the novel's subversiveness: Bakhtin tries to endow the novel with a subversive potential derived from its inscription, through its ancestry, with (lower-)class identity and class resistance.[5] The second concerns the somewhat dehistoricised formal capacity of the modern novel to relativise the official discourses of its own day (even though some novels, Bakhtin concedes, reinforce them). The novel would therefore seem to be subversive partly because of a value or complex of values that it represents and partly because of its capacity to bracket as discourses and thereby undermine whatever values the official (presumably oppressive) regime espouses. The novel's historical associations seem to become part of its identity or being in the first version, whereas in the second version the novel serves as Other to dominant discourses, as a threatening projection of the lacunae in their own identities. Therefore, these two dimensions might be formulated as the essentialist and the reflexive understandings of the novel, respectively.[6]

Julia Kristeva insists that the carnivalesque relativising Bakhtin promotes is always the transgression of a law on behalf of '*another law*'; otherwise, it would be irresponsible and irrelevant linguistic play.[7] And Bakhtin himself, in emphasising the addressivity of the word (its orientation toward its speaker and its audience), would also seem to imply that any subversion takes place along a specific vector, on behalf of a specific speaking position. Yet his main accounts of the novel in 'Discourse in the novel' and *Problems of Dostoevsky's Poetics* tend to obscure this implication. His study of Rabelais (one of the novel's important predecessors) is, however, explicit about the value that Rabelais's central representational mode, the carnivalesque, promotes: it is the body, considered as a slighted partner in meaning.

Carnival subversion, as Bakhtin describes it in *Rabelais and his World*, is directed against an official language that would deny the body, the cyclical nature of human life, and the triumph of the species over the death of the individual. Bakhtin holds the carnivalesque to be an antidote not only to a particular dominant meaning but also, more profoundly, to a particular *form* of meaning: the abstracted, disembodied concept of meaning that the Platonic philosophical tradition has favoured. Carnival laughter is not an abstract negation, a bracketing 'not-x'. It undermines official language in the Renaissance by mocking it, em-bawdying it, and re-connecting it to the life cycle: 'Negation in popular-festival imagery has never an abstract logical character. It is always something obvious, tangible. That which stands behind negation is by no means nothingness but the "other side" of that which is denied, the carnivalesque upside down.'[8]

Carnival laughter challenges traditional concepts of logic and identity. It is ambivalent in that it affirms and denies at once, diminishing the individual but re-ennobling him or her through the medium of the collectivity; it expresses 'the point of view of the whole' on the whole, not private ridicule (p. 416). In addition to its oral genres, which are characterised by hyperbolic praise and abuse, its principal manifestation is the masquerade, in which masks destabilise identities in general and masked surrogates for high figures are ritually degraded and deprived of their official identities. Bakhtin proposes that these sexual or scatological humiliations defy officialdom's pretences to personal power and reassert the power of the metaphorical body of the people, the life cycle that transcends the individual.

The subversion of essentialising, abstract, unitary meaning on behalf of the body holds obvious attractions for feminism, which may be said to have taken the part of the body in several ways. Feminists have asserted the body's role in meaning (in shaping the voice, in providing the spatial modelling for the conceptualisation of the world, in the materiality of the sign). They have also called attention to the ways in which women play the part of the body for male subjectivity, being identified not only with both eerie and celebratory conceptions of reproduction but also with the threatening potential for the body to become a corpse and silence the mind. And they have investigated the reduction of the body to part-objects: to the objectified female erogenous zones, and to the having or not-having of a penis (misconstrued as the Phallus, a signifier of privilege, rather than as a mere bodily organ among others) which becomes symbolically overwritten as gender identity.[9] In the course of creating an abstracted, primarily mental version of subjectivity, Western culture has projected many aspects of the body on to its margins: not only on to women, but also on to the lower classes (Bakhtin's popular culture of pre-capitalism, the proletariat of capitalism) and on to outsiders it deems exotic and Other.[10] Women, like these other groups, have an interest in integrating the body's semantic and organic aspects in order to free themselves from *embodying* the body, symbolically, for their culture(s).

But the myth Bakhtin derives from Rabelais of a larger-than-life folk body, the emblem of material-based class consciousness for the people, raises more problems than it solves for feminists. Even aside from the fact that the 'symbolic, broad meaning' (p. 301) of the carnivalesque body cannot be unmarked by gender – so that women's participation in this myth, historically and figuratively, is problematised[11] – Bakhtin's concept of the carnivalesque folk-body harks back to a golden age in which 'the people' were clearly separate from official culture and therefore capable of making their critique from a conceptually pure 'outside'. Not only could there be no analogous myth of an outside for women, materialist understandings of culture preclude the possibility of any class stratification that is not maintained by the interrelations of classes. Although Bakhtin elsewhere suggests that true understanding from outside (exotopy, *vnenakhodimost'*) must be preceded by a moment of identification, and although he recognises that Rabelais himself participated in both high and low culture, he seems at moments to espouse an ideologically mystified, nostalgic, and historically suspect conception of the lower classes as a monolithically subversive force. At best, his account may be considered to elide the political, economic, and ideological interrelation of the 'high' and the 'low' and the historical proofs of the marketplace genres' subversiveness for heuristic purposes.[12]

But apart from Bakhtin's claims about its social origins, the concept of the carnivalesque provides a useful gloss not only on the semantics of the body in Rabelais's text but also on subsequent shifts in the semantic range of the represented body. As Bakhtin describes it, the modern individual body comprehends both the sublimated (sentimentalised, abstracted) and the degraded (shameful, inert) conceptions of the body in privatised forms. The degraded conception of the body, however, no longer possesses the capacity to enrich the abstracted one because it has been privatised: whereas shit metaphorically attributed to the collective body of the people could symbolise the life cycle and the fertility of decay, personal shit is merely the detritus of individuals whose lives are separate and ephemeral (pp. 301-2). But even though most social forms of carnival have betrayed their popular origins by being (like the body) institutionalised or privatised, some literary traces of carnival forms survive in their true ambivalence: the 'genres of reduced laughter – humor, irony, sarcasm' (p.120); the literary types of the rogue, the clown and the fool, who unsettle identities by parodying them; and the novel's tendency – derived from carnivalesque ridicule – to interanimate and relativise discourses. In each of these cases, the carnivalesque that Bakhtin originally imagined to exist outside official discourses persists only in the form of an 'in between', an interstitial and relativising relationship to other meanings and identities.

Bakhtin's critique of the artificial opposition between meaning and the body that obtains in modernity by no means implies that this binary can be restored, through combination or synthesis, to some semblance of an original totality.[13] The sundering into body and meaning does not divide a whole into halves that may be reconnected, any more than the sublimated and degraded versions of the body could be joined to produce an undistorted whole. In this respect, Bakhtin's attempt to subvert the categories of meaning and identity greatly resembles the project of deconstruction, which de-naturalises binary oppositions by showing that their terms do not cohere. Deconstruction exposes the ways in which binary terms develop in response to each other and in response to the very category of meaning itself; it suggests that the stable definitions abstracted from words, and submitted to logical analysis, are in fact misleading generalisations that occlude the textual and semantic specificity of the differing usages of a word. Bakhtin's emphasis on the primacy of the utterance

– the discursively, historically, and subjectively specific use of language – leads to a similar conclusion about the fraudulence of abstracted definitional categories. Yet an advantage of Bakhtin's approach over deconstruction lies in its greater emphasis on the (socio-)historical and subjective, or intentional, constitution of language.[14] At this juncture, where the social practices of individuals are transmitting and refracting discursive traditions, ideology can be grasped not as a seamless system but as a dynamic and temporal interrelation of utterances.

Because of its emphasis on the intersubjectivity of the utterance, Bakhtin's work reminds us that any attempt at purely semantic subversion addresses itself to another utterance: a particular deployment of a category of meaning that is itself in the process of historical becoming. The logical negation or linguistic transgression of a conceptual category may or may not affect the disposition of power that it justifies or conceals within specific utterances; however, such an assault may probe the digestive power and resilience of the dominant ideologies. In this light, carnivalesque literary form (the grotesque rejoining of separated and transformed categories) and content (the semantic elaboration of biology) can be understood as inextricable and vital protests against the specious separation of form from content, body from meaning – though not as literary encodings of an effective political protest. But even though the carnivalesque's literary and semantic subversion may have exerted a transformative ideological pressure on the dominant discourses it opposed, some of its effects seem to have escaped its original purpose. It was anti-individualist, to the extent that individualism imposes an abstracted and alienating concept of insular personhood. But it also drew upon the concept of organicism – aligning itself with humanism – as an alternative to the abstraction and repression promoted by officialdom, and organicism was subsequently institutionalised under less liberating auspices.

For by the time of Dostoevsky, authoritarian asceticism had given way to an organic version of liberal individualism within dominant political, scientific and literary discourses. The body had by no means been re-integrated with meaning , but a fascination with the body as a site of interchange between the individual and the environment had set in.[15] The new dominant ideology figured the individual as an organic whole whose transactions with the environment were *free*, in at least three senses: intentional, unfettered by significant collective obligations, and without subjective impact or 'cost' for the individual. As a result of this ideological transformation, the embodiment of

Dostoevsky's characters mainly signifies their individuation, not their corporeal existence; Bakhtin does not emphasise the subversiveness of folk-tradition and bawdy laughter in discussing the novels of Dostoevsky. Instead, he locates Dostoevsky's importance in his depiction of characters who are ideologues – who interact with each other, who attempt to persuade each other, who represent certain values for each other. The dialogic novel of Dostoevsky implicitly criticises the *laissez-faire* relations among individuals in a market society by emphasising the mutual constitution of selves and the grounding of subjectivity in ideologically significant languages. This literary imaging of other languages and other persons as engaged and engaging subjectivities – however abstract and mystified their very mode of individuation might be – complicates the model of free human interaction promoted by classical economics. In other words, by the time of Dostoevsky the dominant ideology had come to incorporate certain elements of the carnivalesque forms that Rabelais and others had deployed against it, so that Dostoevsky's counter-hegemonic stance was significantly and appropriately different from that of Rabelais.

Viewed in conjunction, Bakhtin's discussions of Rabelais and Dostoevsky amount to neither an empirical account of the novel's history and form, nor a manifesto about what the novel should become. Rather, Bakhtin uncovers the ideological range of the novel genre we have inherited as a function of its past, and its history might best be understood as the accumulation of a repertory rather than as a linear development.[16] The novel does not simply espouse the values of the body deriving from the carnivalesque, but neither is it a value-free form that relativises all discourses indiscriminately. The heritage of the carnivalesque provides the novel with a set of specific strategies for relativising the discourses it portrays, strategies such as their incarnation in vividly embodied and concretely situated characters and the juxtaposition of discourses marked as high and low, inner and outer. These strategies lend themselves to the purposes of specific historical critiques with varying degrees of receptiveness.[17] Thus, the novel cannot be considered inherently (historically or formally) subversive, but neither is the novel as a genre a politically neutral vehicle for ideology.

The novel's potential to be oppositional without being merely reflexive, qualified by the individual novel's capacity to enforce or undermine dominant ideologies, affords a useful metaphor for conceiving of female identity as a range of particular relationships – subversive or affirmative – to an historically mutating power structure.[18] The example of the novel suggests that the history of women's oppression and resistance by no means guarantees subversiveness to female identity, whether that subversiveness is construed essentially (as the promotion of female values) or reflexively (as the conceptual bracketings of masculinity and phallicism represented by French feminist theories about the transgressive multiplicity of the female genitals and of female *jouissance*).[19] Nevertheless, the concept of 'woman' as an historically produced but ultimately rhetorical identity provides one useful way to reconcile feminist agency in sociopolitical life with the impossibility of essentialised female identity. From a feminist point of view, 'woman' must be disunified as a conceptual category and disavowed as an essential object of knowledge; but women must continue to be recognised as structuring sites, objects, and Others of utterance.[20]

Furthermore, a dialogic and historicised conception of subversion – exemplified by the interaction between the carnivalesque and the discourse of individualism – points to the need for women to redefine themselves continually and polemically due to official culture's propensity to re-annex the values that it has projected, in distorted form, on to its Others.[21] The patriarchal structure whose oppressions feminists combat is always changing, and the terms of feminist attempts at refutation and subversion must respond to these changes. For example, the growing attention paid by the media in recent years to the phenomenon of the 'sensitive man' and in general to men's capacity for nurturance – traditionally a feminine function – by no means implies that feminism has begun to work itself out of a job. On the contrary, feminists must investigate the shifts in political power and redefinitions of socioeconomic allegiances that have made this ideological accommodation possible (and *advantageous*) without its having wrought or reflected a significant change in the general socioeconomic position of women. Just as carnivalesque organicism proved susceptible to drastic reinterpretation, any value that women espouse for oppositional purposes can be not only 'double-voiced' but duplicitous, especially if it originated in the distorted projections and repressions of patriarchy (DN, p. 324).

Ideology as the vanishing-point of dialogue: the case of Gertrude Stein

Bakhtin's dialogic encounter with Dostoevsky's novels led him to develop a celebratory, heroic version of the discursive possibilities for interchange between self-conscious ideologues depicted in Dostoevsky's novels. Locating these ideological discourses in individuals also preserves individual agency. Despite the profound innovations of Dostoevsky's novels, however, the aspects of them that Bakhtin extols mainly fall within the practice of realism, the novelistic mode that predominated in the late nineteenth century: individual accountability was, after all, the byword of realism, even though it was typically understood as a matter of personal ethics rather than of existential authenticity. Therefore, I would like to consider Bakhtin's theory of the novel in the light of one of the stories from Stein's *Three Lives* (1909), a text on the cusp between realist and modernist conceptions of the novel. I claim it as a novelised form because of its engagement with the novelistic tradition and its foregrounded representation of incommensurate discourses; I do not intend to deny any distinction between the short story and the novel by this tactic. Stein's 'The gentle Lena' does not exemplify Bakhtin's theory of the novel but rather serves as an instructive rejoinder to it.

Stein's *Three Lives* undertakes the narration of ordinary, inarticulate lives. This is the problem of Western realism *par excellence* – something many critics have failed to take into account when they have contrasted Stein's attention to the lives of the lowly with a high-culture or patriarchal literary ideal of the heroic or event-filled literary life; the fascination with the ordinary experiences of ordinary people had, in fact, already overtaken Anglo-American prose fiction by the late nineteenth century. The significant innovation of Stein's *Three Lives* was not its subject-matter (which was inspired by Flaubert's *Trois Contes*) but its abandonment of one of the most significant chronotopic characteristics of realism: the time of decision-making and self-awareness.[22]

Classic realism had replaced heroic action with heroic subjectivity by representing the self-consciousness of characters, a textual space of reflection that seemed to endow them with a human potential greater than their circumstances.[23] George Eliot neatly articulated this solution in 1857 while enlisting the reader's sympathies for her ordinary characters: '[T]hese commonplace people – many of them – bear a conscience, and have felt the sublime prompting to do the painful right; they have their unspoken sorrows, and their sacred joys . . . Nay, is there not a pathos in their very insignificance – in our comparison of their dim and narrow existence with the glorious possibilities of that human nature which they share?'[24] Elaborating this human nature became one of the primary concerns of classic realism, accomplished by a narrator who bore the burden of ideology by undertaking to account for the *representativeness* of every action, the illustrative or explanatory value that distinguished it from mere contingency. As a result of this emphasis on typicality, the reader's identification with characters was supposed to take place on a level of common human nature that transcended circumstances. The characters into whose subjectivities the narrator dips try to make generalisations about human nature from their experience, and in turn to apply those rules ethically; this space of ethical reflection is the main token of subjectivity within realism.

In contrast to the play of induction and deduction in the classic realist novel, Stein's narrator and characters in 'The gentle Lena' – the third of her *Three Lives* – seem to be remarkably opaque, slow-witted, and cautious about generalisations. The characters are not ideologues (as in Dostoevsky, and to a lesser extent in typically realist novels), and neither is the narrator an ideologue (as in most realist novels). There is no space of reflection or decision-making, except for the barest reference to what Lena feels or knows on a few rare occasions. It would, in fact, be hard to *characterise* either the narrator's relationship to Lena or our own, precisely because of the narrator's refusal to signal in her own discourse either Lena's subjectivity (with which we could identify) or her secure objectification (which we could pity).

This ambiguity within the representation of Lena appears most strikingly in the narrator's references to 'Poor Lena'. The repetition of the phrase (like many repetitions in Stein) renders it suspect, opening up a casual use of language that could pass for cliché to a more discriminating attention. Furthermore, the phrase is ironised by Mrs Haydon's having warned her daughter Mathilda that 'she [Mathilda] knew her cousin Lena was poor and Mathilda must be good to poor people.'[25] Since Mrs Haydon's perception of Lena as poor allows her to manipulate Lena, and since her daughter Mathilda's perception of Lena as poor contributes to Mathilda's contempt for her, we are made to see that pity for Poor Lena by no means implies sympathy with her.

It is important to differentiate the way in which Stein de-stabilises her narration from the kind of ultimately stable irony that Bakhtin describes in 'Discourse in the novel' as grounding the 'hybrid construction(s)' in a Dickens novel (DN, p. 304). Bakhtin's examples from *Little Dorrit* show how the narrative double-accenting of certain 'official-ceremonial' languages and languages of public opinion expose 'the hypocrisy and greed of common opinion' (DN, p. 307). One of his examples is the narrator's voicing of the general awe at a sumptuous dinner given by Mr Merdle, the climax being, "*O, what a wonderful man*

*this Merdle, what a great man, what a master man, how blessedly and
enviably endowed* – in one word, what a rich man!" Bakhtin explains,
'The whole point here is to expose the real basis for such glorification,
which is to unmask the chorus' hypocrisy: "wonderful", "great",
"master", "endowed" can all be replaced by the single word rich. . . The
ceremonial emphasis on glorification is complicated by a second
emphasis that is indignant, ironic, and this is the one that ultimately
predominates in the final unmasking words of the sentence' (DN,
p. 304).

Despite the complexity of the sentence's multi-addressivity (the
people's address to each other and to Mr Merdle, the narrator's
address to us), the italicised words in the quotation are stably iron-
ised. The truth of social esteem, we see, is money and the self-
interested relation of the have-nots to the haves. The false discourse
of virtue is made to undermine itself for the sake of some unexhibited
(in this example) *true* discourse of virtue. Indeed, Bakhtin's own
references to 'greed' and 'hypocrisy' partake of this language of
individual virtue. Hypocrisy in particular – a concept that permeates
the nineteenth-century realist novel – presupposes an essential moral
character that a represented individual attempts to deny, conceal or
prettify. This judgement of hypocrisy is possible, in fact, only because
the narrator stabilises moral judgement – whether of individual characters or of the straw man, public opinion – through authorial evaluation, or through the presentation of non-public episodes that seem to
illustrate a character's most private and therefore most fundamental
nature.

The lack of interiority in Stein's 'The gentle Lena' takes the story out
of the realm of individual virtue or hypocrisy: similarly, its problema-
tisation of discourses is not usually governed by classic irony. Aside
from these innovations, Stein's parodic revision of realism is most
apparent in the travesty of the central marriage plot. Lena, the main
character, is a German immigrant who is happily established as a
servant in the United States when the story begins. Overwhelmed by
the machinations of her aunt and Herman Kreder's mother, Lena and
Herman submit to being married. But their submission is not enough
for their relatives, who try to convince them to *want* to get married.
Herman's sister, to whom he flees on the date first set for his wedding,
tries to graft a language of bashful sexuality onto the situation: '"I'd be
awful ashamed Herman, to really have a brother didn't have spirit
enough to get married, when a girl is just dying for to have him"'
(p. 266). Herman's father also offers him a language for his situation:

'. . . [S]aying you would get married to a girl and she got everything all ready, that was a bargain just like one you make in business and Herman he had made it, and now Herman he would just have to do it . . . ' (. 263).

Similarly, Mrs Haydon, Lena's aunt, tries to present Lena with a narrative of Herman as a good catch, only to be irritated by Lena's incomprehension:

> 'Answer me, Lena, don't you like Herman Kreder? He is a fine young fellow, almost too good for you, Lena, when you stand there so stupid and don't make no answer. There ain't many poor girls that get the chance you got now to get married.'
> 'Why, I do anything you say, Aunt Mathilda. Yes, I like him. He don't say much to me, but I guess he is a good man, and I do anything you say for me to do.' (pp. 252-3)

What Mrs Haydon is asking of Lena is what Herman's sister and father are asking of him: for the couple to assume ideology, not simply to be subjected to it. Discourses of passion, of honour and of economic advantage are presented to Herman and Lena, discourses that would have them assume responsibility for their marriage. Their refusal to assume these discourses, to express anything but passive obedience, functions in some ways like the fool's polemical incomprehension of convention described by Bakhtin.[26] But they are not tricksters who gleefully elude fixed identities. Rather, they are estranged from the languages available to them.

Not all of the discourses of realism have been unsettled, though. For example, Stein's description of Lena's cousin Mathilda is couched in terms of moral evaluations (evaluations not thematised by the subsequent narrative, in contrast to realist practice) that are naturalised by being figured in Mathilda's body, as well as by being omnisciently pronounced: 'Mathilda was an overgrown, slow, flabby, blonde, stupid, fat girl, just beginning as a woman; thick in her speech and dull and simple in her mind, and very jealous of all her family and of other girls, and proud that she could have good dresses and new hats and learn music, and hating very badly to have a cousin who was a common servant' (p. 248). And Lena herself is given an aesthetic–sensual value in the opening of the story, a trace of romanticisation in the description of her voice being 'as awakening, as soothing, and as appealing, as a delicate soft breeze in midday, summer' (p. 239). Integral character is preserved; however, the use of repeated epithets – in addition to 'poor Lena', there are the 'good German cook' and the 'pleasant, unexacting mistress' – calls attention to the formulaic quality underlying any representation of stable identity in fiction.

Nevertheless, the narrative omniscience inherited from classic realism allows Stein to expose two factors in the constitution of identity that classic realism excludes: the unconscious and the impingement of ideology on the individual. Forgoing classic realist examinations of Lena's interiority (replications of her thoughts), the narrator none the less tells us what Lena does not feel, does not know, or does not know she feels. 'Lena did not really know that she did not like it' in Germany, we are told (p. 246). 'Lena would have liked much better to spend her Sundays with the girls she always sat with' than at Mrs Haydon's (p. 247). 'She did not know that she was only happy with the other quicker girls, she always sat with in the park' (p. 248). Lena 'did not ask if she would like being married any better' than being a servant (p. 254). Once Lena has been established in the Kreder home, 'nobody ever noticed much what Lena wanted, and she never really knew herself what she needed' (p. 269). The effacement of Lena's subjectivity is presented as her estrangement from her feelings and especially from her desires; in order to highlight the way in which other people's utterances appear to Lena as alienating imperatives, the narrator must assure us that Lena has suppressed unconscious desires, even a suppressed capacity *to* desire.

The attempts to appropriate or exclude desire in the story are mediated by the discourse of the *propre*: the relation between propriety and property governing society's demand that the self and its desires be contained and managed as a prerequisite for the individual's being awarded self-ownership.[27] Desire, in its unmanaged form, threatens to disrupt the *propre*: 'Herman all his life never wanted anything so badly, that he would really make a struggle against any one to get it. Herman all his life only wanted to live regular and quiet, and not talk much and to do the same way every day like every other with his working' (p. 271). The implicit opposition between orderly living and desire in this remark has in fact been developed by the story that precedes 'The gentle Lena' in *Three Lives*, in which the title character Melanctha's belief in a 'wisdom' that results from wandering (wandering that is accorded sexual, anti-domestic overtones) is contrasted with Jeff Campbell's endorsement of '"living regular and not having new ways all the time just to get excitement"' (p. 167). 'The good Anna' similarly highlights the efforts of Anna to manage other people, to 'put things in their place' (p. 39), to create orderly households and also to uphold her 'firm old world sense of what was the right way for a girl to do' (p. 24). If the good Anna practises a somewhat empowering (but also self-destructive) internalisation of the *propre*, and if Melanctha and Jeff articulate a struggle between the body's meaning-ful desires and the *propre*, then Lena might exemplify a body's passive and abject acquiescence to the ideological imperative of domestic reproduction that the discourse of the *propre* mediates. Bakhtin writes that in Dostoevsky's novels, '*a specific sum total of ideas, thoughts, and words is passed through several unmerged voices, sounding differently in each*'. But whereas Dostoevsky's method reveals '*the fully signifying word*', the word enriched by repetition, each rendition of the *propre* in Stein's text elaborates its deadening monologism and especially its capacity to set female subjectivity at odds with the female body.[28]

After Lena becomes pregnant, her old friend the 'good German cook' mourns the extent to which she has '"let [herself] go"' (p. 272) – failing to assume the *propre* in two senses. But Herman, in contrast, has found something to desire: 'It was new for Herman Kreder really to be wanting something, but Herman wanted strongly now to be a father, and he wanted badly that his baby should be a boy and healthy' (p. 275). Herman eventually takes upon himself the perpetuation of the *propre* in domestic life: 'He more and more took all the care of their three children. He saw to their eating right and their washing, and he dressed them every morning, and he taught them the right way to do things . . .' (p. 278). Whereas Herman assumes the discourse of the *propre*, channelling his desire into his role as *paterfamilias*, Lena increasingly loses concern for the body that she very clearly does not control. After the third child, Lena 'did not seem to notice very much when they [the babies] hurt her, and she never seemed to feel very much now about anything that happened to her' (p. 278). When her last child is born dead, Lena dies, too, and 'nobody knew just how it had happened to her' (p. 279). Herman subsequently becomes both father and mother, not only assuming Lena's function but also acquiring her personal adjective 'gentle' for himself and the children (pp. 278, 279) – a sinister dispersion of her identity.

Ideology functions in this text as the limits of what can be known, felt, and thought. It is not a positive discourse, embodied in an ideologue who can be refuted (as in Dostoevsky) or represented by the narrator in the inter-arrangement of discourses. Like the carnivalesque understanding of negation, ideology is not simply the abstract opposite of what is said but is rather the obverse, the implicated Other, of what is said. Experienced individually as an unconscious (Lena's failure to feel), it becomes socially intelligible according to what is unspeakable and thereby unthinkable: the unspeakable challenges to the *status quo* or the unspeakable assumptions that make the *status quo* possible. That Lena might have some desire that cannot be channelled into the domestic reproduction of society is unthinkable in the first sense; that Lena's death was the handy disposal of a body that had served its (others') purpose, not an unforeseeable contingency whose cause or logic 'nobody knew', is unthinkable in the second sense.

In contrast to Bakhtin's celebration of the festival of meanings (in which every one 'will have its homecoming')[29] and the liberation of the individual from monologic definitions, Stein's 'The gentle Lena' demonstrates language's potential to appropriate an individual repressively. Working from the realist depiction of characters as liberal and self-constituted individuals, Stein depicts an epistemological gap within the individual between feeling and knowledge that corresponds to the individualised, Freudian unconscious. And working from the realist ironisation of the discourses of common sense, common knowledge, and social propriety, Stein points to a new understanding of the ideological status of these discourses, inhering not in their interested concealment of some deeper truth (as in the hypocritical discourses of classic realism) or in their forthright articulation of existential relations, but rather in their limits, in their suppressions of knowledge and inquiry, and in their ability to obscure the possibility of counter-discourse.

In particular, Stein exposes the contradiction between the form of subjectivity implied by dominant social discourses (of romance, of honour, of economic negotiation) and the desires of the body (especially the female body) that those discourses attempt to order and manage. She exposes the access women have to this form of subjectivity as a kind of self-negation in 'The good Anna', even though the alternative represented by Lena's passive resistance by no means corresponds to a *'joyful relativity'*[30] or creative marginality. The text shows how ideology can function, not by being manipulated consciously by its beneficiaries (since the manipulators, Mrs Haydon and Mrs Kreder, are equally subject to the ideologies that they transmit), but by being internalised and embodied in the desires of the subject (as in Herman's upsurging of paternal desire).

Stein's feminist–modernist response to realism (which I am construing as a response to Bakhtin as well) raises disturbing questions. For example, does the narrator's stabilising knowledge of Lena's feelings have sinister implications in a culture in which women are too often spoken for? And doesn't the representation of a woman whose only choices are between self-alienating acquiescence to society's demands and inarticulate, equally self-alienating resistance to them reinscribe the futility of women's struggling against patriarchal discourses? It seems important, in considering these questions, to remember that Stein's text is not an assertion: not an authoritative answer, not a conclusive allegory in which Lena stands for all women within patriarchial societies. The story interrelates the ideological discourse of the *propre* and the twin projects of biological and ideological reproduction by demonstrating that ideology's discursive power to exclude or encode unconscious desires; it is not a model of all ideology's necessary functioning.

Stein's story hints at the kind of accommodation that Bakhtin's theories might productively make for some modernist novels, construed as an alternative (though not an equivalent) to the Dostoevskian way of representing ideology. And a Bakhtinian reading of 'The gentle Lena' reveals that the story's undeniable subversion of certain aspects of realism – a subversion that highlights the oppression of women in private life but that engages other literary and cultural issues besides feminism as well – is neither a bracketing and unimplicated negation of realism, nor a simple exposure of the ways in which classic realism occludes 'essential' truths about female experience. Rather, Stein's text squarely addresses realism as a polyphonic but ideologically specific artistic practice that has been shaped by the interests of patriarchy, and must be adapted to the purposes of feminism. This dialogic engagement with realism allows her to create a supple narrative that is both a version (a loyal, but not identical, repetition) and a sub-version (a critical version, a version that lurks beneath the surface of realism) of the realist marriage plot, and it aptly dramatises the dialogic relation that every subversion maintains to its opponent.[31]

Notes

1 Bakhtin holds certain conservatively humanist views of literature: he values the coherence and mastery of authorial intentions, 'great time' as the test of the work of art's richness, and the organic unity of the work. Those of us who encountered these concepts within New Criticism or reverentially biographical forms of thematic criticism may sense a contradiction between post-structuralist Bakhtin and humanist Bakhtin; the tension between his aesthetics of organic containment and politics of hegemonic conflict deserves further attention. Nevertheless, it is certain that Bakhtin's emphasis on the social constructedness of authors and artworks disavows the transcendental overtones that claims about intentionality and artistic unity have acquired in twentieth-century Anglo-American criticism.

2 Mikhail Bakhtin, 'Discourse in the novel', in *The Dialogic Imagination,* ed. Michael Holquist, trans. Caryl Emerson and Michael Holquist, Austin, 1981, p. 421; subsequent references are given in the text as DN, followed by page number.

3 Varied generic definitions of the novel appear throughout Bakhtin's work; they are not all transparently in agreement, as I suggest below. The versions I privilege are

most fully articulated in 'Discourse in the novel'.

4 Bakhtin, 'From the prehistory of novelistic discourse', in *The Dialogic Imagination*, p. 44-5.

5 *Ibid.*, p. 50.

6 The complexity of Bakhtin's ideas about the novel might also be reduced to a conflation of description with prescription; this is to some extent Tzvetan Todorov's claim in *Mikhail Bakhtin: The Dialogical Principle*, trans. Wlad Godzich, Manchester and Minneapolis, 1984, p. 90. In general, however, the latter version of the two I propose – the novel as relativising technique – has predominated in criticism on Bakhtin, obscuring his careful attention to typologies of novel subgenres and other marks of formal and historical specificity within the novel. Katerina Clark and Michael Holquist, for example, state that 'Bakhtin assigns the term "novel" to whatever form of expression within a given literary system reveals the limits of that system as inadequate, imposed, or arbitrary' – a statement which reflects only Bakhtin's most extreme claims about the novel's powers of parodic critique and renewal (*Mikhail Bakhtin*, Cambridge, Mass. and London, 1984, p. 276).

7 Julia Kristeva, 'Word, dialogue, and novel', in *Desire in Language*, ed. Leon S. Roudiez, trans. Thomas Gora, Alice Jardine and Leon S. Roudiez, New York, 1980, p. 71.

8 Bakhtin, *Rabelais and his World*, trans. Hélène Iswolsky, Cambridge, Mass. and London, 1968, p. 410; subsequent page references are given in the text.

9 For a sample of the formulations by feminists, mainly working out of a psychoanalytic tradition, that have governed many Anglo-American treatments of the relationship between meaning and the body, see Elaine Marks and Isabelle de Courtivron, eds., *New French Feminisms*, Brighton and New York, 1981.

10 Peter Stallybrass and Allon White describe the further consolidation of this 'sublimated public body' as a specifically bourgeois phenomenon. Their revisionist reading of Bakhtin as the foundation for the study of the social constitution and interrelation of 'high' and 'low' has powerfully influenced my own reading of Bakhtin and subversion (*The Politics and Poetics of Transgression*, London and Ithaca, 1986, p. 93).

11 A detailed reading of the valences of gender in Bakhtin's reading of Rabelais is beyond the scope of this essay; however, it is significant that most of Bakhtin's attempts to explain away any personal misogyny in Rabelais's references to women merely reinscribe the symbolic conceptual burden that 'woman' bears for an implicitly masculine subjectivity in the text. Wayne Booth also addresses the issue of misogyny in Bakhtin's reading of Rabelais, but he implies (construing misogyny as a personal rather than a symbolic offence) that the somewhat democratic inclusion of women's point of view in the text would have solved the problem ('Freedom of interpretation', in Gary Saul Morson, ed., *Bakhtin: Essays and Dialogues on his Work*, Chicago and London, 1986, p. 165).

12 Bakhtin's ideas on 'exotopy' or 'outsidedness' appear in the as yet untranslated 'Author and hero in aesthetic activity' ('Avtor i geroi v esteticheskoi deyatel'nosti'); they are referred to by Todorov in *Mikhail Bakhtin*, p. 99. See also Ann Jefferson's contribution to this volume, especially pp.153-9.

In deriving the carnivalesque as a literary phenomenon from the social practices of the marketplace, Bakhtin hypothesises a closer relationship between literary forms and socio-economic realities than he elsewhere deems defensible; see Todorov, *Mikhail Bakhtin*, p. 58. Moreover, some of Bakhtin's interpreters have suggested that he may have indulged in the myth of the subversive folk for polemical purposes, as a veiled critique of monoglossic Stalinism or as an antidote to sterile, overly abstract readings of Rabelais's work (see Clark and Holquist, *Mikhail Bakhtin*, pp. 295-320, and Richard M. Berrong, *Rabelais and Bakhtin: Popular Culture in 'Gargantua and Pantagruel'*, Lincoln, Nebraska and London, 1986, p. 107 and *passim*). On the problematic subversiveness of carnivals, fairs, and markets, see

Stallybrass and White, *The Politics,* especially pp. 15-18.

13 Feminists who hold certain values (nurturance, sharing, an orientation toward processes, caretaking of the body and the living space) to be essentially female and worthy of being emphasised over the falsely dominant male values (aggression, competition, goal-orientation, abstraction and intellection) succumb to this belief that the sexes possess complementary sets of 'essential' possibilities for human self-realisation. Similarly, any attempt to synthesise the sexes into an androgynous whole merely reinscribes the distortions of the categories themselves.

14 On the relationship between Bakhtin's theories and deconstruction, see Juliet Flower MacCannell, 'The temporality of textuality: Bakhtin and Derrida', *Modern Language Notes,* C: 5, 1985, pp. 968-88; Graham Pechey, 'Bakhtin, Marxism and post-structuralism', in Francis Barker *et al.,* eds., *Literature, Politics and Theory: Papers from the Essex Conference, 1976-1984,* London and New York, 1986, pp. 104-25; and Allon White, 'Bakhtin, sociolinguistics and deconstruction', in Frank Gloversmith, ed., *The Theory of Reading,* Brighton and Totowa, N.J., 1984, p. 133.

Derrida repeatedly emphasises the historicity of the sign and the scene of writing, but the tendency of deconstructive readings thus far has been to undo terms as verbal–conceptual abstractions within the context of intellectual history, at what Bakhtin would call their 'semantic heights' (DN, p. 284).

15 The sublimated interchanges of the body became the object of faculty psychology, which considered the link between cognition and bodily perception in an abstracted form; they also emerged as pathos to be managed in the literature of romanticism and realism. Similarly, the degraded body was posited by Darwinism and naturalism. In these conceptions, the body was thematised as a link to generation and mortality, but only on an individual level.

16 Bakhtin explicitly compares generic tradition to a language in *Problems of Dostoevsky's Poetics,* ed. and trans. Caryl Emerson, Manchester and Minneapolis, 1984, p. 159.

17 For example, nineteenth-century Anglo-American novels readily juxtaposed inner and outer views of character in order to expose individual dissimulation and hypocrisy, but such critiques were always in danger of being reduced to *ad hominem* judgements rather than evaluations of broader social systems.

18 The relationship between women and the novel exceeds mere analogy because of the historical intersection of women's and the novel's concern for the revaluation of the body. Diane Price Herndl also addresses this relationship in the context of theories of feminine writing in 'The dilemmas of a feminine dia-logic' (paper read in the session 'Toward a Theory of Feminist Dialogics' at the 1987 convention of the Modern Language Association).

19 For an elaboration of these theories, see especially the selections by Luce Irigaray, Hélène Cixous, and Julia Kristeva in Marks and de Courtivron, eds., *New French Feminisms,* as well as Kristeva's 'The novel as polylogue', in *Desire in Language.*

20 This double imperative was formulated at least as early as 1974 by Kristeva and re-stated at least as recently as 1985 by Toril Moi. It is worth considering repeatedly because all the resolutions so far proposed to it, to my knowledge, take the form of imperatives, barely grasped metaphors, or necessarily abstract analogies. Discovering a viable articulation of female identity for the post-structuralist era is, arguably, the most urgent task of feminism at this time, and in the meantime every new approach to the problem renders it slightly more conceivable. See Kristeva, 'Women can never be defined', in Marks and de Courtivron, eds., *New French Feminisms,* p. 137, and Toril Moi, *Sexual/Textual Politics: Feminist Literary Theory,* London and New York, 1985, p. 13.

21 Stallybrass and White argue convincingly that transgressive mining of its own symbolic margins is characteristic of the bourgeoisie: transgression can be 'a powerful ritual or symbolic practice whereby the dominant squanders its symbolic capital so as to get in touch with the fields of desire which it denied itself as the price paid

for its political power' (*The Politics*, p. 201). But their account does not address the peculiar position of women who (if they are bourgeois) can be both dominant and marginal.

22 The time of ethical reflection that I describe could be considered a further, specialised development of '*psychological time*', which Bakhtin describes as an innovation of the novel of ordeal; it seems to me to be a distinctive chronotopic hallmark of realism (Bakhtin, 'The *Bildungsroman* and its significance in the history of realism', in *Speech Genres and Other Late Essays*, ed. Caryl Emerson and Michael Holquist, trans. Vern W. McGee, Austin, 1986, p. 15).
23 Catherine Belsey persuasively elaborates a politicised account of the concept of 'classic realism' in *Critical Practice*, London and New York, 1980, especially chapters 3 and 4.
24 George Eliot, *Scenes of Clerical Life*, ed. David Lodge, New York, 1982, pp. 80-1.
25 Gertrude Stein, *Three Lives*, New York, [n.d., reprint of 1909 edtion], p. 249; subsequent page references are given in the text.
26 See Bakhtin, 'Forms of time and of the chronotope in the novel: notes toward a historical poetics', in *The Dialogic Imagination*, p. 164.
27 The French word *propre* can convey not only the sense of 'propriety' but also of 'one's own' (possessions or self) and connects etymologically to 'property'; this significant linkage between bodily conduct, public respectability, ownership, and subjectivity was pointed out by Derrida in 'La parole soufflée', in *Writing and Difference*, trans. Alan Bass, London and Henley, 1978, p. 183.
28 Bakhtin, *Problems*, pp. 265-6 (Bakhtin's italics).
29 Bakhtin, 'Toward a methodology for the human sciences', in *Speech Genres*, p. 170.
30 Bakhtin, *Problems*, p. 124.
31 Consultations with Paul Foster have been invaluable to me in preparing this essay.

Clair Wills

Upsetting the public: carnival, hysteria and women's texts

Reading Bakhtin, it's hard not to envy Rabelais. However much one extols the virtues of *Ulysses*, or the more popular pleasures of Brighton beach or the Costa del Sol, they still lack that combination of critique and indecency typical of the carnival Rabelais could take as his source. So it appears a mostly compensatory gesture when critics enthuse about the 'carnival*esque*' they find in the latest (post-)modernist novel. Surely they can't really confuse reading a good book with the experience of carnival grounded in the collective activity of the people? What seems to be lacking in this textual carnival is any link with a genuine social force. This is an argument made by Peter Stallybrass and Allon White in *The Politics and Poetics of Transgression*, where they reject some of the easy appropriations of Bakhtin's too often populist and utopian theory of carnival, which argue for the 'transgressive' potential of carnivalesque literature.[1] The authors point out that literary carnival doesn't possess the same social force as actual carnival may once have done. Displaced from public sphere to the bourgeois home (let alone to the novel read by its fire), carnival ceases to be a site of actual struggle. Shifting the emphasis slightly, I want to ask whether some women's texts may not have a more productive relationship to carnival, leading to a closer connection between literary transgression and cultural transformation.[2] I will draw an analogy between Bakhtinian carnival, hysteria and women's texts in terms of their capacity to disrupt and remake official public norms, arguing firstly that carnival and hysteria are linked in terms of the 'content' of their representations, as critics such as Stallybrass and White and Catherine Clément have maintained.[3] Moreover, just as the hysteric seems to 'store' the misplaced carnival content, representing the past in the present, so, I will argue, this cyclical return to the past mirrors the relation to the past which Bakhtin takes as the mark of carnival: in opposition to 'official' time, which presents a linear and hierarchical teleology of events, carnivalesque time is aware of 'timeliness' and crisis in the version of history which it presents. But while both carnival and hysteria are excluded from official public norms, the question should be how to dialogise the public realm by bringing the excluded and 'non-official' into juxtaposition with the official. In this essay I want to focus on the crucial transition from private to public discourse for women, and on the importance of the continuing dialogue between these two areas in feminist poetry. Part of my analysis will take the form of a comparison between a discourse designated 'feminine' by certain 'scientific' discourses – the discourse of the hysteric (a victim of the bourgeois home who is not generally considered to be politically progressive) – and the work of a contemporary poet from Northern Ireland, Medbh McGuckian.[4]

In drawing an analogy between popular carnival and 'hysterical' discourse I am wary of the difficulties in using the term 'hysterical' to refer to even quite a specific area of women's writing. One must continually ask, who speaks the name 'hysteric'? Bearing in mind the process by which the word serves to objectify and marginalise certain types of 'feminine' discourse, I want to look at texts which, precisely because they have lain so far outside official public norms, have been designated 'hysterical', not only by conservative theorists, but also by avant-garde critics such as Julia Kristeva. Since these texts are received as 'not quite literature', the imperative must be to investigate the most productive ways to use that position 'outside' the institution, not in order to be permanently disruptive, but in order to undo and remake that institution. As I hope to show, the 'constructive' role of the 'hysterical' text will depend above all on the function which the work performs, both in relation to the writer's private life, and in bringing this private life into conflict with public norms.

Of central importance in any consideration of these questions is the status of popular festive forms within literature. For Bakhtin, in order for popular carnival to become politically effective it must 'enter' the institution of literature. In *Rabelais and his World*, he argues that it is only in literature that popular festive forms can achieve the 'self-awareness' necessary for effective protest. Of carnival he says: 'its wide popular character, its radicalism and freedom, soberness and materiality were transferred from an almost elemental condition to a state of artistic awareness and purposefulness. In other words, medieval laughter became at the Renaissance stage of its development the expression of a new free and critical historical consciousness.'[5]

This concept of 'artistic awareness' is never fully theorised by Bakhtin, but what seems to be at stake is a juxtaposition of 'official' and 'non-official' modes of communication. In the final pages of the Rabelais book he relates the concept of 'awareness' to 'the victory over linguistic dogmatism' (p. 473), which is secured by the introduction of the vernacular into the category of 'great literature'. The power of carnival to turn things upside down is facilitated by bringing it into dialogic relation to official forms. Hence the mixing of popular and official languages which occurs in texts drawing on the vernacular as well as classical and medieval Latin brings an increased awareness of time and the *difference* between historical epochs. The dialogue between the languages 'suddenly disclosed how much of the old was dead and how much of the new was born' (p. 468). It is only by bringing the excluded and carnivalesque into the official realm in a single text that the concept of public discourse may be altered (so texts written solely in the vernacular would be too far outside the official realm to have an effect). It is Rabelais's ability to make use of official forms, including new forms of scientific knowledge, and bring them into dialogic relation with popular knowledge and 'festive' forms which can raise carnival to 'a higher level of ideological consciousness' (p. 473).[6] For in the Middle Ages carnival had been contained – centred in small pockets of activity in provincial towns, it lacked organisation. It was not in a position to 'dialogise' official forms of communication and organisation because, as Bakhtin points out, it remained 'strictly divided' from them:

> And so medieval culture of folk humour was fundamentally limited to these small islands of feasts and recreations. Official serious cultures existed beside them but strictly divided from the marketplace. The shoots of a new world outlook were sprouting, but they could not grow and flower as long as they were enclosed in the popular gaiety of recreation and banqueting, or in the fluid realm of familiar speech. In order to achieve this growth and flowering, laughter had to enter the world of great literature. (p. 96)

The 'opening up' of the carnivalesque is ultimately achieved through literature,[7] but although Bakhtin stresses literature's power to communicate festive forms, to foster the protest that would otherwise remain contained in separate areas, he goes on to chart the narrowing of its potential through subsequent literary epochs. The ability to dialogise popular and official forms isn't the property of a particular text, but importantly depends on the type of institution into which it is inserted. So, and this is a point I shall return to, it's important not to look to individual texts by women to alter literary norms, abstracted from the need to control the way those texts are received.

Similarly contained, but this time within the private sphere of the bourgeois family rather than the public but provincial marketplace, is the hysteric's protest incommunicable? The disruptive possibilities of hysteria and the 'hysterical' text have been debated within feminism, most notably in the discussion between Catherine Clément and Hélène Cixous in *The Newly Born Woman*, where they disagree about the hysteric's ability to 'break' the family mould. Here I want to relate this problem to the particular relationship to time and history which Bakhtin describes as the mark of carnival festivity, and ask, does the hysteric belong to the past? For Bakhtin, carnivalesque time looks to the past and the future. Unlike the official feast in which the link with time has become formal, and change and moments of crisis are relegated to the past, popular festive forms harness the 'timeliness' of past events in order to project a utopian time: 'Carnival was the true feast of time, the feast of becoming, change and renewal. It was hostile to all that was immortalised and completed' (p. 10). While the official feast looks to the past in order to reconfirm hierarchy, the return of the popular feast to the past ('the natural (cosmic) cycle' or 'biological or historic timeliness' (p. 9)) presages a moment of renewal. Like the mixing of languages in Rabelais, and this time outside the institution of literature, what seems to be valuable about carnival is its awareness of the discontinuity of history, or history as crisis.

There are two important questions concerning the hysteric's relationship to the past. Firstly, is she socially and historically bound to the Victorian era (in which case any abstraction in the form of a theory of the 'hysterical' text, or, indeed, the whole of psychoanalytic practice would be called into question)? More specifically, is the hysteric bound to the past, personal and cultural, through 'reminiscence'? In her cyclical return to the crises of her personal history, which she repeats in her symptoms, the hysteric may represent in miniature the relationship of popular festive forms to the past, yet her capacity for turnings things 'upside-down' is contained within the family. The possible 'transgressive' nature of popular festive forms and hysterical discourse are connected not only in their similar relation to history, but also in their content. As Stallybrass and White point out, Freud's descriptions of the hysteric call on popular festive imagery: 'It is striking how the broken fragments of carnival, terrifying and disconnected, glide through the discourse of the hysteric' (p. 171). The

carnival role of the grotesque body in mocking, degrading and inverting high culture has been displaced onto the psyche of the hysteric.
Was the 'madness' of these Viennese women then the belated representation of popular carnival which had been suppressed? For Freud
the repressed past survives in woman. He records in a footnote Frau ·
Emmy von N.'s answer to an inquiry about her age: 'I am a woman of
the last century.'[8]

But for Catherine Clément in *The Newly Born Woman*, the hysteric
does not simply recall childhood events but represents in her symptoms and her discourse the repressed past of patriarchal history. The
culture has a zone for what it excludes, which comprises those who are
'afflicted with a dangerous symbolic mobility. Dangerous for them
because those are the people who are afflicted with what we call
madness, anomaly, perversion, or whom we label, says Mauss, "neurotics, ecstatics, outsiders, carnies, drifters, jugglers, acrobats"' (p. 7).
Stallybrass and White also stress the remembrance not only of a
personal but also of a pantomimic past, as they analyse the hysteric in
terms of carnival. They view hysteria both as a Victorian phenomenon,
and as a 'displacement' from previous history. As such it is simply the
most recent manifestation of the bourgeoisie's contradictory relationship to the 'low' society which it has repressed. Since for them
psychoanalysis, like the institution of art, corresponds to a sublimation of the social force of carnival into representation of carnival, the
presence of an 'upside-down world' in the discourse of the hysteric is
to be specifically linked to the bourgeoisie's attempt to define itself as
a class in opposition to the social terrain of dirt, servants and sexuality.
So, although the social force of carnival may have been displaced and
fragmented, it retains a symbolic importance which is central to post-
Renaissance culture. In the absence of social forms fitting to what they
wish to express, hysterics attempt 'to produce their own by pastiche
and parody in an effort to embody semiotically their distress' (p. 174).
The hysteric's symptoms thus constitute a 'staging' of the carnivalesque: 'Once noticed, it becomes apparent that there is a second
narrative fragmented and marginalised, lodged within the emergent
psychoanalytic discourse. It witnesses a complex interconnection
between hints and scraps of parodic festive form and the body of the
hysteric' (p. 174). Pantomime thus becomes the 'symptomatic locus'
of the bourgeois imaginary as it attempts to represent the unconscious.

This historicised interpretation has a markedly different emphasis
from Clément's feminist reading of the hysteric's 'reminiscence'. For

her the hysteric, in her kinship with the witch and the sorceress (a kinship which Freud also notes), reinscribes the repression of women. Each figure, sorceress and hysteric, articulates the possibilities for protest available at different historical times. They are linked through their repetition of the crises of the women who came before them: the hysteric 'resumes and assumes the memories of the others' (p. 5). And it may be that the contemporary woman writer has been bequeathed the legacy of reminiscence left by the sorceress and hysteric. Just as Bakhtin saw popular festive forms enriched by their introduction into literature, the publication of texts which assume the memories of previous women's crises may be one way to open up the provincial, familial nature of the hysteric's protest. In this way Adrienne Rich dreams of a 'common language' that would draw together the transforming power of women separated by historical and social circumstance, asserting the identity of past and present not so that things should stay the same, but in order to show possibilities for the future.[9] The hope is that by creating a collective past, women will be able to break up the present. But if this is her legacy, how is it possible for the woman writer to make public the protest which in the case of the hysteric was contained within the bourgeois family, without merely becoming a spectacle for the male gaze? Moreover, *can* the past be a source of political change in the present? Clément asks, 'Do the abnormal ones – madmen, deviants, neurotics, drifters, jugglers, tumblers – anticipate the culture to come, repeat the past culture, or express a constantly present utopia?' (p. 8). In the same way we can ask of Bakhtin, what relationship can popular festivity have to the past which doesn't reconfirm hierarchy (like the official feast), and which can at the same time be effective in remaking public norms? The central difficulty concerns the discourse and representations of the hysteric, the power of anachronism. In *Origins of Psychoanalysis* Freud explains the process whereby 'anachronisms' live on in the psyche of the hysteric as a failure of translation. 'The memory behaves as though it were some current event', as the psychic force associated with the early traumatic event increases in its capacity to disrupt in the process of repression:

> Each later transcription inhibits its predecessor and takes over the excitatory process from it. If the later transcription is lacking the excitation will be disposed of according to the psychological laws governing the earlier epoch and along the paths which were then accessible. Thus an anachronism remains: in a particular province fueros are still in force. Relics of the past still survive.[10]

The 'fuero' is an ancient Spanish provincial law. We could read Freud as saying that there has been insufficient centralisation in the 'state' of the hysteric. The crises of the past live on in a separate area of the psyche like the last vestiges of small-town marketplace carnival. When the crisis erupts it will have gathered force, yet the question remains of how to make public the disruptive potential of this experience of crisis so that it doesn't stay enclosed in the familial arena, since for Bakhtin the extended, protruding, secreting grotesque body was able to resist and destabilise the monumental, static, classical body precisely because of its *openness*.

Publicising the private

What power has the past to upset present cultural norms? The question hinges on the status of negativity, on the relationship between the excluded and the law, between, for Clément, the imaginary and symbolic. As Jane Gallop points out in her article 'Keys to Dora', it comes down to the relationship between public and private. Gallop plays on Freud's note to the Dora case, 'Open or shut is naturally not a matter of indifference', in order to ask whether the hysteric opens the family up or is closed by it.[11] Is her protest enclosed within the family, or does it have the power to alter the structure of the symbolic? Bakhtin notes the importance of the 'openness' of the grotesque body even after it has entered 'great literature', where the grotesque images become 'the means for the artistic and ideological expression of a mighty awareness of history and historic change, which appeared during the Renaissance' (pp. 24-5). But the grotesque spasms which play themselves out on the body of the hysteric are enclosed within the family, or the stage atmosphere of Charcot's hysterical spectacles at the Salpêtrière. If, as Bakhtin claims, the 'openness' of the grotesque images has been steadily denied since the Renaissance (so, for example, the Romantic grotesque becomes symbolic of individual isolation, separated from the material world), if the public sphere has been privatised, then the question is how can it be remade as public speech?[12] As I have noted, for Stallybrass and White the transgressive discourse of the hysteric has no power to change anything since it is part of the problem. The very conception of bourgeois individuality, they argue, has been created by a marginalisation and sublimation of the social force of carnival into individual psychic space, as the bourgeoisie attempt to differentiate themselves from the 'low' collectivity of the 'people'. Moreover, it is in the particular institutions of art and psychoanalysis that carnival lives on as the suppression of the material 'body' of festivity leads to its return within symbolic discursive levels.[13] But while this historical thesis makes possible an illuminating narrative of post-Renaissance society, it overlooks the asymmetrical relation of women to literary and psychoanalytic practice.

Stallybrass and White identify the emergence of a notion of authorship with the beginnings of a relationship of observation and representation, instead of participation, between the subject and carnival; the author places himself above the scene of carnival and thereby transforms it into an object of representation (they instance Jonson's *Bartholomew Fair*). But even as he distances the 'low' carnivalesque activity and creates his identity as an author in opposition to it, it becomes all the more symbolically important in his writing: 'What is excluded at the overt level of identity formation is productive of new objects of desire' (p. 25). Thus the bourgeois subject has a 'dialogic' relation to carnival – the differentiation by which the subject creates his identity is dependent on disgust, but disgust in its turn bears the imprint of desire. So the hysteric's illness results from the Victorian middle-class suppression of the body. Hysteria, and Freud's discourse upon it, represent a '*psychic* irruption of *social* practices which had been suppressed' (p. 176). Here the importance of seeing carnival not simply as the underside of the symbolic order but as engaged in a dialogic relation with it becomes clear. The unconscious is not simply the repository of displaced popular carnival, but is constructed out of a fantasy relation of bourgeois ideology to carnival. Bakhtin, claim Stallybrass and White, wavers between a theory of the grotesque of carnival as oppositional, popular festivity which acts as a negation of the social symbolic order, and carnival as 'hybrid' – a mediation between high and low forms of culture rather than the Other of official culture. Emphasising the importance of the later theory, they argue that it is fruitless merely to positivise the various elements of carnival, to celebrate the body. In this respect, although it is clear that much of their theorising is indebted to Lacanian and Kristevan concepts, the authors are keen to distance themselves from what they argue is a dangerous tendency in theorists such as Kristeva and Foucault to analyse carnival in terms of its liberatory qualities. Celebratory claims for the power of the carnivalesque to undo hierarchies are merely a fetishising of the repressed, a repetition of the desire for 'lost' domains which their book analyses as constitutive of bourgeois subjectivity. 'The bourgeoisie . . . is perpetually rediscovering the carnivalesque as a radical source of transcendence', and it is simply misguided 'to associate the exhilarating sense of freedom which transgression affords with any necessary or automatic political progressiveness' (p. 201).

It is important therefore that the question of opening up the hysteric's protest isn't simply reduced to the issue of publicising or publishing a private language, since in those terms it would differ little from literary autobiography, leaving the relationship between the author and the carnival material unchanged. Nevertheless, bearing in mind the gendered nature of the literary and psychoanalytic institutions, women may have a different relationship to carnival, since, as Clément argues, they are both placed together in the zone of the anomalous. Thus the function which the literary work performs for the woman writer may differ in crucial ways from the need to maintain desiring distance from the popular realm which Stallybrass and White analyse as a defining characteristic of authorship. I want to deal with the precise ways in which this relationship might differ in a later section, and here turn instead to an alternative theory of bourgeois distancing, which stresses the importance of the male bourgeoisie's distancing of a specifically female and openly sexual 'low' realm.

In his book *Male Fantasies*, a psychoanalytic study of a group of officers of the Freikorps in Weimar Germany, Klaus Theweleit presents a different history of the creation of bourgeois identity.[14] He stresses the part played by a fantasy construction of womanhood in the evolution of a 'civilised' ego. As important as the 'self-distancing' behaviour by which the bourgeoisie separated themselves from the realm of dirt and servants (here, like Stallybrass and White, he follows Norbert Elias),[15] is the more specific fear of working-class female sexuality, crystallised in the figure of the 'Red Nurse'. Like Clément, Theweleit sees a connection between the figures of the witch and the hysteric, and twentieth-century male fantasies of female sexuality. His history is one of the persecution of female sexuality from burnings to private asylums – there is an internalisation of persecution concomitant with the movement from private to public sphere. For Theweleit, as for Irigaray, the 'unconscious' of bourgeois (and fascist) identity is a historically repressed femaleness. He therefore sees it as 'almost inevitable' that Freud would choose to investigate the psyches of hysterical women because, 'In the course of the repression carried out against women, those two things, the unconscious and femaleness, were so closely coupled together that they came to be seen as nearly identical' (p. 432).

The fantasies of the Freikorps men concerning the 'castrating rifle woman' and 'monstrous' proletarian woman seem to spring from a fear of the free circulation of working-class sexuality. Theweleit points out that the fantasies, though unconnected to women's actual behaviour, did have a bearing on the different sexual mores in working-class communities, notable for the 'conspicuous absence of any Christian bourgeois sexual ethic' (p. 141). The importance of this analysis for the discussion here lies in the soldier males' disgust at the *public* nature of the working-class women's protests and their unashamed displays of sexuality. It was this which inspired their murderous desire:

> The reality of working-class women didn't match the actual experience of soldier males, but it may well have fit in with the horror stories they were fed about erotic, aggressive, 'masculine' women. The war had freed working-class women from the housewife's role they had known beforehand. Forced to become sole providers for their families, many entered the factories. They had organized anti-hunger demonstrations and ransacked display windows. (p. 144)

This freely circulating body of the working-class woman would then be the antithesis of the closed body of the hysteric, contained within the family. But these two worlds are brought together in the figure of the servant girl – the one on the 'threshold' between the family and the world outside. Jane Gallop notes the 'murderous desire' for the servant girl on the part of the male bourgeoisie: 'As a threatening representative of the symbolic, the economic, the extra-familial, the maid must be both seduced (assimilated) and abandoned (expelled).'[16] In the mind of the male bourgeois there is a simple equation between the prostitute and the servant girl. (And Theweleit points out that they were often the same. In Vienna in 1926, seventy percent of registered prostitutes were either servants, unskilled workers or seamstresses. He notes: 'the typical master of the Wilhelmine bourgeois household thought that a kind of right to sexual access went along with the servant girls' (p. 165).) Crucially, of course, there is also an equation between the servant girl and the bourgeois woman. All these women are 'on the market' and any one can be substituted for any other. This is Dora's realisation, and the spur to her hysterical rebellion.[17] Hélène Cixous notes the importance of realising kinship with the other in the circuit of exchange where 'the servant girl is the repressed of the boss's wife' (p. 150). It may be that in order for public protest to be made, the bourgeois woman must realise that she is the same as the maid, for in the masculine economy the hysteric and the prostitute were always the same. In her history of hysteria, I. Veith charts a continuity in the accusation of excessive sexual needs in all these aberrant women, from the witch's copulation with the devil (curable

by burning) to the hysteric's masturbation (curable by clitoridectomy). Even when such drastic measures weren't prescribed, Veith
records the objections of a Dr Carter to the excessive use of the
speculum in consultations with Victorian hysterical women. Frequent
internal examination, he claimed, pandered to their worst instincts
and placed them in the same category as prostitutes. Freud's 'discovery' of the sexual aetiology of neurosis can be read as the logical
continuation of this diagnostic trend.[18]

But if it is the case that 'public' women become associated in male
fantasy with the witch and the prostitute (as in the soldier males'
fantasies of the proletarian women), how is it possible for women to
protest publicly without feeding the network of 'disgust' and 'desire'
described by Stallybrass and White, how can they become public on
their own terms? The danger is that public woman (the woman who
publishes) will merely perform the displaced abjection of the male
bourgeoisie – her text will represent a place where the distance from
carnivalesque content can be charted in the same moment as it is
desired in the act of reading. In making public women's prostitution
the writer will be taken for a prostitute herself (she 'sells herself' within
the male institution). The poet Medbh McGuckian has made this
connection explicit in discussing the difficulties of writing about a
private life: 'I feel that you're going public – by writing the poem you're
becoming a whore. You're selling your soul which is worse than any
prostitution – in a sense you're vilifying your mind. I do feel that must
be undertaken with the greatest possible fastidiousness.'[19] The difficulty is for the woman writer to utilise the myths which have been
associated with her – to 'expose' the history of her exclusion – without
thereby 'making a spectacle' of herself.[20] The transgressive potential
of women's writing hinges on the relationship between the excluded
and the law. I have argued that for Bakhtin carnival must be brought
into dialogue with official forms through the medium of literature, in
order to be politically effective; analogously, the 'lawlessness' of the
witch, the hysteric and the proletarian woman must be brought within
the public sphere, conforming to some extent with its norms, if it is to
become a language which can engage politically with the 'official'
language. At issue is the move from private production to public
'authorship'. Do women writers repeat the distancing of carnival
content in the process of authoring which Stallybrass and White give
as the constitutive moment of the institution of literature?

Although it may be valid to criticise modernism's 'transgression' as
politically illusory, what this account omits is that 'authorship' is

gendered, and for women writers, who were never able to shore up
their identity in the institution of literature, it may be precisely
through access to representation that the sites of discourse could be
altered. Shifted from public sphere to the bourgeois home, carnival
ceases to be a site of actual struggle, but the conflicts of the modern
private sphere may have generated a social force on to which the
bodily energies of carnival have been displaced. Designated marginal
to the dominant forms of culture, the attempt of many contemporary
women writers to introduce the concerns of the private domestic
sphere into the public discourse of literature entails a theoretical as
well as a representational intervention, as it fuses the private (unofficial) side of women's narrative with the public (official literary) norm.
So feminist poetry challenges the dominant literary canon by inscrib-
ing a different relationship to personal history, the body, the history
of women's exclusion. In making a claim for the importance of the
'personal' and experiential nature of recent feminist poetry as a denial
of 'distance', I am aware of the warning made most recently by Jan
Montefiore against criticism of women's texts 'based on the assumption that what makes a poem valuable or interesting is its author's
awareness of her own dilemma as a woman'.[21] Montefiore urges critics
not to read poems for the way they show the writer to have been the
emotional victim of patriarchy; rather it is important to be aware of
what makes the poem *different* from autobiography. But conversely,
the danger is a reading of feminist poetry which would repeat the
canonical critical gesture which denies such 'personal' and experiential testimony its status as literature. The poetry is attempting to make
an intervention on the level of acceptable representations, and any
theoretical approach to feminist writing must allow it to retain its
specificity as literature while being aware that at the same time it aims
to change the sites of discourse. The challenge of feminist poetry is
precisely a *literary* challenge, and only through that a political one; the
text attempts to change the literary norm in formal ways, and through
this the forms of cultural authority which it indirectly figures, as the
literary canon comes to 'stand for' the values of the dominant culture.[22]

But the ability of overtly feminist writing to remake public norms in
this way is denied by theorists such as Julia Kristeva, for whom
women's writing, precisely because of its position outside the dominant literary culture, is destined to remain always a negative, possess-
ing no lever with which to prise open the realm of authoritative values.
It is interesting therefore that Stallybrass and White criticise Kristeva

for investing too much in literary transgression. For them, Kristeva 'confuses the projection of bourgeois desire with the destruction of its class identity' (p. 201). It is her simple positivisation of Bakhtinian carnival which means that she will only be able to alter representations rather than the sites of discourse. But what prevents Kristeva from entertaining radical subversion of the subject is her psychoanalytic orthodoxy; any text which privileges the semiotic without at the same time bolstering the law of the Father, is psychotic. So transgression is no more than a cathartic outlet for the pre-oedipal in the repressed phallic subject. Transgression must accept 'another law', as she says in 'Word, dialogue, and novel', or it will be mere linguistic play.[23] Kristeva warns of the dangers for the woman writer, estranged from language: 'if no paternal "legitimation" comes along to dam up the inexhaustible non-symbolised impulse, she collapses into psychosis and suicide.'[24] With regard to women's writing, her emphasis on the need for the law means that she cannot see it as transgressive at all. Women's texts are too 'hysterical' to be truly disruptive: 'When a woman novelist does not produce a family of her own, she creates an imaginary story through which she constitutes an identity: narcissism is safe, the ego becomes eclipsed after freeing itself, purging itself of reminiscences. Freud's statement "the hysteric suffers mostly from reminiscence" sums up the large majority of novels produced by women.'[25]

So the question of whether the hysteric is contained or not, open or shut, is intimately connected to the question of reminiscence discussed earlier. In representing the past as symptom (which can have no efficacy), she seems destined to remain trapped by the past, rather than to offer a vision of the future. Turned the other way, the question concerns the possibility of entertaining a relationship to the past which isn't simply one of mastery. For Freud and Breuer in *Studies on Hysteria,* the successful cure of the hysteric involves a type of catharsis in which the repressed past (the initial trauma) is led into the light of rationality, and thus diffused. So, just as the persistence of memory is connected to repressed reaction, curing the hysteric may mean killing the past and its innovating force in the present. (Stallybrass and White note that Freud's early method involved reproducing grotesque material in comic form: 'When Frau Emmy can at last look at the "grotesque figures" and "laugh without a trace of fear", it is as if Freud had managed a singular restitution, salvaging the torn shreds of carnival from their phobic alienation in the bourgeois unconscious by making them once more the object of cathartic laughter' (p. 171). But such laughter can be read as the diffusion of the power to protest, a mastery of the psyche of the hysteric.)

Staging hysteria

If the personal and cultural past to which the hysteric is bound is to be effective it must be communicable, representing rather than represented. But if Theweleit is correct in interpreting the figures of mad and possessed women as male fantasies, in what way can they become productive images for women? In historical terms, Natalie Zemon Davies has shown how the image of the disorderly woman was able at certain times to widen behavioural patterns for women, sanctioning riots and political disobedience. There is a certain 'spillover into everyday life' from the inverted carnivalesque activity: thus women are shown ways to protest through 'mimicry' of the 'unruly' roles offered them.[26] The hysteric's reminiscence involves several types of repetition or mimicry.[27] Firstly there is what Stallybrass and White describe as a pantomime of carnival in the psyche, a repetition of social carnival in the unconscious (and, importantly, in the comic cathartic cure). Again, the hysteric's symptoms show a continuity with the past through repetition as symbol (Dora's facial neuralgia reproduces the slap she gives to Herr K). As Clément points out, it is this display of the past which gives the hysteric her power: 'That is how the hysteric, reputed to be incurable, sometimes – and more and more often – took on the role of a resistant heroine: the one whom psychoanalytic treatment would never be able to *reduce*' (p. 8). But this resistance can only act as a limit on the master discourse, especially since it is performed as a spectacle for the master. Mary Russo in her article 'Female grotesques: carnival and theory' examines the problems of female 'spectacle' in relation to hysteria. The staged photographs from the Salpêtrière 'can be read as double somatisations of the women patients whose historical performances were lost to themselves and recuperated into the medical science and medical discourse which maintain their oppressive hold on women'.

Bearing this in mind, Russo asks whether it is possible that the 'display' and 'stagings' of hysteria may be used to 'rig us up (for lack of the phallic term) into discourse'.[28] Is it possible that the recontextualisation of the discourse and representations of the hysteric may be able to overturn the master discourse, to turn the staged play upside-down? Luce Irigaray argues that it is in 'La Mystérique', where she encourages women to mime their hysterisation by the master: 'She is pure at last because she has pushed to extremes the repetition of this abjection, this revulsion, this horror to which she has been condemned, to which, mimetically, she had condemned herself.' Rather than a recontextualisation of the 'high' discourse in the realm of the 'low', as in carnival, this strategy involves a repetition of the woman's speculisation as object of the master discourse, but in a different context. Irigaray puts forward such 'subversive mimesis' as the only possible means for women to speak within patriarchal ideology. Parody takes place not in the way suggested by Bakhtin for the carnivalesque, which inverts the established hierarchy, but by representing the position of the 'low'. Irigaray asserts that women's capacity for resisting the patriarchal order stems not from an ability to take up a masculine subject position (since 'any theory of the subject is always appropriated by the masculine'), but from her ability to disrupt the subject/object split from her position as intractable object, insecure 'ground' of masculine speculations.

'Mimesis' entails taking up the role historically assigned to the feminine – Freud's 'masquerade of femininity'. Irigaray claims that in the reproduction of this role there always remains an excess, a part which is not accounted for in masculine speculations. She sees her task as the interpretation of that irreducible femininity which remains even when the speaker takes part in the masquerade.[29] But she leaves unanswered the important question of the speaker's intentions. Is it the speaker's consciousness that she is being subversive which makes her so, or is every statement by a woman within the masculine economy in fact subversive? Crucial in Irigaray's formulation is that the repetition would differ from the original spectacle in that it would no longer be performed for men. But it is difficult to see how such a 'new' context would be definable or recognisable. How would a truly transgressive hysteria differ from a recuperable one? The woman, Irigaray states, 'still subsists, otherwise and elsewhere than where she mimes so well what is asked of her. Because her own "self" remains foreign to the whole staging. . . Her sex is heterogeneous to this whole economy of representation, but it is capable of interpreting that economy precisely because it has remained "outside".'[30] Can the representation of the self as a riddle in fact avoid mastery and masculine appropriation? Might it not instead reconfirm the Freudian thesis of female sexuality as a dark continent, i.e. precisely the scenario which encourages man to possess and conquer it?

For Irigaray the dreams and riddles of 'La Mystérique' are able to 'recast the roles that history has laid down for subject and object', but there is surely a danger that speaking in riddles, reproducing the discourse of the hysteric, will merely serve to make more complex the veils that are laid over the female. As Sarah Kofman argues, for Freud it was 'by virtue of her sexuality that woman is enigmatic, for sexuality is what constitutes the "great riddle" of life which accounts for the entire difference between men and women'. Female sexuality thus acquires a privileged status as the object of study; the secret of their sex is hidden by the 'shame' and 'modesty' which civilisation expects from them. Kofman describes Freud's investigation into female sexuality as a desire to uncover the whole story:

> Because woman does not have the right to speak, she stops being capable or desirous of speaking: she 'keeps' everything to herself, and creates an excess of mystery and obscurity as if to avenge herself, as if striving for mastery. Woman lacks sincerity; she dissimulates, transforms each word into an enigma, an indecipherable riddle. That is why the patient's narrative is always foreshortened, defective, disconnected, incomplete, lacking in 'links'.[31]

On the one hand, Irigaray would suggest that dissimulation, or covering up the 'truth', may be a means of subverting the existing order. On the other this veiling may differ little from traditional modesty. The male reader/subject is then drawn on by the mystery and disguise with which the object is veiled and spurred on to discover the 'truth' about the female, which in this guise differs little from the traditional 'dark continent' by which she has always been represented. The patient/woman's narrative is probed, opened up for the secrets it can tell about her sex. Here I want to look at two 'riddling' narratives, one author(is)ed by a man, one written and published by a woman, in order to ask if there is a difference when woman 'authors' herself.

The case histories presented by Freud and Breuer in which they document the importance of 'verbal utterance' in the cathartic cure of the hysteric are notable for the way the utterance itself is repressed. The hysteric's text is not present but represented by the texts of the male scientists. In his case history of Anna O, Breuer admires his patient's 'poetical compositions' but presents his own narrative as a substitute for them. He fills in the missing links in her 'defective narrative'. Moreover, the two narratives lead in opposite directions–while Anna O's narrative circles back to the previous year in its repetition of events, Breuer's narrative denies this cyclical movement, replacing it with a linear progression from the onset of the sickness, through a worsening of the symptoms after her father's death, to eventual cure. Unable to write her own diary (Breuer uses her mother's diary to 'check' her creations for accuracy), Anna O instead 'lived through the previous winter day by day'. Her 'poetry' consists of a personal documentation, its content the daily release of 'imaginative products' associated with the events of the day. Breuer describes how things have become 'stuck' inside her, which cause a diffusion of tension on release: 'She knew that after she had given utterance to her hallucinations, she would lose all her obstinacy, and what she described as her "energy".' The things which are stuck are the source of her energy, but Anna O is content at this point to have her energy diffused before an audience of one – so she is 'open' about her secrets (specifically she is open to Breuer in her phantom pregnancy), but closed to the world at the same time.[32]

McGuckian's poetry, by contrast, is enigmatically 'closed' to the reader in its syntactical difficulty, but widely available. McGuckian seems to be looking for a way to speak about women's experience which avoids being 'probed', a riddling discourse which will be public and at the same time distinctively different, disruptive of the normative codes of literary discourse. Her poetry has often been criticised for its obscurity, an enigmatic difficulty which is connected to a tendency to describe personal and political events through the metaphor of the female body. Whether the woman's body is open or closed is of crucial importance to McGuckian: 'open' during sex and pregnancy, is the body thereby closed off to other roles and modes of authority? The antithesis to the opened up body of the mother is the self-sufficient body of the Victorian maid or governess, who becomes symbolic in her poetry of 'single-mindedness'. But this self-sufficiency is contained; like tulips which 'double-lock in tiers as whistle-tight'[33] against the intrusive rain, the Victorian woman is 'dry' and non-reproductive. McGuckian wants to find a way to connect these self-contained units, to link the separate histories of these women in order to make that history itself productive of new possibilities. And this entails the dangerous and ambivalent practice of being 'open'. 'I'm trying to make the dead women of Ireland, who I am the living memory of, I'm trying to give them articulation, if anything. In that sense I'm trying to make their lives not a total waste, that they didn't live in vain, that they have no record at all.' She undertakes this history writing through personal recordings of the 'poetry' of her everyday life. Like Anna O's compositions her poems constitute a diary – the poems are

lies that are no longer true for what I am at the minute. They're like days in a diary which you've crossed out. But you're very involved with them when you need them – they seem so much waste. They've helped you through that day, and that's all they can do. And if they help anyone else who comes after you – you feel that they couldn't because no one else would possibly be in such a terrible state as you were.

The function of the poem is private (a private 'easing' similar to Anna O's compositions), yet once put into circulation the function alters as it bears witness to a private life. The poem 'Sabbath Park' is a battle over reminiscence – a struggle between stifling Protestant Victoriana and an attempt to carve out a space for female, Catholic creativity. Its analogue in the poet's life is when she moved into a large house in a once Protestant area of Belfast; in a gloss on the poem McGuckian has said, 'Louisa is the Victorian ghost who still inhabits the place, the Victorian novelist I sometimes feel tempted or frightened of lapsing into. I'm in battle with the house and my own history, the literary-political history of women, chastity or death.' Read thus the poem is one of affirmation, a celebration of growing strength due to battling with her own, her sex's and her country's history. Rather than attempt to achieve mastery of the past, like Anna O she goes backwards in order to go forwards. Putting into question the notion of history as a progression, her cyclical narrative returns to the hysterical crisis suffered by the Victorian woman, in order to investigate ways out. This entails reciprocity between the Protestant and Catholic women, so she puts 'faith' in a 'less official' entrance as she climbs into the past through the window of the house. She is the opposite of the law as she enters to take control of the house – childish and accidental she 'upsets' the obsolete world of Victoriana gestured towards in 'damask', 'lawn' and 'safari':

> Now, after a year misspent on the ragged
> Garden side of the door, I put faith
> In a less official entrance, the accidental
> Oblongs of the windows that I find
> Have neither catch nor pulley. Broody
> As a seven-months' child, I upset
> The obsolete drawing-room that still seems
> Affronted by people having just gone,
> By astonishing Louisa with my sonnets,
> Almost a hostage in the dream
> Of her mother's hands – that would leave them
> Scattered over their damask sofas after
> Some evening party, filled
> With the radiance of my fine lawn shirt.[34]

This introduction of modern confusion into the conventional femininity of the Victorian house is a byproduct of the speaker's search for her own mother, her own history. For the room she enters, like the mother, is both traditional and 'absent' or 'lost'. Like the Victorian woman she becomes 'almost' a hostage of Louisa's mother, but it is precisely because the house is dragging her 'into its age' that she is able to create. The malady is productive:

> I feel the swaggering beginnings
> Of a new poem flaring up, because the house
> Is dragging me into its age, the malady
> Of fireplaces crammed with flowers, even
> On a golden winter Sunday. No matter
> How hysterically the clouds swing out,
> They may not alter by one drop of rain
> The safari of the garden beds, or make
> Louisa's dress with its oyster-coloured overlay
> Of moss kidnap me kindly for a day,
> As though a second wife were sleeping
> Already in your clothes, the sewn
> Lilies near the ground growing downward.

The final lines effect a break with previous dead history – she will not be trapped by the reversed growth from the shroud of her embattled history. This is because, unlike Louisa and Anna O, she is able to make public the things which are 'stuck' inside her. The woman's psychic upset can be channelled through literature so that it may 'upset' social norms. An earlier poem, 'The seed picture', associates an enigmatic writing with the possibility of 'liberation'. McGuckian makes her portrait with seeds, her picture of Joanna will be able to grow with the body of the girl it represents:

>   the clairvoyance
> Of seed work has opened up
> New spectrums of activity, beyond a second home.
> The seeds dictate their own vocabulary
> Their dusty colours capture
> More than we can plan.[35]

But this opening up is itself contained as the artist again goes backwards into the girl's history:

> Was it such self-indulgence to enclose her
> In the border of a grandmother's sampler,
> Bonding all the seeds in one continuous skin?

It is the connection with previously excluded history (the grandmother's needle-work) which creates that other 'transgressive' language which has its 'own vocabulary'. It is not simply an avant-garde practice but an attempt to open up the protests of the women of the past by seeing their similarity with the feminist protest of the present, just as Bakhtinian carnival brings together the crises of the past and present.

Of course one important consideration which I haven't touched on in this article is the necessity for this literary protest not simply to be contained in individual texts or works, but to be carried out within the framework of other attempts to alter the construction of the dominant literary institution. Developments such as feminist publishing houses are of crucial importance to this enterprise, because of the need to control the way texts are received and read, in order to prevent their objectification and marginalisation within the institution. It is in this respect that Bakhtin's warning that carnival became powerless when contained within texts which had lost the power to dialogise official forms, because of a narrowing of the literary institution, should act as a reminder against the tendency to celebrate the carnivalesque within specific texts.

In *The Female Malady*, Elaine Showalter warns against the dangers of a simple positivisation of women's madness, and the tendency to treat it as an archetypal form of protest when in fact it is a form of containment. And yet she draws a parallel rather than an opposition between the Victorian hysteric and the growing protest of the suffrage movement. Just as suffragettes in Holloway gaol were treated as hysterics (in the same way that Theweleit notes women protesters being treated as witches), so 'the elements of hunger, rebellion and rage latent in the phenomenon of female nervous disorder became explicit in the tactics of the suffrage campaigns'.[36] The suffragettes were able to utilise the link between female protest and madness, a link which was designed to exclude them further, in order to broadcast the contained protest of the hysteric. And so too a literature which draws on the female rebellion of the past may be able to bring it into conflict with official public patriarchal norms.

Notes

1 Peter Stallybrass and Allon White, *The Politics and Poetics of Transgression*, London and Ithaca, 1986; subsequent page references are given in the text.
2 Stallybrass and White implicitly acknowledge the politically progressive nature of women's relationship to transgression when they state, 'Only a challenge to the hierarchy of *sites* of discourse, which usually comes from groups and classes "situated" by the dominant in low or marginal positions, carries the promise of politically transformative power' (p. 201).
3 Hélène Cixous and Catherine Clément, *The Newly Born Woman*, trans. Betsy Wing,

Manchester and Minneapolis, 1986; subsequent page references are given in the text.

4 Although I will be looking specifically at the work of McGuckian, my argument is a more general one; I mean it to hold for radical feminist poetry, and the poetry of female experience, such as work by Adrienne Rich, Audre Lorde, and Muriel Rukseyer.

5 Mikhail Bakhtin, *Rabelais and his World*, trans. Hélène Iswolsky, Cambridge, Mass. and London, 1968, p. 73; subsequent page references are given in the text.

6 See also p. 471: 'The influence of the centuries-old hidden linguistic dogmatism on human thought, and especially on artistic imagery, is of great importance. If the creative spirit lives on in one language only, or if several languages coexist but remain strictly divided without struggling for supremacy, it is impossible to overcome this dogmatism buried in the depths of linguistic consciousness. It is possible to place oneself outside one's own language only when an essential historic change occurs.'

7 Robert Young makes a similar point in relation to heteroglossia and the novel in 'Back to Bakhtin', *Cultural Critique*, 2, 1985-86, pp. 71-92. Young argues against critics who analyse carnival in terms of its 'social force' while neglecting its linguistic dimension, and emphasises Bakhtin's awareness of the need for the 'artistic organisation' of the ordinary languages of the people which takes place in the novel.

8 Sigmund Freud and Joseph Breuer, *Studies on Hysteria*, Pelican Freud Library, vol. 3, London, 1974, p. 107.

9 For poems by Rich memorialising female communities and the women of the past, see especially the volumes *The Dream of a Common Language*, New York, 1978, and *A Wild Patience Has Taken Me This Far*, New York, 1981.

10 Freud, *The Origins of Psychoanalysis*, New York, 1954, p. 175. Freud of course later rejected this theory of the traumatic inception of neurosis on his 'discovery' of infantile sexuality.

11 Jane Gallop, 'Keys to Dora', in Charles Bernheimer and Claire Kahane, eds., *In Dora's Case*, London, 1985, p. 204. See Freud, 'A case of hysteria', in *Case Histories 1: Dora and Little Hans*, Pelican Freud Library, vol. 6, London, 1977, p. 102.

12 Several recent critiques of Habermas, notably by Nancy Fraser and Iris Marion Young, have stressed the importance for feminism and other resistance movements of including some notion of particularism, and values from the private sphere, in rational public discourse. Fraser suggests using the 'private' separate female community as a basis for the construction of a type of discourse which can then enter the public arena: 'separatism, while inadequate as a long-term political strategy, is in many cases a shorter-term necessity for women's physical, psychological and moral survival; and separatist communities have been the source of numerous reinterpretations of women's experience which have proved politically fruitful in contestation over the means of interpretation and communication' ('Habermas and gender', in Seyla Benhabib and Drucilla Cornell, eds., *Feminism as Critique*, Oxford, 1987, p. 54. See also Iris Marion Young's essay on the separation between private and public spheres, 'Impartiality and the civic public', *ibid.*, pp. 57-76).

13 But, as I have argued, for Bakhtin 'actual', nonliterary carnival is unorganised and politically ineffective.

14 Klaus Theweleit, *Male Fantasies*, Cambridge, 1987; subsequent page references are given in the text.

15 See Norbert Elias, *The Civilising Process*, vols. 1 and 2, New York, 1978 and 1982.

16 Gallop, 'Keys', p. 216. On the concept of 'threshold', see p. 215.

17 'No woman tolerates hearing (even if it is about the other woman), "My wife, a woman who is my woman, can be nothing". That is murder. So Dora, hearing it, knowing that the servant-girl had already heard it, sees woman, her mother, the maid, die, she sees woman massacred to make room for her. But she knows she will have her turn at being massacred. Her terrific reaction is to slap Mr. K' (Cixous and

Clément, *The Newly Born Woman*, p. 153).

18 I. Veith, *Hysteria: The History of a Disease*, Chicago, 1965, p. 210. On witches and burning, see also Keith Thomas, *Religion and the Decline of Magic*, London, 1971, pp. 435-86. On clitoridectomy (specifically Isaac Baker Brown's surgeries), see Elaine Showalter, *The Female Malady*, London, 1987, pp. 75-7; for Brown's own testimony, see Sheila Jeffreys, ed., *The Sexuality Debates*, London, 1987, pp. 11-42.

19 Interview of Medbh McGuckian by Clair Wills, Belfast, November 1986; subsequent prose quotations from McGuckian are taken from these interviews. Margaret Homans notes that it was considered scandalous in the early nineteenth century for a woman to write publicly: 'if she did, she was judged not as a writer but as a woman' (*Women Writers and Poetic Identity*, Princeton, 1980, p. 5). This tendency to look for a woman's sex in her words has of course continued.

20 Mary Russo, 'Female grotesques: carnival and theory', in Teresa de Lauretis, ed., *Feminist Studies/Critical Studies*, Basingstoke, 1988, p. 200.

21 Jan Montefiore, *Feminism and Poetry*, London, 1987, p. 5. This is a tendency which marks Sandra Gilbert and Susan Gubar's *The Madwoman in the Attic*. See also, for an argument aimed specifically at poetry, Alicia Suskin Ostriker's analysis of a 'line of feeling' traced through the history of women's poetry in *Stealing the Language*, Boston, 1986.

22 Extending the Russian Formalist idea of 'norm-breaking', John Frow provides an excellent account of the way in which literary norms come to 'stand for' dominant cultural norms: 'The literary canon acts as an exemplary mode of authority and comes to bear a heavy charge of value through which literature comes to "stand for" (though rarely *completely*) the whole realm of authoritative values' (*Marxism and Literary History*, Oxford, 1986, p. 128).

23 Julia Kristeva, 'Word, dialogue, and novel', in *Desire in Language*, ed. Leon S. Roudiez, trans. Thomas Gora, Alice Jardine and Leon S. Roudiez, New York, 1980, p. 71. Whereas for Frow the problem with Kristeva's concept of transgression is that it is not literary *enough*: 'the problem is that the notion of a social text does not allow us to discriminate between the ways in which different kinds of codes or discourse function in the literary text, and in particular to account for the literary code' (*Marxism*, p. 127).

24 Kristeva, *About Chinese Women*, New York, 1986, p. 41.

25 Kristeva, 'Oscillation between power and denial', in Elaine Marks and Isabelle de Courtivron, eds., *New French Feminisms*, Brighton and New York, 1981, p. 166.

26 Natalie Zemon Davies, *Society and Culture in Early Modern France*, London, 1975 (see especially pp. 124-51).

27 Veith notes the hysteric's aptitude for mimicry. Convulsive attacks in hysteria had become rare in Charcot's time, but when, because of lack of space, hysterics had to be housed with epileptic patients in the same wing at the Salpêtrière, they occurred frequently as mimicked epileptic fits (*Hysteria*, p. 230). See also, on the hysteric's 'histrionic' ability, Showalter, *The Female Malady*, pp. 152-4.

28 Russo, 'Female grotesques', p. 223. In some ways, of course, the language of the hysteric was never private, contained discourse, since it only became known and publicised as 'hysterical' through the official public discourse of the scientist.

29 Luce Irigaray, 'La Mystérique', in *Speculum of the Other Woman*, Ithaca, 1985, pp. 191-202. See also in the same volume the sections 'A very black sexuality', pp. 66-73, and 'The avoidance of (masculine) hysteria', pp. 268-78.

30 Irigaray, *This Sex Which Is Not One*, Ithaca, 1985, p. 152.

31 Sarah Kofman, *The Enigma of Woman*, Ithaca, 1985, pp. 36-7, 43.

32 Freud and Breuer, 'Fräulein Anna O', in *Studies*, pp. 74-102. Bertha Pappenheim was later to need both obstinacy and energy in her public reformist career.

33 McGuckian 'Tulips', in *The Flower Master*, Oxford, 1982, p. 10.

34 McGuckian, 'Sabbath Park', in *Venus and the Rain*, Oxford, 1984, p. 54.

35 McGuckian, 'The seed picture', in *The Flower Master*, p. 23.

36 Showalter, *The Female Malady*, p. 162.

Ann Jefferson

Bodymatters: Self and Other in Bakhtin, Sartre and Barthes

I borrow the title of this essay from a British television programme whose underlying premiss is that the body matters primarily as a mechanism whose functioning the programme sets out to exhibit and explain. Human physiology is turned into a spectacle for our admiration and edification, and we are implicitly led to believe that all it takes to achieve psychological and social equilibrium is a proper recognition and management of the needs and workings of the human frame: *mens sana in corpore sano.* But the physiological *corpus* extolled by the TV is not the one that any of the writers discussed in this essay would be prepared to recognise as their own. Indeed Sartre and Barthes both explicitly disown such a body, and they do so in the first instance because it does not correspond to the form in which human subjects actually experience their own bodies. Moreover, they also dissociate themselves from physiological conceptions of the body because it is not physiology which figures in the intersubjective relations without which neither psychology nor sociality would be conceivable. The body matters in the work of the three writers I shall be exploring – Mikhail Bakhtin, Jean-Paul Sartre and Roland Barthes – because it proves to be indispensable both to the undoing and to the salvation of all our dealings with others. In one way or another all three give the lie to the notion propounded by our libertarian culture that repression can be undone by a freeing of the body and a proselytising dissemination of knowledge about its workings. Far from being a self-sufficient mechanism, the body in their conception is treated as the site and focus of a whole variety of problems and conflicts.

There are several reasons for discussing these three writers together. In addition to the fact that they are all theorists of the body in their own right, there is a measure of cross-fertilisation between them:

Sartre's allusion to Bakhtin in one of his last interviews puts an
intriguing gloss on the striking similarities between them on a number
of key issues.[1] And as for Barthes, as Annette Lavers argues so
persuasively, he has an undeniably Sartrian streak; this is made particularly explicit in his *dédicace* to *Camera Lucida* which he presents as
a homage to Sartre's *L'Imaginaire*.[2] But the chief reason is that they all
see self–Other relations in the same underlying terms: quite simply,
these relations are determined by the fact that one does not see
oneself as one is seen by others, and this difference in perspective
turns on the body. More specifically, since the body is what others see
but what the subject does not, the subject becomes dependent upon
the Other in a way that ultimately makes the body the focus of a power
struggle with far-reaching ramifications. Thus in one way or another all
three writers take issue with the popular claim that the body is free and
self-determining: it is not and cannot be so because it is subject to the
grip and grasp of the gaze of the Other.[3]

Taking these three writers together makes it possible to construct
a sequence of argument that begins in the early 1920s with Bakhtin,
proceeds via the Sartre of *Being and Nothingness*, returns to the
Bakhtin of the 1930s and ends with the late work of Barthes in the
1970s, up to and including *Camera Lucida*. In a sense all I am proposing
to do here is to offer an exposition of the ideas of these thinkers on the
topic in hand (the body in self–Other relations), and, by presenting
these ideas in a quasi-narrative sequence, make of them a sort of relay
of argument and counterargument, problems and solutions. At the
very least I hope to show that there has been a continuing and long-
standing debate around this issue, even if the participants themselves
have not all always been aware of each other and their alternative
positions. And, somewhat more ambitiously, if a little more tenta-
tively, I shall also be seeking to explore the implications for literature
and writing that are raised by this issue. The rather mystifying inclusion of the body on the recent literary-theoretical agenda may in part
be explained in terms of the argument whose history it is my more
modest aim to document.

Bakhtin – the body as gift

I shall begin at the chronological beginning of my sequence of ideas –
which is also the point where relations between self and Other are
presented in their simplest and sweetest light – with Bakhtin's early
essay 'Author and hero in aesthetic activity'. Written between 1920
and 1924, it is only the second recorded item in Bakhtin's voluminous

output, and precedes the well-known Rabelais study (which I shall be discussing below) by nearly twenty years.[4]

In this essay Bakhtin sees life largely in terms of the literary metaphors of 'author' and 'hero'. The relations between self and Other are viewed as equivalent to those between hero and author. This is because the self is always 'authored' or created by the Other/author (the near-homophony in English is a nice bonus for Bakhtin's association of the two terms). The identity of the subject–hero is dependent upon the creative activity of the Other; and, in particular, what is authored by the Other, the thing that makes the subject a hero, is the body. Self is placed in relation to Other via the body because the body is not a self-sufficient entity: 'the body is not something self-sufficient, it is in need of *the other*, in need of his recognition and form-bestowing activity' (p. 51). Without the Other the body has neither shape nor form because the self has no direct or coherent access to it.

The self (subject) experiences himself and the world quite differently from the way in which he is experienced and perceived by others, and this difference is centred on his body.[5] The subject's position in the world is determined by his body, and it is from its vantage point that his gaze embraces a world which he sees as if from a frontier: 'I am situated as it were on the border of the world I see; in plastic-pictural terms I have no natural relation to it' (p. 30). The Other, however, has a perspective on the subject that enables him both to see the external body that constitutes the subject's vantage point on the world, and also to see that body as part of that world. This is a perspective that is at once radically different from that of the subject, yet also serves to complete it.

There are other differences too, which also have the body as their focus: living his body from the inside, the self experiences his external body (the one the Other sees and authors) as a series of 'disparate fragments, dangling on the string of [his] inner sensation of self' (p. 30). Self and Other are divided by the fact that what is for one sensation and fragment is for the Other object and whole, and it is this unbridgeable difference in experience that both opposes self to Other, and yet simultaneously creates the dependency of self upon Other. Bakhtin repeatedly emphasises the significance of the author's 'outsidedness' (his necessary otherness) in relation to the object of his authoring. The Other relates to the self by building on that difference – not by attempting to relive the subject's sensations, but by creating external shape and form for the subject's body. This is why the Other is an Author.

Essentially this authoring is an act of *gathering*. The author gathers together all the parts of the body that escape the subject's own visual field ('his head, his face and its expression' (p. 25), and then places the resultant entity in the world where for the author (but not, of course, for the hero) the body appears as an object amongst other objects. In short, he transforms the dispersedness of the subject's experience into the assembled whole that makes him a hero. Thus self–Other relations are essentially active and productive: something is produced (rather than merely being revealed), and furthermore that production is construed primarily as an aesthetic one. For Bakhtin it is the

> *aesthetically productive* [my italics] relation of the author to the hero – a relation of intense outsidedness [*vnenakhodimost'*] of the author to all moments of the hero, . . . an outsidedness which makes it possible to assemble the *whole* hero, who from within is dispersed and scattered . . . to assemble the hero and his life and *complete him, creating a whole* by means of those moments which are inaccessible to him within himself: the plenitude of his external image, his physical appearance, the background to which his back is turned. (pp. 17-18)

Artistic activity 'saves' the subject from his limitations (the limitations of his perspective on himself and on the world) and from his fragmentation. Part of the 'sweetness' of Bakhtin's version of self–Other relations in this essay comes from the fact that the subject doesn't appear to be unduly bothered that the price of his 'salvation' is this dependence upon his author. (It's perhaps also worth drawing attention to another aspect of Bakhtin's optimism, namely the fact that the aesthetic is synonymous with the construction of coherence and wholes: this is a view which we will not find endorsed either by the later Bakhtin or by Barthes.)

The author's production of the hero is not just an aesthetic act, it is also an act of love. Relations between author and hero are conceived as entirely happy and loving relations in which the subject–hero receives the whole that the author makes of him as a gift offered by the (author–)lover to his (hero–)beloved. Love is the culmination – or even the condition – of the aesthetic: 'Only love can be aesthetically productive.'[6] Bakhtin's love is a strikingly one-way process in which the author–lover is the active partner and the beloved–hero his passive counterpart. Bakhtin speaks of them as two 'souls' or two 'activities' of which 'one is living life and has become *passive* for the other, which *actively* gives it form and celebrates it' (p. 113, my italics). Bakhtin makes it clear that the beloved's passivity (tellingly defined as 'feminine') is absolutely essential for the success of the authorial activity and its construction of the physical form of the beloved. But it is only the thoroughly undialectical nature of these relations that makes possible such amorous harmony.

This non-dialectic basis of self–Other relations is indirectly confirmed by the instances of a number of possible hiccups in the system mentioned – though not seriously explored – by Bakhtin. Briefly stated, problems may arise when the hero doesn't like the authorial 'judgement' that has been passed on him; when he internalises an image of his external self; when desire brings the two partners too close; or when the hero's death is acknowledged as a part of the picture the author creates of him. In the first three cases, there is, in one way or another, a blurring of the active and passive roles whose clear demarcation is so necessary for the proper functioning of the aesthetic–loving system. If the hero becomes dissatisfied with his physical appearance (i.e. the authorial judgement – the two are synonymous), the result is a kind of authoring of the author by the hero: 'my [the hero's] frustration, and a certain resentment to which is added my dissatisfaction with my physical appearance, *give a solidity to this other, the possible author of my physical appearance*' (p. 35, my italics). Frustration produces a kind of turning of the tables on the author, and the hero assumes a doubly active role; first as author in his own right, and second in his response to his author/Other which becomes frankly aggressive: 'one may distrust him, hate him, wish to destroy him' (p. 35). This unloving activity on the part of the oxymoronic hero–author has an authoring effect of its own, and it is the hero's very resistance to the authorial portrait of himself that engenders a 'heroic' version of the author: 'in attempting to struggle with someone's [the author's] definitively form-bestowing evaluation, I [the hero] compress it to the point where it becomes autonomous, almost an individual localised in existence' (p. 35). When the hero takes issue with the author over who or what he is, then their roles are not only reversed but also blurred in such a way as to change the whole principle on which their relations function. Bakhtin himself fails to pursue the implications of heroic frustration as far as this, but had he done so he would have found himself working with a concept very like the *dialogic*, which is in essence a mode of conflict (rather than sweetness and light) where (because) all subjects have (at least in principle) equal right of say.

The second of Bakhtin's hiccups – where the external image is fatally internalised by the subject – involves the same crossing of the demarcation line. The implied assumption in Bakhtin's discussion of the author's dealings with his hero is that the hero will not take any active interest in the gift which the author makes of him and to him. Loving relations require a thoroughgoing naivety on the part of the beloved; for instance, the beloved cannot have access to his own beauty (p. 51): beauty is always and only in the eye of the beholder. The case that Bakhtin cites is not one that in the first instance involves the hero's own sense of identity, but it can be extrapolated from the purely sporting example described by Bakhtin:

> When one is faced with executing a difficult, risky leap, it is extremely dangerous to follow the movement of one's legs: one must gather oneself together from within, and likewise from within weigh up one's movements. The first rule in any sport is: look straight ahead, not at yourself. . . .
>
> The external image of the action and its external visual (*vozzritel'noe*) relation to the objects of the external world are never given to the performer of the action. (p. 45)

Looking (at yourself) while you leap is a highly dangerous thing to do, and on the figurative plane the effects of such self-regarding attitudes can be just as devastating, because they empty acts of their substance and purpose, and *action* is, significantly, turned into *play* or *gesture* (p. 46). It is fatal – both to leaping and to any seriousness of purpose – for the hero–subject to adopt an authorial perspective on himself, and the system only works as long as each (but particularly the hero) keeps to his allotted role. If the implications of this example had been pursued any further by Bakhtin he might have come up with something like Sartre's idea of *mauvaise foi* which entails precisely this internalising of such external images. (Bakhtin's emphasis on the word gesture (*geste* in French) may by now have suggested Sartre to anyone who hadn't already anticipated that this was where the argument was heading.)[7] That Bakhtin failed to get as far as the sort of problem implied by *mauvaise foi* can be attributed quite clearly to the absence of any dialectic in Bakhtin's view of self–Other relations. *Mauvaise foi* is an inevitable component of the Sartrian scenario because of his assumption that self and Other are in a relation of reciprocity; for Bakhtin, by contrast, sporting injuries and the occasional lapse into *geste* are mere accidents in a system in which such things are not programmed to happen.

The confusions wrought by desire in the Bakhtinian scenario constitute another variant of the demarcation issue. The problem with desire in a context where self–Other relations are conceived as relations created by an 'outsided' authoring of the human subject is that it brings the two parties too close together. The body of the hero (and remember that his body is the basis of his construction as hero) simply disintegrates on contact with the Other, and becomes indistinguishable from that of the author as subject: 'the outer body of the other [here the hero] disintegrates, becomes no more than an aspect of my inner body' (p. 52). Desire places the two parties on the same side of the boundary, or rather destroys the distance that makes it possible to construct boundaries in the first place, and it must ultimately be for this reason that '[the sexual approach] to the other's body is not in itself capable of developing form-bestowing plastic-pictural energies, that is, it is not capable of creating the body as an external, finished, self-sufficient artistic entity' (pp. 51-2).

The final problematic aspect of Bakhtin's self–Other system can be extrapolated from his remarks about the hero's death. Bakhtin points out that the completedness of the author's 'plastic-pictural' image of the hero implicitly entails the hero's death; for the authorial picture to be truly complete, the hero must be as if dead, which, says Bakhtin, is tantamount to saying that 'death is a form of aesthetic finalisation of the personality' (p. 122). This introduces an entirely new dimension to the authored version of the hero's incarnation: 'the tones of a requiem are to be heard throughout the whole life of the incarnated hero' (p. 123). The lover's gift rings a death-knell for his beloved.

Bakhtin finds his way out of this unhappy state of affairs by saying that the hero's death will be transformed by art: 'this lived life is in art safeguarded, justified, finalised in eternal memory' (p. 123). This is a solution that is very much of its time (the 1920s – think of Proust, for example), and it implies an astonishing acquiescence on the part of the hero. Either the hero remains as unaware of the death predicted by the 'tones of a requiem' accompanying his incarnation as hero as he was of his beauty; or else, in living his incarnation as an immolation upon the altar of art, he consents to his own death. Bakhtin would seem to have carried the logic of his system to its ultimate extreme: for what he is saying is that the hero's passivity has no limits and cannot be galvanised even by the prospect of his own extinction. This is an outcome that one cannot imagine many heroes confronting without some wish to revolt, for on these terms the hero would have every reason to refuse the gift of his incarnation, to refuse to play the role of hero, and to demand that the demarcation line that constitutes his role as hero be crossed or simply erased.

I have dwelt on these examples not only because they provide the basis for a critique of the ideas Bakhtin puts forward in the 'Author and hero' essay, but also because they pave the way both to a more *dialogic* conception of intersubjectivity and to Sartre – which, as I hope to demonstrate, in some senses amounts to the same thing. In addition, what the move on to Sartre will also permit is a proper consideration of the role that language plays in self–Other relations even if the literary dimension (so central in the metaphors of Bakhtin's discussion) ceases for the time being to be a significant part of the issue.

Sartre and the body as theft

In formal terms Sartre's scenario is very similar to Bakhtin's: the subject's position in the world is determined by his physical location in it, and the view he has on that world is the one provided by the vantage point that is his body. He shares with Bakhtin's subject the very limited perspective on his own body which in *Being and Nothingness* Sartre neatly defines as the 'point of view on which he has no point of view'. This limitation means that the Other, like Bakhtin's author, is in a position to perceive him (the subject) as he himself cannot – as an object amongst objects in a meaningful relation to the world – that is to say, to give him flesh and identity. Sartre corroborates Bakhtin in maintaining that it is the body which makes possible the subject's incarnation by the Other: 'I exist for myself as a body known by the Other.'[8] But in spite of the close structural similarity of the situation described by both Sartre and Bakhtin, there is a profound contrast in the evaluation that each of them makes of it.

Whereas in Bakhtin the author/Other's incarnation of the hero/subject is a loving and aesthetically motivated gift, in Sartre this incarnation (which he calls an image) is a negation (p. 228), a theft (p. 225), an alienation (p. 263), an enslavement (p. 267); it represents danger (p. 268); it brings shame (p. 261) and fear (p. 259), and is the harbinger of death – 'the death of my possibilities' (p. 271). The Other lets loose a catalogue of irremediable catastrophes for the subject; and even love itself in Sartre proves to be just one of the necessarily antagonistic modes in which self relates to Other.

The difference between these two evaluations of what is fundamentally the same situation can be explained by the fact that Sartre's subject is much more alive than is Bakhtin's to the content of the Other's authoring (although Sartre does not use this word), and his knowledge of this content obliges him to make some kind of response to it. Sartre's subject cannot sit passively upon his pedestal, or naively busy himself with living a life whose celebration in the eyes of the Other has no effects upon that life.

Significantly, there is never any question that the image of the subject created by the Other might be inaccurate: shame, rage, fear (and the occasional instance of pride) are marks of the subject's recognition of the validity of that image. The role of the Other is to reveal the truth of the subject to himself: 'With the appearance of the Other's look I experience the revelation of my being-as-object' (p. 351). This 'being-as-object' cannot be denied or disowned by the subject, as is shown by Sartre's famous *voyeur* scenario. In Sartre's dramatic illustration of this aspect of self–Other relations he has a jealous subject peeping through a key-hole. The jealousy is something that the subject *is*, but not something that he knows. Such knowledge can only be acquired through the intermediary of the Other. For the subject, the sound of footsteps in the corridor is enough to indicate the presence of an Other who instantly transforms his (the subject's) perception of himself and reveals to him his jealousy. The *in flagrante* quality of the scene serves to support the implication that the verdict is incontrovertible: there is no denying the subject's jealousy because he is caught red-handed being jealous.

Yet true as it is, the verdict, like all verdicts, is alienating; the subject is divided from himself by the image of himself that comes from the Other. He is, but also is not what the Other reveals him to be, and shame, rage and fear are as much a sign of the subject's alienation from what he is as they are an index of his recognition of what he is. 'The person [in this case the jealous person] is presented to consciousness *in so far as the person is an object for the Other*' (p. 260). This means that his identity lies in the hands of the Other: 'all of a sudden I [this is the subject speaking] am conscious of myself *as escaping myself . . . in that I have my foundation outside myself*. I am for myself only as I am a pure reference to the Other' (p. 260, my italics). The Other's image is at once a completion of the kind we encountered in Bakhtin's authoring of the hero, and yet also a theft, a loss; giving here proves to be a form of taking. In particular what is taken from the subject is his sense of mastery: as subject he has to concede that '*I am no longer master of the situation*' (p. 265). The Other's image of the subject's *ego* has an authority which deprives the subject of any authoring capacity of his own. Sartre's 'hero' (to describe him in Bakhtin's terminology for a moment) is keenly aware not only of what is being done to him in his incarnation by the Other, but of the price that he has to pay for its implementation, namely the loss of any active role. Being a hero in Sartre's world is not a gift bestowed by the loving attentions of the Other, but the index of a loss of mastery. The subject only becomes a hero because the Other has contrived to strip him of his status as author.

Passivity and activity are not so unquestionably distinct as they are in Bakhtin: in Sartre passivity (in the subject) is the result of a privation of activity; and (the Other's) activity is the means whereby he brings that privation about. Consequently, passivity is something to be resisted, and resisted through a struggle for active mastery. The result is that self–Other relations are a perpetual see-saw on which neither party can ever achieve permanent ascendancy over the other. The site of this struggle is the body, because it is through the body that one becomes vulnerable to the Other: 'My body is there not only as the point of view which I am but again as a point of view on which are actually brought to bear points of view which I could never take; my body escapes me on all sides. This means first that this ensemble of *senses*, which themselves cannot be apprehended, is given as apprehended elsewhere and by others' (p. 352). The subject is vulnerable to the Other on two counts: in the first place, as Sartre is saying here, he cannot control the image or interpretation that his body constitutes in the eyes of the Other. And in the second place, the Other is liable to reduce the subject to being a mere object, *only* a body, and thus denying what Sartre calls the subject's transcendence. For Sartre one is both one's body and more than one's body. One 'exists one's body', as Sartre puts it (p. 351), and at the same time goes beyond it.

It is this going beyond which the Other's construction negates; the Other reduces one's existence to mere 'facticity': 'to the extent that I am conscious of existing for the Other I apprehend my own facticity . . . The shock of the encounter with the Other is for me a revelation in emptiness of the existence of my body outside as an in-itself for the Other' (pp. 351-2). For Sartre this revelation is experienced by the subject as a terrible degradation whose humiliations are compounded by Sartre's implicit gendering of the situation. In the existential world transcendence tends to be presented in masculine terms, facticity in feminine ones. The concepts of 'active' and 'passive' already carry a latent set of connotations that link activity with masculinity and passivity with femininity, but the material qualities of facticity specifically associate it with the feminine.[9] The intervention of the .Other, then, brings the subject low by depriving him not only of his transcendence but also of his masculinity. There are parallels here with Bakhtin's gendering of author and hero, but the passivity of Bakhtin's hero was so extreme that he appeared oblivious or indifferent even to the implied threat to his virility brought by his authored condition. However, I shall leave the feminist strand in my argument hanging for the time being in order to return to a different aspect of the conflict constituted by self–Other relations as described by Sartre.

I say 'as described by Sartre', but what I have been seeking to demonstrate is that the Sartrian scheme merely makes explicit the conflicts and problems which are bound to be thrown up in the view of self–Other relations which he shares with the early Bakhtin. In Bakhtin they remain latent and only surface on the margins of the argument as unfortunate but supposedly incidental exceptions to the basic optimistic rule. Sartre offers a full descriptive account of what is basically the same situation and shows that Bakhtin's exceptions *are* the rule. But it is to Bakhtin that one has to return for an understanding of the nature of the power that self and Other each lay claim to, as well as for an indication of a possible way out of the dilemma.

In Sartre power is automatically granted to the Other; his very presence guarantees him an ascendancy which the subject then seeks to wrest from him in order to appropriate it for himself. But it cannot just be his apparent priority that gives the Other the whip hand in the confrontations in which the subject encounters him. The power which holds the subject in thrall cannot be ascribed to the simple *fiat* of the Other's imaging of that subject; the authority of the image constructed by the Other derives from his implicit recourse to the superior authority that is language.

Sartre does not linger on the linguistic implication of the question because his largely individualist view of human experience and human relations prevents him from taking on board their full discursive extent. Nevertheless, the following claim opens up a whole new dimension to the problem:

> Language is not a phenomenon added on to being-for-others. It *is* originally being-for-others; that is, it is the fact that a subjectivity experiences itself as an object for the Other . . . [Language] is already given in the recognition of the Other. I *am* language. By the sole fact that whatever I may do, my acts freely conceived and executed, my projects launched toward my possibilities have outside of them a meaning which escapes me and which I experience. (p. 372).

Dialogism is exactly this: for in self–Other relations the subject is translated into linguistic terms over which he has no control and whose meaning is inevitably determined by the Other. At this point, therefore, Bakhtin comes back into the argument – no longer as the author of 'Author and hero' (no pun intended), but as the theorist of dialogism. It might be going too far to suggest that Bakhtin himself could have written the following, but the author of *Problems of*

Dostoevsky's Poetics and of 'Discourse in the novel' would have appreciated (and I can't help thinking wholly endorsed) every word of the following lines from Sartre:

> the 'meaning' of my expressions always escapes me. I never know exactly if I signify what I wish to signify ... For lack of knowing what I actually express for the Other, I constitute my language as an incomplete phenomenon of flight outside myself. As soon as I express myself, I can only guess at the meaning of what I express – *i.e.* the meaning of what I am – since in this perspective to express and to be are one. *The Other is always there, present and experienced as the one who gives to language its meaning.* (pp. 373-4, my italics)

The self is constituted by the language of the Other which draws its power from the simple fact that it is language. It is not actually the otherness of the Other which gives him priority in the confrontation between self and Other, but language. It is precisely this linguistic priority that gives the constructions that the Other places on the subject the force of their conviction. The subject's awareness that the Other has access to a language that lies beyond his (the subject's) control exemplifies precisely what Bakhtin means by dialogism.[10] If relations between self and Other can be conceived of as dialogic, then Bakhtin's concept of dialogism could be taken as an implicit acknowledgement on his part that the scenario of 'Author and hero in aesthetic activity' does have its darker side, and that author and hero are linked as much by the kind of conflict described by Sartre as by the love adduced by the early Bakhtin.[11]

Once the relationship between self and Other has been set up in the terms that I have been outlining, there is no real possibility of any exit from it.[12] Sartre's galvanising of Bakhtin's hero into a more active role only compounds the problems inadvertently raised by Bakhtin, so that every form of human relations proves to be merely one of two equally unsatisfactory alternatives. As Sartre says at the end of his discussion of the various manifestations of 'concrete relations with Others' (love, language and masochism on the one hand, and indifference, desire, hatred and sadism on the other):

> ceaselessly tossed from being-a-look to being-looked-at, falling from one to the other in alternate revolutions, we are always, no matter what attitude is adopted, in a state of instability in relation to the Other ... and we shall never place ourselves concretely on a plane where the recognition of the Other's freedom would involve the Other's recognition of our freedom. The Other is on principle inapprehensible; he flees me when I seek him and possesses me when I flee him. (p. 408)

The recognition of the role of language in the situation exacerbates it still further because the weight of the linguistic system seems to remove all possibility of any individual initiative as a means of getting out of the dilemma.

However, the factor that both Sartre and the Bakhtin of 'Author and hero' overlook is that they are limiting themselves to seeing things entirely in terms of *representation*. Or at least, while they acknowledge that what they are propounding takes representation as its basis, they do so very fleetingly and without pausing to consider whether there might not be an issue here worth exploring at greater length. Bakhtin mentions in passing that the distance he establishes between author and hero makes the activity of representation the key to the relations that exist between the two protagonists: 'what expresses . . . the reality of the aesthetic event is the term . . . "representation" . . . , a word which shifts the centre of gravity from the hero to the aesthetically active subject – the author' (p. 80). The underlying determination of the situation is ultimately attributable to the fact that it is conceived in terms of a representation: the author acquires his status through his authoring of a representation of which the hero is both object and passive recipient.

Equally for Sartre, the effect of the gaze of the Other is to produce an image of the subject which he may experience as an inadequate representation, but which is none the less precisely that, a representation.[13] The subject may suffer from the representation constructed by the Other, but his responses – be they evasive or aggressive – still show him to be thinking in terms of representation. Either he longs for a better, more adequate representation of himself or he retaliates by making the Other the object of his own representation.

But the later Bakhtin – the Bakhtin who theorises carnival in the Dostoevsky and particularly the Rabelais book – demonstrates that there is another world outside and beyond representation. And in this other world, self–Other relations do not have to involve the ascendancy of one protagonist over another, because they do not have to be restricted to the roles that representation entails (notably author, object and recipient). Crucially, what carnival reveals is that relations of representation can be reconstituted as relations of participation, or at the very least that the specular basis of classical representation can be transformed into one which implies an involvement with representation, its objects and its recipients. For the sake of simplicity I shall use the term 'representation' for the former and 'participation' for the latter.

Carnival: representation versus participation

Bakhtin and many of his commentators have tended to portray carnival as a kind of Renaissance Eden from which modern bourgeois man has fallen into representation in a one-way historical process. But I shall be arguing here that carnival is also a concept and a practice which comprise an alternative to – rather than just a predecessor of – representation.

Peter Stallybrass and Allon White have shown that there is nothing that inherently protects carnival from its potential vulnerability to an observing gaze. Its participants can always be transformed from active and equal subjects into the objects of a representation constructed by an author who chooses to place himself above or beyond the scene of carnival.[14] In fact authoring is by its very nature a decarnivalising activity, for the authorial perspective and the demarcations between observer and participants are against the whole spirit of carnival. Carnival 'does not acknowledge any distinction between actors and spectators . . . Carnival is not a spectacle seen by the people; they live in it and everyone participates because its very idea embraces all the people.'[15] The unattainable equality between subjects whose absence is so lamented by Sartre in his scheme of things proves, all of a sudden, to be the cornerstone of Bakhtin's carnival. This indicates, first, that carnival does indeed create a different order of human relations from those constructed by and associated with representation, and second, that carnival may therefore constitute some kind of a solution to the *impasse* of representation. Indeed, Sartre may be trying to grope his way towards some such idea in the post-script to his discussion of 'concrete relations with Others', where he addresses the issue of the togetherness implied in '*Mitsein*'. But he makes no real headway with the idea because he is unable to conceive of a 'we' except as a variation on the basic representational schema, that is to say as either 'co-spectator' or collective object of the gaze of the Other.

One index of the difference between representation and carnival is the thoroughgoing difference in construction of the body that is involved. The represented body is roughly what Bakhtin in *Rabelais and his World* calls the 'classical body': a completed entity sealed off both from the world which is its context and from other bodies. In the 'Author and hero' essay the author's function is to 'gather' the fragments through which the subject experiences himself into a completed whole, the whole which simultaneously constitutes him as a hero. Similarly, in Sartre the subject may be split, but only in the sense that he is alienated from the being that he is for the Other – not in the sense that the image produced by the Other is not complete. (The problem is even – perhaps – that the image is *too* complete: the subject's anguish comes from the way that jealousy is 'added' to his sense of himself through the intervention of the gaze of the Other.) The corollary of this image of the body as whole and complete is its isolation. In the Rabelais book Bakhtin speaks of the 'atomisation' of the being in this conception (p. 24), and comments on the way that in its expression as realism 'boundaries' are drawn between bodies and objects (and thus between body and body) and serve to 'complete each individual outside the link with the ultimate whole' (p. 53).

The carnival body – or what Bakhtin calls the body of 'grotesque realism' – is quite different. It loses its individual definition and is collectivised at a transindividual level:

> In grotesque realism . . . the bodily element is deeply positive. It is presented not in a private, egotistic form, severed from the other spheres of life, but as something universal, representing all the people . . . [T]his is not the body and its physiology in the modern sense of these words, because it is not individualised. The material bodily principle is contained not in the biological individual, not in the bourgeois ego, but in the people, a people who are constantly growing and renewed. (p. 19)

The 'bodily element' (it becomes difficult to speak of 'the body' in the context of carnival) is epitomised by events and activities in which boundaries between bodies, and between bodies and the world, are at their most obscured and eroded: birth, death, copulation, defecation, eating, etc.

At the same time the individual body is frankly dismembered into a series of focal points through which or from which bodies make contact with what lies outside them. The carnival body is a collectivised jumble of protruberances and orifices: bellies, noses, breasts, buttocks, assorted genitalia, mouths, guts, and so on, in which what belongs to whom is both irrelevant and impossible to determine. It is a body whose character is best expressed by the 'senile pregnant hags' in the terracotta collection which Bakhtin discusses. In these figurines is combined 'a senile, decaying and deformed flesh with the flesh of new life, conceived but as yet unformed' (pp. 25-6). (The figures point to an aspect of the corporeal that neither the earlier Bakhtin nor Sartre had addressed in their consideration of the body and its relation to the Other, namely pregnancy.) And at the same time they also suggest a completely different evaluation of factors that they did consider: death, the feminine, and degradation in general (death and woman constituting particular forms of degradation). Death in the collective body of the people is not the unmitigated disaster that it was for both Bakhtin's hero (who was 'saved' only by the art of the author), and for Sartre's subject (whose experience of the death-in-life of the gaze of the Other was so destructive of his own possibilities). In the blurring of boundaries that accompanies death, death and life become indistinguishable: 'Death and death throes, labor and childbirth are intimately interwoven' (p. 151).

Equally, the evaluation of woman in carnival is completely transformed. In his association of the feminine and facticity Sartre is continuing what Bakhtin here calls the ascetic tradition of medieval Christianity which saw woman as 'the *incarnation* of sin, the temptation of the *flesh*' (p. 240, my italics). But carnival derives from a quite other tradition, the popular one, which puts an entirely different value on flesh, and in particular on the flesh of 'the material bodily lower stratum':

> The popular tradition is in no way hostile to woman and does not approach her negatively. In this tradition [as indeed in the other] woman is essentially related to the material bodily lower stratum; she is the incarnation of this stratum that degrades and regenerates simultaneously. She is ambivalent. She debases, brings down to earth, lends a bodily substance to things, and destroys; but, first of all, she is the principle that gives birth. (p. 240)

The destructive/regenerative quality of woman here is exactly the quality which characterises carnival in general, and as such its degradations bring joy rather than the dreadful humiliation suffered by Sartre's subject in his experience of his own facticity. If Sartre's subject is brought low by his objectivation as flesh this ought – at least in the carnival world-view it ought – to be a matter of rejoicing rather than the *malaise*, shame, rage or fear that constitute the Sartrian response. In all forms of grotesque realism things are 'degrade[d], br[ought] down to earth, their subject [turned] into flesh'. And the laughter associated with carnival is singled out by Bakhtin as being particularly effective in 'degrading' and 'materialising' (p. 20). In other words, the process which in the context of representation creates a terrible trauma for the Sartrian subject is turned around and re-evaluated to become an enabling and regenerative one in the context of carnival.

Finally, these differences may be summarised in an opposition between the finished and the unfinished: the body of Bakhtin's hero, like the body of Sartre's subject, in short, the body of representation is a *finished* construction, whereas the body of carnival and the grotesque is by definition *un*finished. In so far as the grotesque body has identifiable shape (comprising its various protruberances and orifices), that shape serves primarily to draw attention to the unfinished processes of becoming and regeneration, as it does so typically for Bakhtin in the figure of the senile, pregnant hag. This is essentially what carnival is about. The distinction contained in the two kinds of body is thus ultimately one between process and product: carnival is a process, representation makes a product.

Comparing and contrasting representation and carnival has yielded a picture of quite precise parallels and inversions, suggesting the existence of underlying structural similarities which enable one to see how each might succeed in gaining purchase on the other. As I have already said, the story is usually told so as to suggest that representation undoes and betrays carnival, sealing up the body's orifices, removing its 'protruberances and its offshoots', smoothing out its 'convexities', and moving it away from the thresholds at which the body either enters or leaves life (i.e. birth and death) (p. 29), so that representation is presented as a repression of carnival, as something which necessarily follows rather than precedes it.[16] Nevertheless, in Bakhtin's occasional glimpses of the broader historical view, he does seem to be implying that there has been a series of cultural shifts between something like representation and something like carnival: the literary and artistic canon of antiquity was focused on the 'classical body' that I have associated with specular representation, in contrast to which he cites Doric comedy, '"satyric"' drama, Sicilian comic forms, Aristophanes and other writings of 'nonclassic' antiquity as an alternative perspective (p. 31). Similarly, he contrasts the Renaissance and its (carnivalesque) view of the body with the body as it appears in the canons of the Middle Ages, thus establishing a chronology in which carnival follows rather than precedes representation. What the motor behind this sequence is Bakhtin doesn't say, but it would be rather extraordinary if carnival did not succeed on some occasions in actively ousting representation rather than leaving the initiative permanently with the classicism that supports specular representation.

To get some idea of how it might be possible for carnival to turn the tables on representation in this way, I propose to conclude by raising the – perhaps – unlikely-looking question of reading. I do so because in his discussion of reading Roland Barthes seems to be sketching out an exemplary strategy for using carnival as a means of resisting representation, and moreover to be making the body the linchpin of the whole enterprise.

Barthes and the body in the text

The relevance of carnival to reading is not immediately obvious in Bakhtin's own account of carnival but there is, nevertheless, a glancing acknowledgement of its role in his brief synopsis of the history of Rabelais's reception in France in and after the Renaissance period. What Bakhtin is seeking to demonstrate here is that with the passing of the carnival era, reading Rabelais became more or less impossible: La Bruyère in the age of classicism, for example, could see him only as an irreconcilable combination of genius and obscenity; Voltaire in his Enlightenment context was able to appreciate in Rabelais only what he saw as overt satire, and found the rest simply unintelligible; and while the Romantics were more attuned than their predecessors to the grotesque in Rabelais, they (most notably Victor Hugo) could see laughter only in a negative and destructive light. As for the moderns, their positivist bent restricts them to a mere assembling of scholarly material. In the age of representation Rabelais becomes unreadable to an audience which had lost contact with the 'tradition of popular–festive laughter' that informed Rabelais's work. 'The authentic and common interpretation of Rabelaisian images was lost, together with the tradition that had produced them' (p. 115). In other words, to read Rabelais aright you have to place him back in his carnival context. But significantly, the question that Bakhtin does not address is whether the *manner* in which one reads Rabelais's carnivalesque text will be affected by its carnivalesque context. This is because underlying Bakhtin's discussion of Rabelais is an assumption that – even in his own terms – is a kind of self-contradiction: namely, that Rabelais's text is a *representation* of *carnival*. In the perspective of Bakhtin's discussion, Rabelais is deemed to be making a spectacle of carnival [17] which only those who understand what carnival is can properly interpret; but it is an understanding and an interpretation that is ultimately conceived in a representational mould. The question one should ask – and it is the question that I believe Barthes is trying to answer – is: what if Rabelais's carnival extended to the reading of Rabelais himself?

However, before going any further I should also explain how reading fits into an argument that began with self–Other relations and the relation of those relations to the body. It fits – or at least it fits in Barthes – because the reading strategy he is seeking to promote is a response to a problem created by the existence of the Other and by the effects that the Other has on the subject. Barthes's conception of the Other is a sort of mixture of Sartrian antagonisms and Bakhtinian dialogism: that is to say, while he would seem to be adopting a broadly Sartrian view of self–Other relations, he picks up Sartre's cue about the linguistic dimension of these relations and recasts them as a problem of discourse. This is how he does it.

Like Sartre, Barthes is exquisitely sensitive to the hold that the Other has over the subject through his ability to represent the body of the subject. As he says in *Roland Barthes*: 'You are the only one who can never see yourself except as an image . . . : even and especially for your body, you are condemned to the repertoire of its images [à l'imagi-naire]' – that is to say, condemned to a repertoire that lies in the hands of the Other.[18] The situation takes one of its most extreme and painful forms in the experience of being photographed as Barthes describes it in *Camera Lucida*: 'I feel that the Photograph creates my body or mortifies it, according to its caprice.'[19] In other words, photography performs the Sartrian trick of transforming 'subject into object'. But this transformation is above all a linguistic one because effectively what it does is to translate the subject into the terms of the *doxa*, the *déjà-dit* (the already-said), the platitudes of public opinion. The Other constitutes a threat to the Barthesian subject not because he (the Other) has the whip hand in a Sartrian single-handed combat of self–Other relations, but because it is through the Other that the subject falls prey to a representation that constructs him in terms of the stereotype. The Barthesian subject is alienated not merely by becoming an image in the eyes of the Other but through this assimila-tion into the *doxa*.

The problem thus becomes explicitly a dialogic one in that the conflict between self and Other is conceived ultimately as a conflict of discourses. The Barthesian subject's experience of the Other is painful because it reveals to him (the subject) the prior existence of the *doxa*, a discourse which precedes him and to which he is supremely vulner-able. He cannot fight his way out of the tyranny of the *doxa* by adopting or asserting an alternative discourse of his own; he can do so only through a certain *practice* of language which Barthes calls writing and whose effectiveness depends on its being precisely that – a practice – rather than a particular characterisable style.

In this practice the body's relation to language is altered from being the object of its representation to becoming the support and condition of a certain linguistic activity. Or as Barthes rather elliptically puts it, 'Writing proceeds through the body [L'écriture passe par le corps]' (*RB*, p. 80). When the body sides with the subject, then it becomes possible to counter the finished and static representations of the *doxa*, a discourse which Barthes describes as being without a body, even if it takes the body as its object.[20] A *doxa* is no longer a *doxa* if it is no longer finished and complete, if its structures are opened up. The body is a kind of wild-card that slides and also creates slide – like Barthes's own use of the word, 'floating, never *pigeon-holed*, always *atopic*' (*RB*, p. 133). The body is 'the principle of all structuration' and as such opens up the way for a politics directed against the *doxa*: 'If I managed to talk politics *with my own body*, I should make out of the most banal of (discursive) structures a structuration' (*RB*, 175).

There is something distinctly carnivalesque involved in Barthes's use of the body here: it is not the object of a representation, and it is committed to process and practice rather than being defined as a product. There are a number of other aspects of Barthes's use of the body that confirm this impression. The body first makes a substantial and serious appearance in Barthes's work in association with the rather unserious topic of pleasure in *The Pleasure of the Text* (and as a consequence has been an aspect of Barthes's thinking that some critics have been unable to take at all seriously).[21] The pleasure of *jouissance* is a bodily pleasure and is much closer to the joyful corporality of carnival than to the humiliations of facticity that are thrown up by Sartrian desire. Also, the Barthesian body is a dismembered body: it is only as fragment and fetish that it interests and excites. The body that gives pleasure is 'split into fetish objects, into erotic sites', not a whole body.[22] Similarly, Barthes is drawn by the body's ability to blur boundaries. For Barthes an erogenous zone is one between two borders (the gap between jeans and sweater), or as he says in *The Pleasure of the Text*, 'Is not the most erotic portion of a body *where the garment gapes?* . . . It is intermittence . . . which is erotic' (*PT*, pp. 9-10). It is precisely this lifting or questioning of boundaries that is carnivalesque.

What is also carnivalesque is the sliding between bodies that my own listing of the carnivalesque in Barthes has illustrated: it began with a focus on the subject's use of his own body in practice, structuration and the pleasures of *jouissance*, but pleasure also entails a drift that links the body of the subject to other bodies, bodies that give pleasure as fetish and as fragments of erogenous intermittence. And it is at this point that we can at last begin to home in on the question of reading. For in Barthes it seems to be the carnivalesque features of the body that enable self–Other relations to be altered from the fundamentally Sartrian form that is associated with their dependence upon the *doxa* to something more positive and enabling. And this shift is best exemplified for him in the processes of reading and writing. When these are operating as Barthes would ideally wish them to, both body and text are carnivalised, and there finally ceases to be any distinction between subject and object, spectator and representation, distinctions that are entailed by the order of the *doxa*.

Representation is abolished as the body comes out of the frame within which representation seeks to confine it. This abolition is the effect of what Barthes calls *figuration*. Figuration is everything that representation is not: 'Figuration is the way in which the erotic body appears . . . in the profile of the text' (*PT*, pp. 55-6), creating an erotic rather than a specular relationship with its recipient. In representation, by contrast, any desire that there is remains firmly on the diegetic plane: 'such desire never leaves the frame, the picture; it circulates among the characters; if it has a recipient, that recipient remains interior to the fiction'. And Barthes concludes: 'That's what representation is: when nothing emerges, when nothing leaps out of the frame: of the picture, the book, the screen' (*PT*, p. 57). The leap out of the frame that is figuration creates a connection between bodies which completely transforms the relations between what would otherwise be the subject and object of a representation.

Self–Other relations in Barthes have been recast from those that exist between author and hero, between the subject and the object of a representation, to those that exist between a writer and his reader, a reader and a text. The Other is stripped of his authorial potential by a subject who conceives of his other (with a small 'o', perhaps, to distinguish him from the Sartrian one) as the recipient rather than the represented object of his text. In the process reading too is carnivalised.

The key to the Barthesian carnival is what he begins by calling, in an essay by the same title, 'the third meaning', and which in *Camera Lucida* he calls the *punctum*. In the earlier essay he makes the connection with carnival quite explicit when he writes: 'the obtuse meaning [another term for the 'third meaning'] . . . belongs to the family of puns, jokes, useless exertions; indifferent to moral or aesthetic categories (the trivial, the futile, the artificial, the parodic), *it sides with the carnival aspect of things* [*il est du côté du carnaval*].'[23] Being 'du côté du carnaval' means that the third meaning bursts out of the frame, and this puts reading itself on the side of carnival as well.[24] In *Camera Lucida* Barthes works his way towards an understanding of the *punctum* not by trying to describe what the *punctum* is, but by describing its effects. The presence of a *punctum* in a photograph triggers 'tiny jubilations' in its reader, 'an internal agitation' which in French he also calls 'une fête'.[25] It sets the reader in motion, casts him loose; in short, it launches him into carnival.

The value of this readerly 'fête' for Barthes is primarily in its capacity to counter the *doxa* and open up representations. The 'obtuse meaning' is an active resistance to the pre-established and pre-existing *doxa*. It 'disturbs' the representational discourse that is metalanguage, it 'baffles [and] subverts . . . the entire practice of meaning'.[26] It is a kink in the order of representation, the bug in its system. It shows, in a word, what carnival can do to representation, that carnival is not the passive victim of the predations of representation, that it can fight back.

It should, nevertheless, be admitted that Barthes's 'fête' does not restore the full-blooded Renaissance carnival that Bakhtin describes in Rabelais. In the first place, Barthes's is a very ungregarious carnival in which the subject discovers the singularity of his own body rather than the collective embrace of the people.[27] And in so far as the whole thrust of the Barthesian carnival is designed to disengage the subject from the *doxa* (which is the language of the public, the masses) it could be seen as an attempt to positively extricate the subject from any collective (linguistic) embrace. Equally, the tone of Barthes's carnival is one of elegy (self-confessedly so in the case of *Camera Lucida*), and not that of the uproarious epic exemplified in Rabelais. But for all that it is still carnival. And it does still counter the nefarious effects of representation.

There does, however, remain a question about the efficacy of Barthes's largely literary solution as it might apply both to the personal and to the political sphere. Does Barthes's carnival of reading offer solutions to the problem of how to live in the face of the Other (a question which might pose itself for a woman)? Or to the problem of how to counter politically the politically undesirable constructions of the Other (a question which might pose itself for a feminist)? Stallybrass and White argue that the trangressions of modernism and its successors (amongst whom one must surely number Barthes) are in political terms purely illusory because 'Only a challenge to the hierarchy of the *sites* of discourse . . . carries the promise of politically transformative power'.[28] And indeed, Barthes himself seems to acknowledge something of the kind when he suggests that the political effects of his strategy of structuration are quite likely to go unnoticed: 'The problem is to know if the political apparatus would recognise for very long this way of escaping the militant banality by thrusting into it . . . my own unique body' (*RB*, p. 175).

It would seem that the problem of self–Other relations is at once solved and re-opened by the explicit inclusion of language and literature into the frame of reference. For the early Bakhtin (who, it will be remembered, excludes any serious consideration of language from his discussion), literature offers a unique and highly efficacious solution to self–Other relations – but this is a solution that is offered before there is any real problem. The significance of literature is most evident in the metaphors that Bakhtin uses in his discussion, and their justification is provided by the fact that he is proposing aesthetic activity as the model for self–Other relations. With Sartre, for whom these relations can only be construed as problematic, the possibility of a solution to the see-saw of power relations between self and Other is fairly decisively removed when language is added into the balance. In enlarging the scope of the problem through the inclusion of the linguistic dimension Sartre shows the scales to be unavoidably tipped in favour of the Other. At this stage of Sartre's argument literature is neither here nor there.

The implicit synonymy between the carnivalesque and the novelistic in Bakhtin is explicitly developed by Barthes in his festival of reading. But in providing a convincing way out of the dilemmas posed by Sartre in a sphere that was apparently expanded to include language, Barthes paradoxically pays the price of a dramatic reduction in the scope of the arena in which the battles are now fought and won. His lonely carnival of reading may have dissolved the antagonisms between the subject and his Other, but it has done so through a tactics of subversion that is liable to escape the attention of that Other, particularly in his overtly political guise. So that the feminist and even the plain old human subject living out her/his life is unlikely to be able to extend the solution from the purely literary domain, in the manner that the early Bakhtin took for granted.

The difficulty seems to rest on this paradoxical expansion and reduction of the sphere of the literary. On the one hand the field has been enlarged by modernism, and (especially) its successors from the dimensions of the classical work to the infinitely extensible text, and within this text solutions to the problem of the Other have been found. But at the same time, there has been a parallel trivialising of the literary precisely, perhaps, on the part of the Other. It would appear that he (the Other) may have escaped the stratagems that the carnivalesque subject has been trying to coopt him into, and simply removed himself to his traditional and powerful distance. From this distance his gaze can operate in the way that Sartre describes so well, and simply constitutes literature as what he will – trivial or whatever. Literature may provide the arena for a solution for self–Other relations, but it is one which is unable to determine how it in turn may be determined. Literature cannot provide the means for a solution unless it is empowered by the Other to do so, since it is caught up in the very problematic for which it seemed – momentarily – to have provided the solution.[29]

Notes

1 Interview with Michel Contat and Michel Rybalka in *Le Monde,* 14 May 1971, pp. 17 and 20-1. Sartre mentions having recently read the Dostoevsky book, but is somewhat dismissive of it as an example of the 'new formalism' which, he says, 'does not lead anywhere' (p. 21). Bakhtin alluded to Sartre with tantalising brevity in a couple of later interviews. In one he refers to the polyphonic qualities of Sartre's fiction, but finds that although there is a lot of Dostoevsky in Sartre, it is 'profounder' in Camus ('O polifonichnosti romanov Dostoevskogo', *Rossiya,* 2, 1975, pp. 189-98). In the other he mentions Sartre as a 'brilliant' example of the thinker as distinct from the philosopher or sage (see Maya Kaganskaya, 'Shutovskoi khorovod', *Sintaksis,* 12, 1984, pp. 139-90).

2 See Annette Lavers, *Roland Barthes: Structuralism and After,* London, 1982.

3 When I speak of the Other here I shall be using the word largely in the sense shared by the three writers under discussion, borrowing from Sartre the capitalisation that designates his special role. There are, I am aware, psychoanalytic dimensions to the problem which I shall not be pursuing.

4 Mikhail Bakhtin, 'Avtor i geroi v esteticheskoi deyatel'nosti', in *Estetika slovesnogo tvorchestva,* 2nd ed., Moscow, 1986, pp. 9-191. For the place of this essay in Bakhtin's work, see the bibliography of his writings in Katerina Clark and Michael Holquist, *Mikhail Bakhtin,* Cambridge, Mass. and London, 1984, pp. 353-6. Clark and Holquist discuss this essay in their chapter devoted to 'The architectonics of answerability', which they see as laying the groundwork for all that followed in Bakhtin's thought. Holquist's English translation of the essay is still forthcoming, but there is already a French one under the title 'L'auteur et le héros', in Mikhail Bakhtine, *Esthétique de la création verbale,* trans. Alfreda Aucouturier, Paris, 1984. The translations here have been provided by David Shepherd; page references in the text are to the Russian edition. In these and all subsequent quotations italics are the authors' own unless otherwise indicated.

5 I shall be using the masculine pronoun in referring to the subject. In this context *she* is not strictly interchangeable with *he,* since the topic of the body in self–Other relations entails quite particular (cultural and political) problems for the female subject. Any gendering of the situation raises issues which, regrettably, are not directly confronted by any of the authors in question. There will be more discussion of the feminine dimension of the problem below.

6 Bakhtin, [Untitled], ed. S. G. Bocharov, in *Den' poezii 1984,* Moscow, 1985, p. 130, quoted in Ann Shukman, 'Reading Bakhtin with a stiff upper lip', *Scottish Slavonic Review,* 6, 1986, p. 123.

7 Holquist and Clark mention the similarities (and one of the differences) between Bakhtin and Sartre in their chapter devoted to 'Author and hero', but these are only fleeting (if suggestive) allusions whose implications I am seeking to draw out here (*Mikhail Bakhtin,* pp. 63-94).

8 Jean-Paul Sartre, *Being and Nothingness,* trans. Hazel Barnes, London, 1957, p. 351;

subsequent page references are given in the text.

9 For further discussion of this see Toril Moi, 'Existentialism and feminism: the rhetoric of biology in *The Second Sex'*, *Oxford Literary Review*, VIII: 1-2, 1986, pp. 88-95.

10 For a short-hand definition one could do worse than refer to that given by Michael Holquist in the appendix to *The Dialogic Imagination*: 'Dialogism is the characteristic epistemological mode of a world dominated by heteroglossia. Everything means, is understood, as part of a greater whole – there is a constant interaction between meanings, all of which have the potential of conditioning others. Which will affect the other, how it will do so and in what degree is what is actually settled at the moment of utterance. The dialogic imperative is mandated by the preexistence of the language world relative to any of its current inhabitants' (Glossary, in Bakhtin, *The Dialogic Imagination*, ed. Michael Holquist, trans. Caryl Emerson and Michael Holquist, Austin, 1981, p. 426).

11 Ann Shukman points out – quite rightly – that the 'radical change in Bakhtin's approach to the problems of personal interrelationships came in the mid-Twenties when language entered his purview and henceforth was treated as the main bonding element between the self and the world of others' ('Reading Bakhtin', p. 123). By contrast, Tzvetan Todorov's discussion of the importance of 'alterity' in 'Author and hero' fails, I think, to follow through fully the implications of the linguistic dimension of self–Other relations, and for this reason somewhat misrepresents Bakhtin's 'philosophical anthropology' (see *Mikhail Bakhtin: The Dialogical Principle*, trans. Wlad Godzich, Manchester and Minneapolis, 1984, pp. 94-112).

12 Sartre's most thorough – and also his gloomiest – exploration of self–Other relations in the theatre, *Huis clos* (the play in which he uses the famous phrase 'Hell is other people'), has as its English title *No Exit*.

13 'Objectivation is a radical metamorphosis. Even if I could see myself clearly and distinctly as an object, what I should see would not be an adequate *representation* of what I am in myself and for myself' (p. 273, my italics).

14 See especially the last part of the discussion of 'Authorship in the eighteenth century' and the account of the city in Peter Stallybrass and Allon White, *The Politics and Poetics of Transgression*, London and Ithaca, 1986, pp. 118-24 and 125-48. It is, of course, enormously relevant to my own argument that Stallybrass and White identify the emergence of the notion of authorship with that of a relationship of observation and representation between subject and carnival, instead of one of participation. They also rightly contest the view that carnival was exclusively a feature of the Renaissance, and their account is designed to show, among other things, that carnival has been displaced and fragmented, but not lost or destroyed, by post-Renaissance culture. A final accolade for their study: Stallybrass and White are rare among Bakhtin commentators in their understandng of how far the ramifications associated with the body extend.

15 Bakhtin, *Rabelais and his World*, trans. Hélène Iswolsky, Cambridge, Mass. and London, 1968, p. 7; subsequent page references are given in the text.

16 This is also the implication behind the account by Stallybrass and White, who in effect have written a history of the way in which the bourgeoisie, authorship and its concomitant representational strategies have been constituted through the carving out of a differentiating distance from the phenomenon that is carnival. In other words, while they describe representation's relation to carnival, they don't have much to say about carnival's relation to representation.

17 Rather as Ben Jonson does in *Bartholomew Fair*? See Stallybrass and White, *The Politics*, pp. 61-79.

18 Roland Barthes, *Roland Barthes*, trans. Richard Howard, London, 1977; subsequent references are given in the text as *RB*, followed by page number. There is a telling (and no doubt deliberate) echo of Sartre in Barthes's comment that 'the image system [l'imaginaire] is the very thing over which others have an advantage [cela

même sur quoi les autres ont barre]' (*RB*, p. 82). The term 'l'imaginaire' is adopted, but also adapted, by Barthes from Sartre as much as it is derived from Lacan's Imaginary. More telling is the 'avoir barre'; it echoes the following sentence from *Being and Nothingness*, which sums up the basic problem in Sartrian relations between self and Other: 'And as the Other's existence reveals to me the being which I am without my being able either to appropriate that being or even to conceive it, this existence will motivate two opposed attitudes: First – the Other *looks* at me and as such he holds the secret of my being, he knows what I *am*. Thus the profound meaning of my being is outside of me, imprisoned in an absence. The Other has the advantage over me [*autrui a barre sur moi, my italics*]' (p. 363).

19 Barthes, *Camera Lucida*, trans. Richard Howard, London, 1982, p.11. In this context, I should mention another telling echo in Barthes, this time from Bakhtin's 'Author and hero': describing his own experience of his body in the two forms of migraine and sensuality, Barthes writes, 'my body is not a hero' (*RB*, p. 60). (This is not, of course, an echo in the strict sense of the word, since dates of publication rule out any possibility of influence.)

20 The stereotype is that emplacement of discourse *where the body is missing*, where one is sure the body is not' (*RB*, p. 90).

21 This is especially true of Jonathan Culler in his otherwise exemplarily illuminating *Barthes*, London, 1983. Culler is highly suspicious of Barthes's appeal to his body in the later work, which he regards as a symptom of an underlying regression in Barthes's thought. He accuses Barthes of introducing a latent mystification that makes the body the repository of 'Nature' as an ideal truth. While Culler acknowledges the strategic function of the body in Barthes, I think he underestimates the significance of such a strategy. He might also have been a little less dismissive of it had he paused to consider (as I am seeking to do) the extent of the intellectual tradition and the sheer weight of the arguments that lie behind the strategy. See especially chapter 8.

22 Barthes, *The Pleasure of the Text*, trans. Richard Miller, London, 1976, p. 56; subsequent references are given in the text as *PT*, followed by page number. Barthes is actually talking about the text as body here, but I shall be returning to the question of the bodily fragment at greater length in my discussion of Barthes's *punctum*.

23 Barthes, 'The third meaning', in *The Responsibility of Forms*, trans. Richard Howard, Oxford, 1986, p. 44 (my italics).

24 Barthes is actually talking about Eisenstein in this essay, and the discussion of the *punctum* in *Camera Lucida* is about photography, but I think it is in the spirit of Barthes's thinking to use 'reading' as a term to cover the experience of seeing a film and looking at a photograph as well as what is normally understood by the word.

25 Barthes, *Camera Lucida*, pp. 16, 19. Howard translates 'une fête' as 'an excitement', a choice of word which fails to capture the carnivalesque connotations of the original.

26 Barthes, 'The third meaning', pp. 55, 56.

27 E.g. in *Roland Barthes*, where Barthes writes of the way that migraines and sensuality serve to 'individuate my own body' (*RB*, p. 60).

28 Stallybrass and White, *The Politics*, p. 201.

29 I am indebted for inspiration and advice, intellectual as well as bibliographical, to Ken Hirschkop, Mike Holland, Rhiannon Goldthorpe, David Shepherd and Elizabeth Wright.

Terry Eagleton

Bakhtin, Schopenhauer, Kundera

Few modern critical concepts have proved more fertile and sugges-tive, more productively polymorphous, than the Bakhtinian notion of carnival. Indeed it would be a brave critic nowadays who did not at least reverently tip his or her hat in the direction of the concept, when the topic comes up. It is a seriously limiting comment on the work of a critic as superb as the late Paul de Man that it is almost impossible to imagine him being in the least enthused by the idea. In the austere, humourless, astringently negative world of a de Man, none of the emphases we customarily associate with carnival – a certain pleasur-able grossness, a plebeian crudity, knockabout iconoclasm and orgi-astic delight – would seem to have the least place, as they might in some sense in the worlds of F. R. Leavis and William Empson. The bulging, grotesque, excessively replete subjects of carnival could only, one feels, appear as repellently logocentric, obscenely over-pres-ent, to the tragic, sober, emptied subjecthood of de Man's criticism. There is absolutely no feel in de Man, as there is in an Empson, for the vulgar health of the senses, of all that follows from our most banal, biological insertion into the world. For all his epistemological scepti-cism, there is little sense of an intellect which has come to doubt its own sovereignty by glimpsing itself, with a cackle of derisive laughter, from the standpoint of the guts or genitals. De Man's daring subver-sions of reason remain impeccably academic affairs, rendered more in the tones of northern European high seriousness than southern Euro-pean high spirits. Perhaps de Man should be praised rather than censured for his puritan resistance to such scandalous carryings on, for the ruthlessness with which he expels the human body from his discourse. For the concept of carnival, looked at in another light, may be little more than the intellectual's guilty dues to the populace, the soul's blood money, to the body; what is truly unseemly, indecent even, is the apparent eagerness of deans, chaired professors and presidents of learned societies to tumble from their offices into the streets, monstrous papier mâché phalluses fixed in place. Perhaps the remorselessly anti-sentimentalising de Man had sniffed all this out, punitive Fury of bad faith that he was, and was prepared to sit soberly at his desk rather than to risk appearing dishonest, which is not the same as being afraid of appearing ridiculous.

In *Beyond Good and Evil*, Nietzsche opposes 'the stupidity of moral indignation' to what he calls a 'philosophical sense of humour'. 'Cynicism', he remarks, 'is the only form in which common souls come close to honesty; and the higher man must prick up his ears at every cynicism, whether coarse or refined, and congratulate himself whenever a buffoon without shame or a scientific satyr speaks out in his presence.' Whenever anyone speaks 'badly but not ill' of human beings, as bellies with two needs and a head with one, crudely deflating metaphysical solemnities, then 'the lover of knowledge should listen carefully, and with diligence'. The *buffo* and the satyr, Nietzsche laments, are strangers to the ponderous German spirit, lacking as it does 'the liberating scorn of a wind that makes everything healthy by making everything *run!*'[1]. If Bakhtin is the *buffo*, then Marx and Brecht might be proposed as the scientific satyrs, as scornful in their own ways as Nietzsche of high Germanic seriousness. To trace some of the roots of Nietzsche's preoccupation with the body in the work of Schopenhauer, however, is to be rather less persuaded of its spontaneous blessedness – to turn this somatic cynicism on the body itself. It is a striking thought that, had Arthur Schopenhauer not studied medicine and physiology as a university student, the course of Western philosophy, all the way from Nietzsche's praise for the *buffo* to Jean-François Lyotard's points of libidinal intensity, might have been different. No thinker has been more attentive to the body than Schopenhauer, and none less the dupe of its seductive immediacies. Yet it is from Schopenhauer's coarsely materialist meditations on the pharynx and the larynx, on cramps, convulsions, epilepsy, tetanus and hydrophobia, that Nietzsche will derive some of his own affirmations of bodily life; and all that solemn, archaic nineteenth-century discourse of Man in terms of the ganglions and lumbar regions, which survives at least as long as Lawrence, then forms the hinterland for some of our contemporary eulogists of physicality, which includes the exponents of carnival.

Schopenhauer is quite unembarrassed to detect his celebrated Will, that blindly persistent desire at the root of all phenomena, in yawning, sneezing and vomiting, in jerkings and twitchings of various kinds, and seems wholly oblivious of the bathos with which his language can veer without warning in the space of a few pages from high-flown reflections on free will to the structure of the spinal cord or the excrescences of the caterpillar. There is a kind of Bakhtinian bathos or Brechtian *plumpes Denken* about this sudden swooping from *Geist* to genitalia, from the oracular to the orificial, which in Bakhtin's hands at least is a political weapon against ruling-class idealism's paranoid fear of the flesh. With Schopenhauer it is less a question of political revolt than of a kind of thumping cracker-barrel crassness, as when he solemnly illustrates the conflict between body and intellect by pointing out that people find it hard to walk and talk at the same time: 'For as soon as their brain has to link a few ideas together, it no longer has as much force left over as is required to keep the legs in motion through the motor nerves.'[2] Elsewhere, Schopenhauer suggests that a short stature and neck are especially favourable to genius, 'because on the shorter path the blood reaches the brain with more energy' (p. 393). All of this vulgar literalism is a kind of theoretical posture in itself, a sardonic smack at high-toned Hegelianism from one who, though a full-blooded metaphysician himself, regards Hegel as a supreme charlatan and most philosophy except Plato, Kant and himself as a lot of hot air. Crotchety, arrogant and cantankerous, a scathing Juvenilian satirist who professes to believe that Germans need their long words because it gives their slow minds more time to think, Schopenhauer's work reveals a carnivalesque coupling of the imposing and the commonplace evident in his very name.

Indeed incongruity becomes in Schopenhauer's hands the basis for a full-blown theory of comedy which is not without relevance to the work of Bakhtin. The ludicrous, so Schopenhauer argues, springs from the paradoxical subsumption of an object under a concept in other ways heterogeneous to it, so that an Adorno-like insistence on the non-identity of object and concept can come to explain why it is that animals cannot laugh. Humour, in this speciously generalising view, is by and large high words and low meanings, and so like Schopenhauer's own philosophy has an ironic or dialogical structure. This is in itself, however, profoundly ironic, since the discrepancy between percept and concept which occasions the release of laughter is exactly that disjuncture between experience and intellect, or will and representation, which lies at the very core of Schopenhauer's disgusted view of humanity. The inner structure of this bleakest of visions is thus the structure of a joke. Schopenhauer's comic theory is here strikingly close to Freud:

> [Perception] is the medium of the present, of enjoyment and cheerfulness; moreover it is not associated with any exertion. With thinking the opposite holds good; it is the second power of knowledge, whose exercise always requires some, often considerable exertion; and it is the concepts of thinking that are so often opposed to the satisfaction of our immediate desires, since, as the medium of the past, of the future, and of what is serious, they act as the vehicle of our fears, our regrets, and all our cares. It must therefore be delightful for us to see this strict, untiring, and most troublesome governess, our faculty of reason, for once convicted of inadequacy. Therefore on this account the mien or appearance of laughter is very closely related to that of joy. (p. 98).

Comedy is the will's mocking, malicious revenge on the representation, the strike of the Schopenhauerian id against the Hegelian superego; but this source of hilarity is also, curiously, the root of our utter hopelessness. For reason, that crude, blundering servant of the voracious, imperious will, is always pathetic false consciousness, a mere reflex of desire which believes itself absurdly to present the world just as it is. Concepts, in that familiar brand of nineteenth-century irrationalism not wholly irrelevant to the world of a Bakhtin, cannot cling to the rich intricacies of experience but appear as maladroit as a surgeon in boxing gloves.

If humour and hopelessness lie so close together, it is because human existence for Schopenhauer is less grand tragedy than squalid farce. Writhing in the toils of the implacable will, driven on by a relentless appetite they idealise, men and women are less tragic protagonists than pitiably obtuse. The most fitting emblem of the human enterprise is the shovel-pawed mole: 'to dig strenuously with its enormous shovel-paws is the business of its whole life; permanent night surrounds it . . . What does it attain by this course of life that is full of trouble and devoid of pleasure? Nourishment and procreation, that is, only the means for continuing and beginning again in the new individual the same melancholy course' (pp. 353-4). Nothing could be more obvious to Schopenhauer than the fact that it would be infinitely preferable if the world did not exist at all, that the whole project is a ghastly mistake which ought long ago to have been called off, and that only some crazed idealism could possibly believe the pleasures of human existence to outweigh its pains. Only the most blatant self-delusion – values, ideas, the rest of that pointless paraphernalia – could blind individuals to this laughably self-evident truth. It is hard for Schopenhauer to restrain a burst of hysterical laughter at the sight of this pompously self-important race, gripped by a remorseless will-to-live which is secretly quite indifferent to any of them, piously convinced of their own supreme value, scrambling over each other in the earnest pursuit of some goal which will turn instantly to ashes in their mouths. There is no grand *telos* to this 'battleground of tormented and agonised beings', only 'momentary gratification, fleeting pleasure conditioned by wants, much and long suffering, constant struggle, *bellum omnium*, everything a hunter and everything hunted, pressure, want, need and anxiety, shrieking and howling; and this goes on *in saecula saeculorum* or until once again the crust of the planet breaks' (p. 354). If Hegel is the ultimate high-minded mystifier of bourgeois civil society, Schopenhauer is the *buffo* who mouths the truths of the marketplace.

There is something amusing about the very relentlessness of this Schopenhauerian gloom, a perpetual grousing with all the monotonous, mechanical repetition of the very condition it denounces. If comedy for Schopenhauer involves subsuming objects to inappropriate concepts, then this is ironically true of his own pessimism, which stamps everything with its own inexorable colour and so has the funniness of all monomania. The monological has its own unwitting humour, of which the dialogical knows nothing. Any such obsessive conversion of difference to identity is bound to be comic, however tragic the actual outlook. To see no difference between roasting a leg of lamb and roasting a baby, to view both as mere indifferent expressions of the metaphysical will, is as risible as mistaking one's left foot for the notion of natural justice. In another sense, however, Schopenhauer's intense pessimism is not in the least outrageous – is, indeed, no more than the sober realism he himself considers it to be. Absurdly one-sided though this viewpoint may be, it is a fact that throughout class history the fate of the great majority of men and women has been one of suffering and fruitless toil. The dominant narrative of history to date has been one of carnage, wretchedness and oppression; and any Bakhtinian celebration which has not in some sense gone through this belief and emerged somewhere on the other side is politically futile. Moral virtue has never flourished as the decisive force in any historical society, other than briefly and untypically. The monotonous driving forces of history have indeed been enmity, appetite and dominion (the Schopenhauerian Will); and the scandal of that sordid heritage is that it is indeed possible to ask of the lives of innumerable individuals whether they would not in fact have been better off dead. Liberal humanists have the option of either denying this truth, or acknowledging it but hoping that, for some obscure reason, the future might turn out rather better. Such pious wishful thinking is unlikely to withstand the coarse cackle of a Schopenhauerian materialism. There is absolutely no reason why the future should turn out any better than the past, unless there are *reasons* why the past has been as atrocious as it has. If the reason is simply that there is an unsavoury as well as a magnificent side to human nature, then it is hard to explain, on the simple law of averages, why the unsavoury side has apparently dominated almost every political culture to date. Part of the explanatory power of historical materialism is its provision of good reasons for why the past has taken the form it has, and its resolute opposition to all vacuous moralistic hope. Those liberal humanists who have now enlisted the joyous, carnivalesque Bakhtin to their cause need perhaps to explain rather more rigorously than they do why the experience represented by carnival is, historically speaking, so utterly untypical. Unless the carnivalesque body is confronted by that bitter, negative, travestying style of carnivalesque thought which is the philosophy of Schopenhauer, it is difficult to see how it signifies any substantial advance on a commonplace sentimental populism, of a kind attractive to academics.

The confrontation between those two kinds of body is perhaps nowhere so graphically demonstrated as in the fiction of Milan Kundera. His novel *The Unbearable Lightness of Being* sees an intolerable lightness and frailty in anything unique, as though anything which happens only once might as well have not happened at all. *Einmal ist keinmal.* If history can be dissolved into pure difference, then it suffers a massive haemorrhage of meaning; because past events only happen once, they fail to take firm root in our lives and can be expunged from memory, having about them the ineradicable aura of pure accident. The past thus perpetually threatens to dissolve beneath the heel of the present, and this plays straight into the hands of the totalitarian state, adept as it is at airbrushing disgraced politicians out of photographs. What imbues persons and events with unique value, then, is precisely what renders them insubstantial, and Kundera's writing is deeply gripped by this sense of sickening ontological precariousness. It contrasts in this sense with the writing of most of our current fetishists of difference. Pure difference for Kundera cannot be valuable, for value is a relational term; but the paradox is that repetition is an enemy of value too, since the more a thing is repeated the more it tends to fade into meaninglessness.

The point where difference and identity converge most undecidably for Kundera is in the body and sexuality. For sexual love links the unrepeatable experience of a particular, unique relationship with the ceaselessly repetitive, tediously predictable character of the bodily drives. What might be thought to be most deviant, stimulating, shockingly unconventional – a sexual orgy – turns out in the novel in question to be hilariously comic in its endless mechanical repetitions, the supposed singularity of erotic love uproariously repeated in a wilderness of mirrors, each individuated body mockingly mimicking the next. Kundera recognises the profound comedy of repetition, which is one reason why sex is usually the funniest part of his novels; his laughter is that release of libidinal energy which comes from momentarily decathecting the utterly self-identical love object, the magnificent *non-pareil,* in the moment of wry recognition that we all share a common biology. The traditional name of this emancipatory moment is, of course, the carnivalesque, that aggressive onslaught on the fetishism of difference which ruthlessly, liberatingly reduces back all such metaphysical singularities to the solidarity of the flesh.

Kundera's attitude to such emancipation, however, is a good deal more ambiguous and dialectical than that of some official exponents of carnivalesque affirmation. For how is one to use this fleshly solidarity of the species as a demystifying force while avoiding that brutal erasure of difference which is Stalinist uniformity? How to stay faithful to the positive political therapy of carnival without lapsing into biologistic cynicism, or, as Kundera himself might put it, crossing over that hair-thin border which distinguishes 'angelic' meaning from the demonic cackle of meaninglessness? Reproduction, in every sense of the word, may be a source of liberatory humour, which is no doubt one thing Marx meant by suggesting that all tragic events repeated themselves as farce; but the farce in question can be destructive as well as redemptive, which was another of Marx's meanings. The bureaucratic state for Kundera is itself a contradictory amalgam of romantic idealism and cynical materialism: if its discourse is the pure *kitsch* of high-flown sentiment (more evident perhaps these days in the USA than the Soviet Union), its practices render individual bodies and events indifferently exchangeable. The political problem is then to know how to subvert the state's lying romantic idealism without lapsing into a version of its own lethal levelling. One must remember here that for Kundera the image of ungainly naked bodies crowded into a single space, repeating one another endlessly, suggests not only the hilarity of the sexual orgy but the concentration camp.

Every time something is repeated, it loses part of its meaning; the unique, on the other hand, is a romantic illusion. This contradiction in Kundera can be rephrased as a tension between too much meaning and too little. A political order in which everything is oppressively meaningful buckles under its own weight: this is the realm which Kundera names the 'angelic', an intolerable existence since a degree of non-meaning is essential for our lives. The demonic exists to puncture this stifling logocentrism: it is the laughter which arises from things being suddenly deprived of their familiar meanings, a kind of estrangement effect akin to Heidegger's broken hammer, and which a monstrous proliferation of the supposedly singular, as in the sexual orgy, can bring about. Such meaninglessness may be a blessed moment of release, a temporary respite from the world's tyrannical, compulsive legibility in which we slip serenely into the abyss of silence. The demonic is thus closely associated in Kundera with the death drive, a spasm of deconstructive mockery which, like carnival, is never far from the cemetery. But that is enough to remind us that this blessed meaninglessness is by no means wholly to be celebrated. It has about it a malicious, implacable violence, the pure negativity of a Satanic cynicism. Carnival releases us from the terrorism of excessive significance, multiplying and so levelling meanings; but as such it is never far from Schopenhauer's grossly somatic vision of empty futility. Kundera is, I think, right to associate evil, or the demonic, with a radical loss of meaning. Evil, unlike simple immorality, is not hostile or indifferent to particular values but to the whole idea of value as such. It is driven to incredulous mocking laughter, like the compassionate Schopenhauer, by the sheer deceitful hollowness of human beings' pathetic belief that there is ever anything more than facts, than the body, and like Iago relieves the intolerable frustration of this cynicism by reaping malicious delight from destroying value wherever it finds it. This is why evil is traditionally conceived of as radically motiveless: it is not this or that delusion of value which drives it to despair but just a faith in value as such. One of the most unthinkable aspects of the concentration camps is that they were quite unnecessary. It is significance as such that the demonic finds an insupportable scandal; and it is therefore, as Kundera well sees, a tempting lure for the opponents of angelic–authoritarian order, who will be led by it to their doom. The savage irony of the demonic is that it finally dismantles the antithesis of the angels only to conflate the whole of reality together in a levelling not far from the angels' own. Bodies are indifferently interchangeable for both Stalinism and carnival, transgression prized by both revolutionary and cynic. The liberal humanist prizes uniqueness and difference, and supports a bourgeois order which has time for nothing but exchange-value.

Just as we are precariously positioned by our very bodiliness on some indeterminate frontier between sameness and difference, biology and history, so for Kundera we must seek to position ourselves on some wellnigh invisible border between too much meaning and too little, embracing all that the angels reject – 'shit' is the blunt term Kundera gives to the angelically unacceptable – without settling for that sheer shitlike amorphousness which is Stalinism, nihilism, the demonic or (to add a term about which the Eastern European exile is curiously silent) the levelling exchanges of the capitalist marketplace. Happiness is the yearning for repetition, but repetition is what fatally erodes it; the male sexual drive, rather like the authoritarian states of both East and West, is cripplingly divided between a romantic idealism of the uniquely particular (the wife, the permanent mistress) and a promiscuous exchangeability of bodies. *Kitsch* is the name Kundera gives to all 'shitless' discourse, all idealising disavowal of that fundamental meaninglessness which belongs to our biological condition. In the realm of *kitsch*, the dictatorship of the heart reigns supreme: *kitsch* is all smiles and cheers, relentlessly beaming and euphoric like an aerobics class, marching merrily onward to the future shouting 'long live life!'. The Gulag, Kundera comments, is the septic tank *kitsch* uses to dispose of its refuse. If the authoritarian state cannot be opposed by romantic idealism, it is because it actually has a monopoly of it; and this is one reason why Kundera's own critique is inevitably bent back towards a materialism of the body very close to the Bakhtinian notion of carnival. But the endless couplings and exchanges of the carnivalesque body are also terrifyingly close to what is worst about modern political regimes; and there is thus no way in which Kundera can uncritically celebrate some romantic image of plebeian riot. Those who can no longer tolerate shitless discourse are always likely to end up in the shit, boomeranging from angels to devils, pitched helplessly from one metaphysical pole to another. Those who find hierarchies, divisions and distinctions rather too oppressively elitist, too smugly rational, might prefer instead some release of bodies and actions to the same level, of the kind that Schopenhauer describes at one point: 'To enter at the age of five a cotton-spinning or other factory, and from then on to sit there every day first ten, then twelve, and finally fourteen hours, and perform the same mechanical work, is to purchase dearly the pleasure of drawing breath' (p. 578). It is hard to know how much necessary non-meaning, how much free-wheeling contingency, can be embraced by any system of meaning without it collapsing into the demonic. 'We insist that everything must have meaning', writes Vincent Descombes,

> otherwise nothing would have meaning. But there is an alternative hypothesis. Certain defects in meaning are perhaps to be welcomed at the same time as certain defects in the intelligence of meaning are to be deplored. It could be a misfortune to find meaning in everything, for it would then become impossible to understand a meaning in this or in that. Here then is an alternative hypothesis: It is not the case that everything has meaning which claims it, otherwise nothing could claim to have meaning'.[3]

A situation where everything is meaningful is certainly oppressive: the logical extreme of such an attitude is paranoia, a condition in which reality becomes so pervasively, ominously meaningful that its slightest fragments operate as signs in some sinisterly coherent text. Kundera tells the story in *The Book of Laughter and Forgetting* of a Czech being sick in the middle of Prague, not long after the Soviet invasion of the country. Another Czech wanders up to him, shakes his head and says: 'I know just what you mean'.

Derek Parfitt argues in his *Reasons and Persons* that what differentiates human beings from one another is just not significant enough a basis on which to build an ethics. Or, one might add, a politics. It is ironic that radicals must spend as much time as they do emphasising the vital distinctions of class, nation, gender and race to a political antagonist who can afford to ignore them, since none of these distinctions is in the end very important, and the only political strategy likely to dismantle the oppressions they involve is one which is aware of this truth. It is not only tragic but farcical that biological differences of race and gender should have been made the basis of whole systems of brutal dehumanisation, since no serious theoretical defence of their significance has ever been, or can be, advanced. It is not true that there is any isolable, identifiable condition known as 'being Irish', 'being female', 'being Jewish'. Being Irish, female or Jewish may most certainly, in specific social times and places, be associated with highly particular ways of feeling, ways of feeling which may even be peculiar and exclusive to such appellations; but nobody has yet brought off the difficult epistemological trick of peering into themselves and discovering, by introspection, an isolable state of being, independent of all other determinations, which simply was a matter of being one of these things. They are not, in this sense, *identities* at all, any more than 'being human' is. Radical political strategies, of the kind one imagines Bakhtin would have approved, need continually to adjust the tension between the urgent angelic significance of such oppressed subject-positions, and that kind of demonic cynicism which would reduce them to sheer amorphousness. The interesting point about Bakhtinian carnival, in this respect, is that it at once cavalierly suppresses hierarchies and distinctions, recalling us to a common creatureliness not irrelevant to an age gravely threatened with common biological extinction, and at the same time does so as part of a politically specific, sharply differentiated, combatively one-sided practice – that of the lower classes, who incarnate some utopian 'common humanity' at the very moment they unmask their rulers' liberal-minded ideology of 'common social interests' for the shitless, self-interested rhetoric it is. Much of the critical discourse by which Bakhtin has currently been appropriated would seem to me, in Kundera's precise meaning, strikingly shitless – the demonic cackle raised to the service of an angelic ideology. It is very hard to believe that Bakhtin spilt so much ink just to inform us that we should listen attentively to one another, treat each other as whole persons, be prepared to be corrected and interrupted, realise that life is an endless unfinished process, that too much dogma makes you narrow-minded, that nobody has a monopoly of the truth and that life is so much richer than any of our little ideas about it. He was not, after all, George Eliot or E. M. Forster or a liberal Democrat. Those who believe that 'being human' is indeed an identifiable condition of being, whereas being female or Irish is of course not, can no doubt reap solace from parts of Bakhtin's writing, but will need to engage in a fair bit of rewriting elsewhere. Schopenhauer certainly believed in a common human condition; it is just that he also believed that this was the problem, not the answer. It may be that, as a concept, carnival has fought its way through the demystifying pessimism of a Schopenhauer and the dialectical ambivalences of a Kundera, to emerge somewhere on the other side; but this is a hypothesis to be demonstrated rather than assumed.

Notes

1 F. Nietzsche, *Beyond Good and Evil,* Harmondsworth, 1979, pp. 40, 42.
2 A. Schopenhauer, *The World as Will and Representation,* vol. 2, trans. E. F. J. Payne, New York, 1969, p. 284; subsequent page references are given in the text.
3 Vincent Descombes, *Objects of All Sorts,* Oxford, 1986, pp. 15-16.

Key to abbreviations used in the glossary and bibliographical essay

BSP *Bakhtin School Papers,* ed. Ann Shukman, Russian Poetics in Translation, vol. 10, Oxford, 1983

DI Mikhail Bakhtin, *The Dialogic Imagination,* ed. Michael Holquist, trans. Caryl Emerson and Michael Holquist, Austin, 1981

FM P. N. Medvedev, *The Formal Method in Literary Scholarship: A Critical Introduction to Sociological Poetics,* trans. Albert J. Wehrle, Baltimore and London, 1978, and Cambridge, Mass., 1985

FR V. N. Voloshinov, *Freudianism: A Marxist Critique,* trans. I. R. Titunik, New York, 1973

MPL V. N. Voloshinov, *Marxism and the Philosophy of Language,* trans. L. Matejka and I. R. Titunik, New York, 1973

PDPE Mikhail Bakhtin, *Problems of Dostoevsky's Poetics,* ed. and trans. Caryl Emerson, Manchester and Minneapolis, 1984

PDPR Mikhail Bakhtin, *Problems of Dostoevsky's Poetics,* trans. R. W. Rotsel, Ann Arbor, 1973

RW Mikhail Bakhtin, *Rabelais and his World,* trans. Hélène Iswolsky, Cambridge, Mass. and London, 1968, and Bloomington, Indiana, 1984

SG Mikhail Bakhtin, *Speech Genres and Other Late Essays,* ed. Caryl Emerson and Michael Holquist, trans. Vern W. McGee, Austin, 1986

DP Tzvetan Todorov, *Mikhail Bakhtin: The Dialogical Principle,* trans. Wlad Godzich, Manchester and Minneapolis, 1984

MB Katerina Clark and Michael Holquist, *Mikhail Bakhtin,* Cambridge, Mass. and London, 1984

Glossary: alternative translations of key terms

One of the problems facing the student of Bakhtin with no knowledge of Russian is the frequent disparity between translations of a number of key terms in the standard English editions of his work. Indeed, different renderings of the same term are often encountered within the same translation. The effect of this is sometimes to obscure Bakhtin's constant recontextualisation and refinement of crucial concepts. The following list is intended as a guide to some of the most important variants encountered not only in translations of Bakhtin but also in the two best known studies of his work. It is not exhaustive, covering neither the full range of Bakhtin's idiosyncratic terminology nor every instance of variation, but will, we hope, provide a certain measure of clarification, especially if consulted in conjunction with the glossaries contained in *Bakhtin School Papers* and *The Dialogic Imagination*. No attempt is made to express preferences for some translations over others, although the simple juxtaposition of variants may in some cases indicate the undesirability of trying to make Bakhtin's terminology more varied in English than it is in Russian.

The arrangement of such a guide presents obvious difficulties. To list terms in alphabetical order of the English versions would be intolerably repetitive and cumbersome. We have chosen instead to arrange entries broadly in alphabetical order of the transliterated Russian term, departing from this order where it seemed more appropriate to put together words or concepts regularly paired or opposed by Bakhtin. Where a noun appears alongside the related adjective, the noun is given first. The English translations are arranged alphabetically within each entry. The resulting greater brevity, together with the probable familiarity of readers with at least some of the Russian terms in question, should make the guide reasonably easy to use.

Glossary

chuzhoi	alien (*BSP, DI, PDPE, RW*)
	another('s) (*BSP, DI, MPL, PDPE*)
	another person('s) (*PDPR*)
	other (*DI, FM*)
	(the) other's/ others' (*DI, SG, DP, MB*)
	other person's (*MPL*)
	reported (speech) (*MPL, MB*)
	someone else's (*BSP, DI, PDPE*)
dannost'	datum (*FM, FR*)
	givenness (*MB*)
	mode of existence (*MPL*)
	the given (*BSP, SG*)
	what is given (*BSP*)
dannyi	given (*DI, FM, FR, MPL, DP, MB*)
zadannost'	the posited, what is posited (*BSP, MB*)
zadannyi	achieved (*MB*)
	conceived (*MB*)
	posited (*DI*)
izbytok	lavishness (*RW*)
	superabundance (*RW*)
	superiority of information (*PDPR*)
	surplus (*DI, PDPE, SG, MB*)
krugozor	belief system (*DI*)
	conceptual horizon (*DI*)
	conceptual system (*DI, MB*)
	cultural horizon (*DI*)
	field of vision (*PDPE, PDPR*)
	horizon (*DI, FM, DP, MB*)
	point of view (*DI*)
	purview (*BSP, DI, FM, MPL, PDPR, MB*)
	world view (*DI*)
napravlennost'	direction (*PDPR*)
	impulse (*DI*)
	intention (*PDPE*)
	orientation (*DP*)
otsenka	evaluation (*BSP, DI, FM, FR, MPL, PDPE, PDPR, RW, SG, DP, MB*)
	value (*FR, RW*)
	value judgement (*FR, MPL*)

tsennost'	value (*DI, FM, MPL*)
tsennostnyi	axiological (*DI, DP, MB*)
	evaluating (*DI, MB*)
	evaluative (*BSP, DI, FR, MPL*)
	ideological (*DI*)
	judgemental (*DI*)
	valorised (*DI*)
	valuational (*BSP, FM*)
	value- (*DI*)
postupok	act (*FR, SG*)
	action (*BSP, FR*)
	activity (*MB*)
	behaviour (*FR, MPL*)
	deed (*SG, MB*)
	instance of behaviour (*MPL*)
raznorechie	heteroglossia (*DI, SG, DP, MB*)
	heterology (*DP*)
	social diversity of speech types (*DI*)
raznorechivost'	heteroglossia (*DI*)
	mix of varied and opposing voices (*DI*)
	speech diversity (*DI*)
slovo	discourse (*BSP, DI, FR, PDPE, RW, SG, DP, MB*)
	language (*RW*)
	word (instead of 'discourse') (*FM, FR, MPL, PDPR, RW*)
sobytie	co-being (*BSP, MB*)
	event (*FM, FR, MPL, PDPE, PDPR, RW, SG*)
	event/situation (*MB*)
	sharing/event (*MB*)
sobytiinyi	full of event potential (*PDPE*)
	having the nature of an event (*PDPR*)
stanovlenie	becoming (*BSP, DI, MPL, RW, SG, MB*)
	coming-to-be (*BSP*)
	development (*DI*)
	emergence (*SG*)
	evolution (*DI*)
	formation (*MB*)
	generation (*FM, MPL*)
	generative process (*MPL*)
	psychological evolution (*PDPE, PDPR*)
	spirit of process (*DI*)

stanovyashchiisya	becoming (*DI, RW*)
	(ever-)developing (*DI*)
	(ever-)evolving (*DI*)
	generating (*FM*)
	in the making (*DI*)
	in the process of generation (*FM, MPL*)
vnenakhodimost'	being located outside/external to (*PDPE, SG*)
	exotopy (*DP*)
	external location (*PDPR*)
	external position (*PDPE*)
	extralocality (*MB*)
	outside(d)ness (*SG*)
zavershennost'	completedness (*DI*)
	completeness (*DI*)
	completion (*BSP, DP*)
	conclusiveness (*DI*)
	finalisation (*BSP, FM, PDPE, SG*)
	finalisedness (*PDPR*)
	finished quality (*DI*)
zavershennyi	closed off (*DI*)
	complete (*DI*)
	completed (*DI, RW, SG, DP, MB*)
	finalised (*DI, FM, PDPE, PDPR, SG, MB*)
	finished (*DI, FM, MB*)
	finite (*DI*)
nezavershennost'	incompletedness (*MB*)
	inconclusiveness (*DI*)
	non-completion (*BSP*)
	open-endedness (*DI, PDPE, MB*)
	unfinalisability (*PDPE*)
	unfinalised nature (*PDPE, PDPR*)
	unfinalisedness (*PDPR*)
	unfinishedness (*SG*)
nezavershennyi	incomplete (*DI*)
	inconclusive (*DI*)
	open-ended (*DI*)
	unconcluded (*DI*)
	unfinalised (*MB*)
	unfinished (*RW, MB*)
	unresolved (*DI*)

nezavershimost'   open-endedness (*PDPE*)
                           unfinalisability (*PDPE, PDPR*)
  nezavershimyi   uncompletable (*SG*)
                           unfinalised (*SG*)
                           unresolvable (*DI*)
                           unresolved (*DI*)

znachenie   connotation (*RW*)
                           denotation (referential) (*MPL*)
                           formal definition (*SG*)
                           formal meaning (*SG*)
                           meaning (*BSP, FM, FR, MPL, RW, MB*)
                           significance (*FM, SG*)
                           value (semiotic or ideological) (*MPL*)
smysl   (contextual) meaning (*SG*)
                           idea (*MPL*)
                           meaning (*FM, RW, DP*)
                           semantic property (*MPL*)
                           sense (*BSP, MPL, SG*)
                           significance (*MPL*)
                           signification (*MPL*)
                           theme (*MB*)
                           thought (*FM*)

Ken Hirschkop

Critical work on the Bakhtin circle: a bibliographical essay

The Bakhtin snowball is about to turn into an avalanche, so it seems
like a good time to take stock of the existing critical literature. Although
Rabelais and his World was published in English translation in 1968, it
was only in the 1980s that a substantial English-language secondary
literature on Bakhtin emerged, undoubtedly the consequence of the
appearance of the essays collected under the title *The Dialogic Imagination* (a title which, as one reviewer pointed out, might have implied
that Bakhtin's work was not too distant from the traditional preoccupations of the Anglo-American humanities). At the time I am writing
there exist only two book-length works in English, the biography
Mikhail Bakhtin by Katerina Clark and Michael Holquist (*MB*, 1984) and
the introductory work *Mikhail Bakhtin:The Dialogical Principle* by
Tzvetan Todorov (*DP*, 1984) but there are plenty of indications that
this too will change in the near future.

What follows is a relatively complete bibliography of the literature
in English up to 1988 (although there may be items missing for the
years 1987 and 1988), prefaced by a description of the principal
concerns and points of argument which have emerged. The bibliographical list itself includes articles, substantial discussions in books,
and reviews, only some of which are discussed in this essay. I have
excluded articles which explore the Bakhtin circle's work by bringing
it to bear on a particular text or historical problem. This does not
reflect a belief that such pieces are mere 'applications'; on the contrary, in many cases they have provided the most interesting theoretical insights. But to have included them would have made this project
almost impossible.

Anyone with a serious and continuing interest in Bakhtin should
subscribe to *The Bakhtin Newsletter*, which comes out every two years
and includes a very thorough annotated bibliography of works on

Bakhtin in all languages. Inquiries should be addressed to Professor Clive Thomson, Department of French, Queen's University, Kingston, Canada K7L 3N6.

Before passing on to the important questions of interpretation and theory, however, we have to confront what might seem to be a rather pedantic issue: how and by whom were the texts published under the names of Medvedev and Voloshinov written? This problem has had an ambiguous effect on Bakhtin scholarship. On the whole it has clearly been an obstacle to interesting work on Bakhtin and company, because it has licensed a shift of attention away from the theoretical and historical issues posed in the texts to questions about the lives and personal motivations of the authors. But this question of attribution is made more interesting by the fact that it is so obviously a political question as well. The writings of Voloshinov and Medvedev attack the same problems with much the same weapons as the writings of Bakhtin, and each of the texts can be read as a gloss on the others. If one is interested in uncovering the 'real' Bakhtin it matters a great deal whether or not the formulations of Voloshinov and Medvedev can be treated as deviations from Bakhtin's intentions. It mattered, one has to assume, in the Soviet Union in the late 1920s and 1930s, and again when Bakhtin's works were rediscovered in the 1960s (during Khrushchev's tenure, it is worth bearing in mind), for at both times publication could depend on the interpretation placed on ambiguous concepts. In the 1970s and 1980s, in the United States and England, it clearly mattered again, as the case against Bakhtin's authorship of the disputed texts often formed part of a larger argument as to why Bakhtin could not be considered a Marxist like Voloshinov and Medvedev.

The initial spark for this debate was provided by a footnote asserting Bakhtin's authorship in Ivanov (1976: a translation of an article published in 1973). This was then supplemented by scraps of evidence from Soviet sources cited by Wehrle (1978), Clark and Holquist (*MB*), Kozhinov (1977), Winner (1976) and Carden (1979). In each case a different explanation was offered, and in each case the explanation involved rather a great deal of speculation. The Clark and Holquist thesis, that the names of Voloshinov and Medvedev were flags of convenience, is questioned by Titunik (1986 and 1984) and has given rise to alternative conjectures by Todorov (*DP*), Godzich (1985) and Tribe (1986). (Unfortunately for those without Russian, one of the most interesting hypotheses – that the works were attributed to Bakhtin in order to ease their publication in the 1970s, in so far as he, and not Voloshinov and Medvedev, had been effectively rehabilitated

– is made in an editorial preface to a reprint of *The Formal Method* in Russian: 'Ot izdatel 'stva', in Mikhail Bakhtin [*sic*], *Formal'nyi metod v literaturovedenii*, New York, 1982, pp. 4-7.) Shukman (1983), Parrott (1984), Perlina (1983) and Titunik (1984) have all attempted to solve the problem by analysing the language, structure and terminology of the texts in question. This 'internal' approach to the question can often lead (as in Titunik) to an overemphasis on questions of vocabulary, as if Marxism was just a lexical twitch, but it has provided analyses of the rephrasings of key theoretical ideas in the different texts of Bakhtin *et al.*

Another rather old-fashioned scholarly concern – the intellectual and social conditions in which these texts were composed – also has a particular significance for the analysis of the Bakhtin circle. It must surely be obvious that their ideas have become prominent not only on their own merits but also because they dovetail so neatly with current literary concerns. It sometimes seems as if Bakhtin, Medvedev and Voloshinov will be torn to shreds in the struggle between 'humanist' and 'anti-humanist' scholars in the West. In such a situation, historical interpretation is even more important than usual, for without it there is a real danger that the theoretical work will be translated into a series of propositions about 'humanity' as such, 'language' as such, even 'sociality' as such. The fact that Slavic studies – where those in a position to understand the historical context work – has been relatively less engulfed by the theoretical onslaught only makes things worse: theoretical and historical concerns are thereby institutionally separated. However, there is now a great deal of useful work on Bakhtin's intellectual predecessors and interlocutors, which will make it possible to restore the historical dimension of the Bakhtin circle's work.

Interestingly, discussions of theoretical context have tended to either of two poles. Some, wishing to establish Bakhtin's place in the Western philosophical tradition, stress his philosophical kin; others want to describe him as a bridge between Russian Formalism and contemporary semiotics, and so emphasise his connections with linguists and with the Formalists. The danger with the former is that the values Bakhtin enunciates (dialogue, etc.) will be divorced from his 'scientific' analysis of the social sphere of language: a political or ethical Bakhtin with no teeth. Those arguing for a more strictly linguistic version of Bakhtin get the scientific content but in a positivist, and therefore non-political, form.

In the philosophical camp Clark and Holquist (*MB*) spend a great deal of time on what are presented as a few key neo-Kantian and religious sources, and there is good reason to think the end result is a skewed picture. Todorov (*DP*) concentrates on Bakhtin's place in nineteenth-century epistemological and aesthetic debates. Shukman (1984b), Averintsev (1977), Clark and Holquist (1984) and Perlina (1984) all point out significant philosophical influences, in particular, neo-Kantian, existential and Christian ones. While these articles run the risk of turning Bakhtin into an idealist philosopher who dabbles in linguistics and social theory, there is no doubt that the dimension they emphasise is crucial if we are to avoid the Charybdis of an apolitical 'semiotic' Bakhtin (see also Frank 1986 and Belknap 1982). Shukman (1986a, 1984a, 1984b, 1983), has developed a philosophical interpretation of Bakhtin very different from that of Clark and Holquist, and to her work one should add the philosophical suggestions made by Patterson (1985) and Baran (1974). This general picture of Bakhtin changes radically if one takes into account an article by Curtis (1986) on Bakhtin's relation to Nietzsche, which is especially important given the philosophical preferences of the 1970s. A discussion which seems to combine literary and philosophical concerns in a useful way can be found in an article by Jauss (1985).

Morson (1978), Titunik (1973) and Matejka (1973), in contrast to the above, argue that Bakhtin's work should be interpreted as an elaboration of the theoretical moves of Russian Formalism; the first, in opposition to an emphasis on Bakhtin as a philosophical writer, the last, as a way of detaching Bakhtin from any Marxist affiliation. Holquist has described Bakhtin's relation to the Formalists (1985a); Danow (1986) and Galan (1987) compare Bakhtin to the Prague School, the latter claiming to find almost complete agreement on the basic case; Pomorska (1968 and 1978) describes Bakhtin as a 'structuralist *avant la lettre*'. Ivanov (1976) and Segal (1974) make the case for Bakhtin as precursor of Tartu semiotics: here we find the beginnings of the Soviet equivalent of the division of opinion I described above. For a description of how Bakhtin stood among the Formalists and philosophers of the 1920s and 1930s see Matejka (1973, on linguistics), Seduro (1957, on Dostoevsky scholarship) and an excellent article by Aucouturier (1983, on the theory of the novel in the 1930s and Lukács in particular). For a description of the Soviet reception in the 1960s, typified by similar struggles, see again Clark and Holquist (*MB*) and Ivanov (1976), but also Seduro (1975). Kagarlitsky (1988) describes the influence of Bakhtin on socialist intellectuals in the Soviet Union.

One way to balance the critical, evaluative elements in the circle's texts with the analytical, linguistic ones is to interpret them as some kind of interweaving of Marxism and Formalism, thus combining the concerns of a critical social theory, with problems of technical linguistic analysis. It was the Bakhtin circle's ability to combine these two kinds of intellectual work which made them exemplars of 'significant cultural theory' for Raymond Williams (1986). Bennett (1979), however, made this case first, although he limited his argument to *Rabelais* and *Dostoevsky* and relied heavily on Althusser (see the review by Sharratt 1979). It has been advanced in excellent theoretical articles by Pechey (1980), Godzich (1985), Walton (1981) and Zima (1981), but receives what is unquestionably its most systematic and technical treatment in Frow's recent book (1986).

Although these last works have a particular case to make, they are also representative of the reception of Bakhtin by the wider world of literary and cultural analysis. This is, of course, bound to be an uneven process, producing bad work as well as good, but the result so far has been a great deal of theoretically interesting and rigorous work. The interpretation of the works of Bakhtin and Voloshinov in particular has been an important part of the renaissance of Marxist cultural theory: Voloshinov was given pride of place by Williams (1977) in his discussion of language, and Bakhtin has been analysed and extended in Eagleton (1981), La Capra (1983), Polan (1983) and Stam (1988), in addition to the works cited in relation to Formalism. Although it does not present itself as an exercise in Marxist theory, Stallybrass and White's *The Politics and Poetics of Transgression* (1986), on the demise of carnival, is probably the most important work yet on Bakhtin for anyone on the left, distinguished by a rare attention to historical argument. Among its arguments is a sustained polemic against what it regards as the political pretensions of post-structuralism, in this respect extending an earlier article by White (1984).

White's was only the first of several articles by left critics advancing Bakhtin as a materialist alternative to deconstruction and Lacanian or Kristevan analysis. Eagleton (1982) and Sprinker (1986) make the case for Bakhtin almost against Derrida, and there are excellent attempts to bring together these very different traditions in Pechey (1986) and in Weber's extended review of Voloshinov (1985). Kristeva, of course, has spoken for herself in two significant pieces on Bakhtin (1973 and 1980), and her work has been compared to Bakhtin's by Bové (1983), Yaeger (1986) and Danow (1985a). A very interesting discussion of Bakhtin in relation to Derrida and Lacan is found in MacCannell (1985), while perhaps the most extended post-structuralist critique of Bakhtin is that of Carroll (1983), who compares his work to that of Lyotard.

The attempt to replace Derrida with Bakhtin has not gone unchallenged: Young (1985) sees this as an evasion, and one does not have to part with Marxism or social theory to acknowledge the legitimacy of his objections. A reply to Young, against deconstruction, was made by White (1987-8). One obvious point of contention is Bakhtin's concept of history, which deserves more scrutiny than it has so far received. This was one point of Young's article, to which one should add important pieces by Anchor (1985), DeJean (1984) and Howes (1986). Another issue which is basic to any question of cultural theory is that of the establishment and maintenance of authority in language. For a treatment of this via reader-response criticism see Shepherd (1986a); there is an excellent article on cultural authority and the conventions of ethnographic writing by Clifford (1983).

There has recently been a marked attempt by feminists to assimilate Bakhtin's work. Besides the essays in the present volume there are articles by Lanser (1986) on narratology, and by Holden (1985) and Russo (1986) on the carnivalesque. Booth (1982), despite his gender, actually managed to publish the first piece on this topic; Cerquiglini (1986), with a similar disability, still provides an extremely interesting and technical linguistic analysis along feminist lines. Dale Bauer's *Feminist Dialogics* (1988) is the first book-length treatment of the topic, unfortunately unavailable to me at the time I write.

As for more particular theoretical issues, most articles have concentrated on either dialogism and its implied philosophy of language, the theory of the novel, or the theory of the carnivalesque (so, for example, discussion of the concept of the chronotope is rare by comparison). There are a great many discussions of dialogism and polyphony – it tends to receive the lion's share of attention in every introductory article – but there is a tendency not to push Bakhtin too hard, and to leave the concept in the same ambiguous state in which we received it. While theoretical work cannot be an end in itself, this is a case in which the careful analysis of a concept is required, for otherwise dialogism seems to appear as simply a new word for justifying established literary and cultural preferences. The most theoretically distinctive articles I know of are those by Pechey (in the present volume), de Man (1983), and Malcuzynski (1983). A superb and rarely cited article, discussing the relation of polyphony, narrative and linguistic stratification, is Segre (1985). From dialogism we can pass to two closely related concepts, intertextuality and 'finalisation'. The former was formulated by Kristeva (1973) and is discussed at length by Jefferson (1980), Zima (1981) and Frow (1986). 'Finalisation' (*zavershe-nie*) is discussed in Gossman (1979), Markiewicz (1984), Howes (1986) and in Todorov (*DP*). In Bakhtin and Medvedev the idea of 'finalisation' leads to the concept of genre, on which see Thomson (1984a).

There is obviously a great deal in Bakhtin's account of the novel which is open to dispute and to historical counter-example. The more interesting theoretical discussions of the theory of the novel are Wasiolek (1975), Kristeva (1980) and the Aucouturier article cited above (1983). The latter compares Bakhtin to Lukács and finds something more significant than the easily available antithesis. There are also good pieces on this comparison by Corredor (1983) and Kovács (1980).

'Carnivalesque' has been used as a term of praise as loosely as 'dialogical', and this carelessness should point up the need for the definition of these concepts in historical terms. Stallybrass and White (1986) are obviously the main point of reference here, but carnival has also been specified in historical terms by Berrong (1986), Flaherty (1986) and Lotman (1976). Henning (1981) concentrates on the definition of the grotesque. There is, however, also an argument to be made for regarding the carnivalesque as something which needs to be resurrected or invented in the twentieth century, on which see Hayman (1983a), Eagleton (1981) and Berrong again.

Even the most positivist historian must recognise that Bakhtin's theory of the carnivalesque is to some degree a theory of modernism, and none of the contributors cited above is likely to maintain otherwise. Jameson (1973) has a few words to say about the relation of 'dialogism' to a larger modernist project, and Sheppard (1983) compares carnival to Dada. Hutcheon (1983) has used Bakhtin in her defence of post-modernism as a radical practice, although I think Malcuzynski's article on collage and polyphony (1983) is an effective rebuttal. Davidson (1983) also takes dialogism to imply collage, but discusses Bakhtin in relation to postwar poetry.

Certainly the least discussed book of the Bakhtin circle is Voloshinov's *Freudianism,* although now the situation is beginning to change. Ivanov (1976) maintains that this text is central to the Bakhtin circle's project; Emerson (1983b) discusses it in connection with the work of Vygotsky, a theorist with a clear and generally unanalysed relation to Bakhtin; Bruss (1976) compares Voloshinov's critique to Lacan's reconstruction of Freud; Byrd (1987) looks for Freudian themes in *Rabelais.* A very recent article by Pirog (1987) connects Voloshinov's critique of Freud to that of Habermas. All of these works indicate what should be a welcome shift in the focus of Bakhtin scholarship, from attempts to interpret the works on their own to the task of integrating them into larger theoretical and cultural projects.

There remain very few discussions of the circle's writings from a strictly linguistic perspective. Raymond Williams (1977) tackled the issue at a very high level of abstraction, and there are very well informed discussions from the perspective of Soviet semiotics in Matejka (1973) and Ivanov (1976); to these early works one can now add those of Stewart (1983), Fowler (1981) and Pateman (1982). No doubt this is an effect of the predominance of literary theorists and critics in the assimilation of Bakhtin.

Finally, there is the matter of the textual and stylistic organisation of the works of Bakhtin himself. The most detailed account of these matters is found in Emerson's preface to *PDPE* (1984a) and in an earlier article (1983a), but there are also comments by Bové (1983) and Sprinker (1986). We have included a guide to the translation of key concepts in the present volume, but the translation problems are also discussed in Erlich (1979), Carden (1979), Gossman (1979) and Baran (1974).

Anchor, Robert 1985. 'Bakhtin's truths of laughter', *Clio*, XIV: 3, pp. 237-57.

Aucouturier, Michel 1983. 'The theory of the novel in Russia in the 1930s: Lukács and Bakhtin', in John Garrard, ed., *The Russian Novel from Pushkin to Pasternak,* New Haven.

Averintsev, Sergei 1977. [Untitled], *Soviet Literature,* 1, pp. 145-51.

Bagby, Lewis 1982. 'Mikhail Bakhtin's discourse typologies: theoretical and practical considerations', *Slavic Review*, XLI: 1, pp. 35-58.

Baran, Henryk 1974. Review of *PDPR, Slavic and East European Journal*, XVIII: 1, pp. 77-9.

Bauer, Dale M. 1988. *Feminist Dialogics: A Theory of Failed Community,* Albany, N.Y.

Beaujour, Elizabeth K. 1969-70. Review of *RW, The French Review,* XLIII: 1, pp. 190-1.

Belknap, Robert 1982. Review of *DI, Slavic Review,* XLI: 3, pp. 580-1.

Bennett, Tony 1979. *Formalism and Marxism,* London and New York, pp. 75-97.

Bennett-Matteo, Susan 1986. 'Bakhtin: the disputed texts', in R. Kirk Belknap, ed., *Deseret Language and Linguistic Society,* Provo, Utah.

Bernstein, Michael Andre 1983. 'When the carnival turns bitter: preliminary reflections upon the abject hero', *Critical Inquiry*, X: 2, pp. 283-306 (reprinted in Morson 1986a).

Berrong, Richard M. 1986. *Rabelais and Bakhtin: Popular Culture in 'Gargantua and Pantagruel',* Lincoln, Nebraska and London.

Bialostosky, Don 1986. 'Dialogics as an art of discourse in literary criticism', *PMLA,* CI: 5, pp. 788-97.

Bialostosky, Don 1985. 'Booth's rhetoric, Bakhtin's dialogics and the future of novel criticism', *Novel*, XVIII: 3, pp. 209-16.

Bialostosky, Don 1983. 'Bakhtin versus Chatman on narrative: the habilitation of the hero', *The University of Ottawa Quarterly*, LIII: 1, pp. 109-16.

Booth, Wayne C. 1984. 'Introduction', in *PDPE*, pp. xiii-xxvii.

Booth, Wayne C. 1982. 'Freedom of interpretation: Bakhtin and the challenge of feminist criticism', *Critical Inquiry*, IX: 1, pp. 45-76 (reprinted in Morson 1986a).

Bové, Carol Mastrangelo 1983. 'The text as dialogue in Bakhtin and Kristeva', *The University of Ottawa Quarterly*, LIII: 1, pp. 117-24.

Bové, Carol Mastrangelo 1982. Review of *DI*, *The Minnesota Review*, 18, pp. 158-62.

Brittain, Celia 1974. 'The dialogic text and the *texte pluriel*', *Occasional Papers* (Language Centre, University of Essex, Colchester), 14, pp. 52-68.

Bruss, Neil A. 1976. 'V. N. Voloshinov and the structure of language in Freudianism', in *FR*, pp. 117-48.

Bruss, Neil A. and I. R. Titunik 1976. 'Preface', in *FR*, pp. vii-xiv.

Byrd, Charles L. 1987. 'Freud's influence on Bakhtin: traces of psychoanalytic theory in *Rabelais and his World*', *Germano-Slavica*, V: 5-6, pp. 223-30.

Carden, Patricia 1979. Review of *FM*, *Slavic and East European Journal*, XXIII: 3, pp. 411-12.

Carroll, David 1983. 'The alterity of discourse: form, history and the question of the political in M. M. Bakhtin', *Diacritics*, XIII: 2, pp. 65-83.

Cerquiglini, Bernard 1986. 'The syntax of discursive authority: the example of feminine discourse', *Yale French Studies*, 70, pp. 183-98.

Clark, Katerina and Michael Holquist 1986. 'A continuing dialogue', *Slavic and East European Journal*, XXX: 1, pp. 96-102.

Clark, Katerina and Michael Holquist 1984. 'The influence of Kant in the early work of M. M. Bakhtin', in Joseph P. Strelka, ed., *Literary Theory and Criticism*, New York.

Clifford, James 1983. 'On ethnographic authority', *Representations*, I: 2, pp. 118-46.

Conway, Jeremiah P. 1983. 'The retreat from history: a Marxist analysis of Freud', *Studies in Soviet Thought*, XXV: 2, pp. 101-12.

Cornwell, Neil 1986. Review of *MB*, *Irish Slavonic Studies*, 7, pp. 169-70.

Corredor, Eva 1983. 'Lukács and Bakhtin: a dialogue on fiction', *The University of Ottawa Quarterly*, LIII: 1, pp. 97-107.

Curtis, James M. 1986. 'Michael Bakhtin, Nietzsche, and Russian pre-revolutionary thought', in Bernice Glatzer Rosenthal, ed., *Nietzsche in Russia*, Princeton.

Danow, David K. 1986. 'Dialogic perspectives: the East European view (Bachtin, Mukařovský, Lotman)', *Russian Literature* (Amsterdam), XX: 2, pp. 119-41.

Danow, David K. 1985a. 'M. M. Bakhtin in life and art' (Review of *MB*, *DP*), *American Journal of Semiotics*, III: 3, pp. 131-41.

Danow, David K. 1985b. 'Dialogic perspectives: Bakhtin and Mukařovský', in John Deely, ed., *Semiotics 1984*, Lanham, Maryland.

Danow, David K. 1984. 'M. M. Bakhtin's concept of the word', *American Journal of Semiotics*, III: 1, pp. 79-97.

Davidson, Michael 1983. 'Discourse in poetry: Bakhtin and extensions of the dialogical', in Michael Palmer, ed., *Code of Signals: Recent Writing in Poetics,* Berkeley.

DeJean, Joan 1984. 'Bakhtin and/in history', in Benjamin A. Stolz, Lubomir Doležel and I. R. Titunik, eds., *Language and Literary Theory,* Ann Arbor.

de Man, Paul 1983. 'Dialogue and dialogism', *Poetics Today,* IV: 1, pp. 99-107.

Donoghue, Denis 1985. 'Reading Bakhtin', *Raritan,* V: 2, pp. 107-19.

Eagleton, Terry 1982. 'Wittgenstein's friends', *New Left Review,* 135, pp. 64-90.

Eagleton, Terry 1981. *Walter Benjamin, or Towards a Revolutionary Criticism,* London, pp. 143-56.

Ehre, Milton 1984. Review of *DI, Poetics Today,* V: 1, pp. 172-7.

Elsworth, J. D. 1985. 'A festival of resurrection' (Review of *MB), Times Higher Education Supplement,* 14 June, p. 19.

Emerson, Caryl 1985. 'The Tolstoy connection in Bakhtin', *PMLA,* C: 1, pp. 68-80.

Emerson, Caryl 1984a. 'Editor's preface', in *PDPE,* pp. xxix-xliii.

Emerson, Caryl 1984b. 'Bakhtin and intergeneric shift: the case of Boris Godunov', *Studies in Twentieth Century Literature,* IX: 1, pp. 145-68.

Emerson, Caryl 1983a. 'Translating Bakhtin: does his theory of discourse contain a theory of translation?', *The University of Ottawa Quarterly,* LIII: 1, pp. 23-51.

Emerson, Caryl 1983b. 'The outer word and inner speech: Bakhtin, Vygotsky and the internalization of language', *Critical Inquiry,* X: 2, pp. 245-64 (reprinted in Morson 1986a).

Emerson, Caryl and Gary Saul Morson 1987. 'Penultimate words', in Clayton Koelb and Virgil Lokke, eds., *The Current in Criticism,* West Lafayette, Indiana.

Erlich, Victor 1979. Review of *FM, Slavic Review,* XXXVIII: 1, pp. 154-5.

Flaherty, Peter 1986. 'Reading carnival: towards a semiotics of history', *Clio,* XV: 4, pp. 411-28.

Fowler, Roger 1981. 'Anti-language in fiction', in *Literature as Social Discourse,* London, pp. 142-61.

Frank, Joseph 1986. 'The voices of Mikhail Bakhtin' (Review of *MB, DP, PDPE), New York Review of Books,* October 23, pp. 56-60.

Friedberg, Maurice 1984. 'Fighting oblivion and distortion', *Present Tense,* XI: 2, pp. 59-60.

Friesner, Scott 1985. Review of *DP, Rubicon,* V, pp. 154-7.

Frow, John 1986. *Marxism and Literary History,* Oxford, pp. 125-69.

Galan, F. W. 1987. 'Bakhtiniadi Part II: the Corsican Brothers in the Prague School, or the reciprocity of reception', *Poetics Today,* VIII: 3-4, pp. 565-77.

Gasparov, M. L. 1984. 'M. M. Bakhtin in Russian culture of the twentieth century', *Studies in Twentieth Century Literature,* IX: 1, pp. 169-76.

Godzich, Wlad 1985. 'Foreword', in *FM,* 1985 reprint, pp. vii-xiv.

Goodison, A. C. 1987. 'Structuralism and critical history in the moment of Bakhtin', in Joseph Natoli, ed., *Tracing Literary Theory,* Urbana, Illinois.

Gossman, Lionel 1986. 'Mikhail Bakhtin' (Review of *MB), Comparative Literature,* XXXVIII: 4, pp. 337-49.

Gossman, Lionel 1979. Review of *FM, Comparative Literature,* XXXI: 4, pp. 403-12.

Haas, Wilbur A. 1976. 'The reported speech of Valentin N. Voloshinov', *Dispositio,*

I: 3, pp. 352-6.

Hall, Jonathan 1985. 'Falstaff, Sancho Panza and Azdak: carnival and history', *Comparative Criticism,* 7, pp. 127-46.

Hall, Jonathan 1984-5. 'Totality and the dialogic: two versions of the novel', *Tamkang Review,* XVI: 1-4, pp. 5-30.

Hall, Jonathan 1981. 'Mikhail Bakhtin and the critique of systematicity', in M. A. Abbas and Tak-Wai Wong, eds., *Literary Theory Today,* Hong Kong.

Hayman, David 1983a. 'Toward a mechanics of mode: beyond Bakhtin', *Novel,* XVI: 2, pp. 101-20.

Hayman, David 1983b. 'Bakhtin's progress' (Review of *DI), Novel,* XVI: 2, pp. 173-7.

Henning, Sylvia Debevec 1981. '*La forme in-formante:* a reconsideration of the grotesque', *Mosaic,* XIV: 4, pp. 107-20.

Hirschkop, Ken 1989a. 'The classical and the popular: musical form and social context', in Christopher Norris, ed., *Music and Politics,* London.

Hirschkop, Ken 1989b. 'Dialogism as a challenge to literary criticism', in Catriona Kelly, Michael Makin and David Shepherd, eds., *Discontinuous Discourses in Modern Russian Literature,* London and New York.

Hirschkop, Ken 1986a. 'Bakhtin, discourse and democracy', *New Left Review,* 160, pp. 92-113.

Hirschkop, Ken 1986b. 'The domestication of M. M. Bakhtin', *Essays in Poetics,* XI: 1, pp. 76-87.

Hirschkop Ken 1986c. 'Bakhtin and liberalism', *The Bakhtin Newsletter,* 2, pp. 139-46.

Hirschkop, Ken 1986d. Review of *FM, Scottish Slavonic Review,* 6, pp. 145-6.

Hirschkop, Ken 1985a. 'The social and the subject in Bakhtin' (Review of *PDPE), Poetics Today,* VI: 4, pp. 769-75.

Hirschkop, Ken 1985b. 'A response to the forum on Mikhail Bakhtin', *Critical Inquiry,* XI: 4, pp. 672-8 (reprinted in Morson 1986a).

Holden, Kate 1985. 'Women's writing and the carnivalesque', *LTP* (Journal of Literature Teaching Politics), 4, pp. 5-15.

Holquist, Michael 1987. 'Inner speech as social rhetoric', *Dieciocho,* X: 1, pp. 41-52.

Holquist, Michael 1986a. 'The surd heard: Bakhtin and Derrida', in Gary Saul Morson, ed., *Literature and History: Theoretical Problems and Russian Case Studies,* Stanford.

Holquist, Michael 1986b. 'Introduction', in *SG,* pp. ix-xxiii.

Holquist, Michael 1985a. 'Bakhtin and the Formalists: history as dialogue', in R. L. Jackson and Stephen Rudy, eds., *Russian Formalism: A retrospective Glance,* New Haven.

Holquist, Michael 1985b. 'The carnival of discourse: Bakhtin and simultaneity', *Canadian Review of Comparative Literature,* XII: 2, pp. 220-34.

Holquist, Michael 1984. 'Introduction', *Studies in Twentieth Century Literature,* IX: 1, pp. 7-12.

Holquist, Michael 1983a. 'Answering as authoring: Mikhail Bakhtin's translinguistics', *Critical Inquiry,* X: 2, pp. 307-19 (reprinted in Morson 1986a).

Holquist, Michael 1983b. 'Neotextualism: an anti-humanist threat to comparative literature', *Neohelicon,* X: 2, pp. 47-61, 81-8.

Holquist, Michael 1982-3. 'Bakhtin and Rabelais: theory as praxis', *Boundary,* XI: 1-2, pp. 5-19.

Holquist, Michael 1982a. 'Bad faith squared: the case of M. M. Bakhtin', in Evelyn Bristol, ed., *Russian Literature and Criticism: Selected Papers from the Second World Congress for Soviet and East European Studies,* Berkeley.

Holquist, Michael 1982b. 'The irrepressible I: the role of linguistic subjectivity in dissidence', *Yearbook of Comparative and General Literature,* 31, pp. 30-5.

Holquist, Michael 1981a. 'The politics of representation', in Stephen J. Greenblatt, ed., *Allegory and Representation,* Baltimore.

Holquist, Michael 1981b. 'Introduction', in *DI,* pp. xiii-xxxiv.

Holquist, Michael 1978. 'Bakhtin, Mikhail Mikhailovich', in Victor Terras, ed., *Modern Encyclopedia of Russian and Soviet Literature,* New Haven.

Howes, Craig 1986. 'Rhetorics of attack: Bakhtin and the aesthetics of satire', *Genre,* XIX: 3, pp. 25-43.

Hoyles, John 1982. 'Radical critical theory and English', in Peter Widdowson, ed., *Re-Reading English,* London.

Hutcheon, Linda 1983. 'The carnivalesque and contemporary narrative: popular culture and the erotic', *The University of Ottawa Quarterly,* LIII: 1, pp. 83-96.

Ivanov, Viacheslav V. 1976. 'The significance of M. M. Bakhtin's ideas on sign, utterance and dialogue for modern semiotics', in Henryk Baran, ed., *Structuralism and Semiotics,* White Plains, N.Y.

Jackson, Robert 1987. Review of *RW, Georgia Review,* XLI, pp. 415-20.

Jameson, Fredric 1974. Review of *MPL, Style,* VIII: 3, pp. 535-43.

Jameson, Fredric 1973. 'Wyndham Lewis as Futurist', *Hudson Review,* XXVI: 2, pp. 303-6.

Jauss, Hans Robert 1985. 'The identity of the poetic text in the changing horizon of understanding', in Mario J. Valdes and Owen Miller, eds., *Identity of the Literary Text,* Toronto.

Jefferson, Ann 1986. 'Realism reconsidered: Bakhtin's dialogism and the "will to reference"', *Australian Journal of French Studies,* XXIII: 2, pp. 169-84.

Jefferson, Ann 1980. 'Intertextuality and the poetics of fiction', *Comparative Criticism,* 2, pp. 235-50.

Jha, Prabhakara 1985. 'Lukács, Bakhtin and the sociology of the novel', *Diogenes,* 129, pp. 63-90.

Jones, Malcolm V. 1975. 'Scholar of the carnival' (Review of Bakhtin *Festschrift* published in Saransk, USSR), *Times Literary Supplement,* 25 July, p. 857.

Kagarlitsky, Boris 1988. *The Thinking Reed,* London, pp. 278-80.

Kaiser, Mark 1984. 'P. N. Medvedev's "The collapse of Formalism"', in Benjamin A. Stolz, Lubomir Doležel and I. R. Titunik eds., *Language and Literary Theory,* Ann Arbor.

Kibler, William 1970. Review of *RW, Style,* IV: 1, pp. 73-5.

Kijinski, John 1987. 'Bakhtin and works of mass culture: heteroglossia in *Stand By Me*', *Studies in Popular Culture,* X: 2, pp. 67-81.

Kinser, Samuel 1984. 'Chronotopes and catastrophes: the cultural history of Mikhail Bakhtin' (Review of *DI* and *DP*), *Journal of Modern History,* LVI: 2, pp. 301-10.

Kloepfer, Rolf 1980. 'Dynamic structures in narrative literature: the dialogic principle', *Poetics Today,* I: 4, pp. 115-34.

Kochis, Bruce and W. G. Regier 1981. Review of *DI, Genre,* XIV:4, pp. 530-5.

Kovács, Árpád 1980. 'On the methodology of the theory of the novel: Bakhtin, Lukács, Pospelov', *Studia Slavica Academiae Scientiarum Hungaricae,* XXVI: 3-4, pp. 377-93.

Kozhinov, Vadim 1977. 'The world of M. M. Bakhtin', *Soviet Literature,* 1, pp. 143-4.

Kristeva, Julia 1980. 'Word, dialogue, and novel', in *Desire in Language,* ed., Leon S. Roudiez, trans. Thomas Gora, Alice Jardine and Leon S. Roudiez, New York.

Kristeva, Julia 1973. 'The ruin of a poetics', in Stephen Bann and John E. Bowlt, eds., *Russian Formalism,* Edinburgh.

La Capra, Dominick 1983. 'Bakhtin, Marxism and the carnivalesque', in *Rethinking Intellectual History: Texts, Contexts and Language,* Ithaca, N.Y.

Lanser, Susan S. 1986. 'Towards a feminst narratology', *Style,* XX: 3, pp. 341-63.

Le Charite, Ray 1986. *Rabelais's Incomparable Book,* Lexington, Kentucky.

Lechte, John 1986. 'Fiction and polyphony', in Terry Threadgold *et al.,* eds., *Semiotics, Ideology, Language,* Sydney.

Liao, Ping Hui 1984. 'Intersection and juxtaposition of wor(l)ds', *Tamkang Review,* XIV: 1-4, pp. 395-415.

Lodge, David 1988. 'The novel now: theories and practices', *Novel,* XXI: 2-3, pp. 125-38.

Lodge, David 1987. 'After Bakhtin', in Nigel Fabb *et al.,* eds., *The Linguistics of Writing,* Manchester and New York.

Lodge, David 1984. 'Mimesis and diegesis in modern fiction', in Anthony Mortimer, ed., *Contemporary Approaches to Narrative,* Tubingen.

Lokke, Virgil 1987. 'Contextualizing the either/or: invariants/ variation and dialogue in Jakobson/Bakhtin', in Clayton Koelb and Virgil Lokke, eds., *The Current in Criticism,* West Lafayette, Indiana.

Lotman, Yuri 1976. 'Gogol and the correlations of "the culture of humour" with the comic and serious in the Russian national tradition', in Henryk Baran, ed., *Semiotics and Structuralism,* White Plains, N.Y.

MacCannell, Juliet Flower 1985. 'The temporality of textuality: Bakhtin and Derrida', *Modern Language Notes,* C:5, pp. 968-88.

McHale, Brian 1978. 'Free indirect discourse: a survey of recent accounts', *PTL,* III, pp. 249-87.

McKenna, Andrew J. 1983. 'After Bakhtin: on the future of laughter and its history in France', *The University of Ottawa Quarterly,* LIII: 1, pp. 67-82.

McKinley, Mary B. 1987. 'Bakhtin and the world of Rabelais criticism', *Degré Second,* XI, pp. 83-8.

Malcuzynski, M.-Pierrette 1984. 'Polyphonic theory and contemporary literary practices', *Studies in Twentieth Century Literature,* IX: 1, pp. 75-87.

Malcuzynski, M.-Pierrette 1983. 'Mikhail Bakhtin and contemporary narrative theory', *The University of Ottawa Quarterly,* LIII: 1, pp. 51-65.

Markiewicz, Henryk 1984. 'Polyphony, dialogism and dialectics: Mikhail Bakhtin's theory of the novel', in Joseph P. Strelka, ed., *Literary Theory and Criticism,* New York.

Matejka, Ladislav 1973. 'On the first Russian prolegomena to semiotics', in *MPL,* pp. 161-74.

Miller, Stephen 1969. Review of *RW, New York Times Book Review,* 19 January, p. 36.

Monas, Sidney 1985a. 'Verbal carnival: Bakhtin, Rabelais, *Finnegans Wake* and the Growthesk', *Irish Slavonic Studies,* 6, pp. 35-45.

Monas, Sidney 1985b. Review of *PDPE, Partisan Review,* LII: 4, pp. 452-6.

Morson, Gary Saul 1986a. *Bakhtin: Essays and Dialogues on His Work,* ed. (includes preface by Morson, Morson 1983, Morson 1981a, Bernstein 1983, Booth 1982, Emerson 1983b, Holquist 1983a, Stewart 1983, Hirschkop 1985b, Morson 1985 and extracts from *SG,* introduced by Morson), Chicago and London.

Morson, Gary Saul 1986b. 'The Baxtin industry', *Slavic and East European Journal,* XXX: 1, pp. 81-90.

Morson, Gary Saul 1985. 'Dialogue, monologue and the social: a reply to Ken Hirschkop', *Critical Inquiry,* XI: 4, pp. 679-86 (reprinted in Morson 1986a).

Morson, Gary Saul 1983. 'Who speaks for Bakhtin?', *Critical Inquiry,* X: 2, pp. 225-44 (reprinted in Morson 1986a).

Morson, Gary Saul 1981a. 'Tolstoy's absolute language', *Critical Inquiry,* VII: 4, pp. 667-87 (reprinted in Morson 1986a).

Morson, Gary Saul 1981b. *The Boundaries of Genre: Dostoevsky's 'Diary of a Writer' and the Traditions of Literary Utopia,* Austin, pp. 107-42.

Morson, Gary Saul 1978. 'The heresiarch of META', *PTL,* III, pp. 407-27.

Natoli, Joseph 1987. 'Tracing a beginning through past theory voices', in Joseph Natoli, ed., *Tracing Literary Theory,* Urbana, Illinois.

Parrott, Ray 1984. '(Re)capitulation, parody or polemic?', in Benjamin A. Stolz, Lubomir Doležel and I. R. Titunik, eds., *Language and Literary Theory,* Ann Arbor.

Pateman, Trevor 1982. 'Discourse in life: V. N. Voloshinov's *Marxism and the Philosophy of Language',* *University of East Anglia Papers in Linguistics,* 16-17, pp. 26-48.

Patterson, David 1987a. 'Dostoevsky's poetics of spirit: Bakhtin and Berdyaev', *Dostoevsky Studies* (Austria), VIII, pp. 220-31.

Patterson, David 1987b. 'Signification, responsibility and spirit: Bakhtin and Levinas', *Cithara,* XXVI: 2, pp. 5-19.

Patterson, David 1985. 'Mikhail Bakhtin and the dialogical discussion of the novel', *Journal of Aesthetics and Art Criticism,* XLIV: 2. pp. 131-8.

Pechey, Graham 1986. 'Bakhtin, Marxism and post-structuralism', in Francis Barker *et al.,* eds., *Literature, Politics and Theory: Papers from the Essex Conference, 1976-1984,* London and New York.

Pechey, Graham 1980. 'Formalism and Marxism' (Review of *FM* and Bennett 1979), *Oxford Literary Review,* IV: 2, pp. 72-81.

Perlina, Nina 1984. 'Bakhtin and Buber: problems of dialogic imagination', *Studies in Twentieth Century Literature,* IX: 1, pp. 13-28.

Perlina, Nina 1983. 'Bakhtin–Medvedev–Voloshinov: an apple of discourse', *The University of Ottawa Quarterly,* LIII: 1, pp. 35-47.

Pirog, Gerald 1987. 'The Bakhtin circle's Freud: from positivism to hermeneutics', *Poetics Today,* VIII: 3-4, pp. 591-610.

Polan, Dana 1989. 'Bakhtin, Benjamin, Sartre: toward a typology of the intellectual cultural critic', in Catriona Kelly, Michael Makin and David Shepherd, eds., *Discontinuous Discourses in Modern Russian Literature,* London and New York.

Polan, Dana 1983. 'The text between dialogue and monologue', *Poetics Today,* IV: 1, pp. 145-83.

Polzin, Robert 1984. 'Dialogic imagination in the Book of Deuteronomy', *Studies in Twentieth Century Literature*, IX: 1, pp. 135-44.

Pomorska, Krystyna 1984. 'Mikhail Bakhtin and his dialogic universe', *Semiotica*, XLVIII: 1-2, pp. 169-74.

Pomorska, Krystyna 1978. 'Mixail Baxtin and his verbal universe', *PTL*, III, pp. 379-85.

Pomorska, Krystyna 1968. 'Foreword', in *RW*, pp. v-x.

Ponzio, Augusto 1986. 'On the methodics of common speech', *Differentia*, 1, pp. 137-66.

Ponzio, Augusto 1984. 'Semiotics between Peirce and Bakhtin', *Semiotic Inquiry/Recherches Sémiotiques*, IV: 3-4, pp. 273-92.

Raskin, Marina 1981-2. Review of *DI*, *Modern Fiction Studies*, XXVII: 4, pp. 667-9.

Regier, W. G. 1985. Review of *MB*, *PDPE*, *DP*, *Genre*, XVIII: 1, pp. 74-81.

Reid, Robert 1985. Review of *BSP*, *Irish Slavonic Studies*, 6, pp. 160-1.

Reilly, Ann and Prospero Saiz 1981. 'Voloshinov, Bennett and the politics of writing', *Contemporary Literature*, XXII: 4, pp. 510-43.

Richter, David H. 1986. 'Bakhtin in life and art' (Review of *MB*, *DP*), *Style*, XX: 3, pp. 411-19.

Russo, Mary 1986. 'Female grotesques: carnival and theory', in Teresa de Lauretis, ed., *Feminist Studies/Critical Studies*, Bloomington, Indiana.

Schuster, Charles I. 1985. 'Mikhail Bakhtin as rhetorical theorist', *College English*, XLVII: 6, pp. 594-607.

Seduro, Vladimir 1975. *Dostoevsky's Image in Russia Today*, Belmont, Mass., pp. 307-32.

Seduro, Vladimir 1957. *Dostoyevski in Russian Literary Criticism 1846-1956*, New York, pp. 202-32.

Segal, Dmitri 1974. *Aspects of Structuralism in Soviet Philology* (University of Tel Aviv Papers on Poetics and Semiotics, 2), Tel Aviv.

Segre, Cesare 1985. 'What Bakhtin left unsaid: the case of the medieval romance', in Kevin Brownlee and Marina Scordiles Brownlee, eds., *Romance: Generic Transformations from Chrétien de Troyes to Cervantes*, Hanover, N.H. and London.

Seidel, Michael 1983. 'Satire and metaphoric collapse: the bottom of the sublime', in J. D. Browning, ed., *Satire in the Eighteenth Century*, New York.

Sharratt, Bernard 1979. 'The play of the book' (Review of Bennett 1979), *The Literary Review* (Edinburgh), 4, 16-29 November, pp. 13-14.

Shepherd, David 1988. Review of *SG*, *Modern Language Review*, LXXXIII: 3, pp. 808-9.

Shepherd, David 1986a. 'The authority of meanings and the meanings of authority: some problems in the theory of reading', *Poetics Today*, VII: 1, pp. 129-45.

Shepherd, David 1986b. Review of *BSP*, *Quinquereme*, IX: 2, pp. 246-8.

Sheppard, R. W. 1983. 'Tricksters, carnival and the magical figures of Dada poetry', *Forum for Modern Language Studies*, XIX: 2, pp. 116-23.

Shukman, Ann 1986a. 'Reading Bakhtin with a stiff upper lip', (Review of *MB*) *Scottish Slavonic Review*, 6, pp. 122-6.

Shukman, Ann 1986b. 'Bakhtin, theorist of dialogue' (Report on Cagliari conference), *The Bakhtin Newsletter*, 2, pp. 134-6.

Shukman, Ann 1985. Review of special Bakhtin issue of *The University of Ottawa Quarterly, Irish Slavonic Studies,* 6, pp. 161-2.

Shukman, Ann 1984a. 'Bakhtin and Tolstoy', *Studies in Twentieth Century Literature,* IX: 1, pp. 57-74.

Shukman, Ann 1984b. 'M. M. Bakhtin: notes on his philosophy of man', in William Harrison and Avril Pyman, eds., *Poetry, Prose and Public Opinion,* Letchworth.

Shukman, Ann 1983. 'Editor's introduction', in *BSP,* pp. 1-4.

Shukman, Ann 1980. 'Between Marxism and Formalism: the stylistics of Mikhail Bakhtin', *Comparative Criticism,* 2, pp. 221-34.

Shukman, Ann 1979. Review of *MPL, Language and Style,* XII: 1, pp. 74-5.

Silverman, David and Brian Torode 1980. *The Material Word: Some Theories of Language and Its Limits,* London and Boston, pp. 305-10.

Singer, Alan 1988. 'The voice of history/the subject of the novel', *Novel,* XXI: 2-3, pp. 173-9.

Smith, Brittain 1988. Review of *DP, Russian Literature Triquarterly,* 21, pp. 241-2.

Solomon, Maynard 1973. 'Mikhail Bakhtin: introduction', in Maynard Solomon, ed., *Marxism and Art,* Brighton.

Sprinker, Michael 1986. 'Boundless contexts: problems in Bakhtin's linguistics', *Poetics Today,* VII: 1, pp. 117-28.

Stallybrass, Peter and Allon White 1986. *The Politics and Poetics of Transgression,* London and Ithaca, NY.

Stam, Robert 1988. 'Mikhail Bakhtin and left cultural critique', in E. Ann Kaplan, ed., *Postmodernism and its Discontents,* London.

Stam, Robert 1987. 'Bakhtin, eroticism and the cinema: strategies for the critique and transvaluation of pornography', *Cineaction,* X.

Steiner, George 1981. 'At the carnival of language', (Review of *DI*), *Times Literary Supplement,* 17 July, pp. 799-800.

Stewart, Susan 1987. Review of *SG, New York Times Book Review,* 22 March, p. 31.

Stewart, Susan 1983. 'Shouts on the street: Bakhtin's anti-linguistics', *Critical Inquiry,* X: 2, pp. 265-81 (reprinted in Morson 1986a).

Sturrock, John 1987. 'Concluding dialogue' (Review of *SG*), *Times Literary Supplement,* 21 August, p. 892.

Sturrock, John 1982. Review of *DI* and *DP* (original French edition), *Modern Language Review,* LXXVII: 2, pp. 398-402.

Thaden, Barbara Z. 1987. 'Bakhtin, Dostoevsky and the status of the "I"', *Dostoevsky Studies* (Austria), VIII, pp. 199-207.

Thibault, Paul 1984. 'Narrative discourse as a multi-level system of communication: some theoretical proposals concerning Bakhtin's dialogic principle', *Studies in Twentieth Century Literature,* IX: 1, pp. 89-118.

Thomson, Clive 1984a. 'Bakhtin's "theory" of genre', *Studies in Twentieth Century Literature,* IX: 1, pp. 29-40.

Thomson, Clive 1984b. 'Bakhtinian methodologies', *Semiotic Inquiry/Recherches Sémiotiques,* IV: 3-4, pp. 372-87.

Thomson, Clive 1983. 'The semiotics of M. M. Bakhtin', *The University of Ottawa Quarterly,* LIII: 1, pp. 11-21.

Titunik, I. R. 1986. 'The Baxtin problem: concerning Katerina Clark's and

Michael Holquist's *Mikhail Bakhtin'*, *Slavic and East European Journal*, XXX: 1, pp. 91-5.

Titunik, I. R. 1984. 'Bakhtin &/or Voloshinov &/or Medvedev: dialogue &/or doubletalk?', in Benjamin A. Stolz, Lubomir Doležel and I. R. Titunik, eds., *Language and Literary Theory*, Ann Arbor.

Titunik, I. R. 1981. 'Bakhtin and Soviet semiotics: a case study', *Russian Literature* (Amsterdam), X: 1, pp. 1-16.

Titunik, I. R. 1976. 'M. M. Baxtin (the Baxtin School) and Soviet semiotics', *Dispositio*, I: 3, pp. 327-38.

Titunik, I. R. 1973. 'The formal method and the sociological method (M. M. Baxtin, P. N. Medvedev, V. N. Voloshinov) in Russian theory and study of literature', in *MPL*, pp. 175-200.

Todorov, Tzvetan 1985. 'Humanly plural' (Review of *MB*), *Times Literary Supplement*, 14 June, pp. 675-6.

Tribe, Keith 1986. 'Mikhail Bakhtin: word and object' (Review of *MB*), *Economy and Society*, XV: 3, pp. 403-13.

Tribe, Keith 1980. 'Literary methodology' (Review of *FM* and Pierre Macherey, *A Theory of Literary Production*), *Economy and Society*, IX: 2, pp. 241-9.

Ulmer, Gregory 1980. Review of *FM*, *Clio*, IX: 2, pp. 314-17.

Wall, Anthony 1986. 'Bakhtin as seen in the German Democratic Republic', *The Bakhtin Newsletter*, 2, pp. 137-8.

Wall, Anthony 1984. 'Characters in Bakhtin's theory', *Studies in Twentieth Century Literature*, IX: 1, pp. 41-56.

Walton, William Garrett, Jr. 1981. 'V. N. Voloshinov: a marriage of Formalism and Marxism', in Peter Zima, ed., *Semiotics and Dialectics*, Amsterdam.

Wasiolek, Edward 1987. Review of *PDPE*, *Comparative Literature*, XXXIX: 2, pp. 187-9.

Wasiolek, Edward 1982 . Review of *DI*, *Comparative Literature*, XXXIV: 2, pp. 174-6.

Wasiolek, Edward 1975. Review of *PDPR*, *Slavic Review*, XXXIV: 2, pp. 436-8.

Weber, Samuel M. 1985. 'The intersection: Marxism and the philosophy of language', (Review of *MPL*), *Diacritics*, XV: 4, pp. 94-112.

Wehrle, Albert J. 1982. Review of *DI*, *Slavic and East European Journal*, XXVI: 1, pp. 106-7.

Wehrle, Albert J. 1978. 'Introduction: M. M. Bakhtin/P. N. Medvedev', in *FM*, pp. ix-xxiii.

White, Allon 1987-8. 'The struggle over Bakhtin: fraternal reply to Robert Young', *Cultural Critique*, 8, pp. 217-41.

White, Allon 1984. 'Bakhtin, sociolinguistics and deconstruction', in Frank Gloversmith, ed., *The Theory of Reading*, Brighton and Totowa, N.J.

White, Hayden 1983. 'The authoritative lie' (Review of *DI*), *Partisan Review*, L: 2, pp. 307-12.

Williams, Raymond 1986. 'The uses of cultural theory', *New Left Review*, 158, pp. 19-31.

Williams, Raymond 1977. *Marxism and Literature*, Oxford, pp. 35-42.

Wilson, Robert R. 1987. Review of *MB* and Morson 1986a, *Canadian Review of Comparative Literature*, XIV: 2. pp.260-7.

Winner, Thomas 1976. 'Jan Mukařovský: the beginnings of structural and semiotic aesthetics', in Ladislav Matejka, ed., *Sound, Sign and Meaning:*

Quinquagenary of the Prague Linguistic Circle, Ann Arbor.

Yaeger, Patricia 1986. 'Emancipatory discourse' (Review of *MB* and *DP*), *Contemporary Literature*, XXVII: 2, pp. 246-56.

Yates, Frances 1969. Review of *RW, New York Review of Books,* 9 October, pp. 16-21.

Yengoyan, Aram A. 1977. Review of *MPL, American Anthropologist,* LXXIX: 3, pp. 700-1.

Young, Robert 1985. 'Back to Bakhtin', *Cultural Critique,* 2, pp. 71-92.

Zelnick, Stephen 1979. Review of *FM, Journal of Aesthetics and Art Criticism,* XXXVII: 3, pp. 366-7.

Zima, Peter V. 1981. 'Semiotics, dialectics and critical theory', in Peter Zima, ed., *Semiotics and Dialectics,* Amsterdam.

Notes on the contributors

Tony Crowley is a lecturer in the Department of English at the University of Southampton. He has taught at universities in Britain and America, and has published articles on language and cultural theory. *The Politics of Discourse: The Standard Language Question in British Cultural Debates,* a study of issues related to those discussed in his contribution to this volume, is to be published in 1989. His current research interests are centred on Joyce and war in discourse.

Terry Eagleton, formerly fellow in English at Wadham College, Oxford, is now a fellow of Linacre College, Oxford and university lecturer in Critical Theory. His many publications include *Literary Theory: An Introduction* and a novel, *Saints and Scholars.* His latest book, *The Ideology of the Aesthetic,* will appear in 1989.

Nancy Glazener is a graduate student at Stanford University. Her main research interests are feminist theory and materialist theories of culture, and she is completing a dissertation entitled *The Realist Imperative: Realism as Form and Social Value in Nineteenth-Century American Literature.*

Ken Hirschkop is lecturer in the history and theory of communication at the University of Southampton. He has written on Bakhtin, discourse theory and the politics of modern culture for *New Left Review, Poetics Today, News from Nowhere* and *Essays in Poetics,* and is completing a book entitled *Bakhtin and Democracy.* His current research interests are theories of democracy and communication, and the politics of twentieth-century culture in the Soviet Union, England and the United States.

Ann Jefferson is a fellow in French at New College, Oxford. She is the author of *The Nouveau Roman and the Poetics of Fiction* (1980) and *Reading Realism in Stendhal* (1988), and co-editor of *Modern Literary Theory: A Comparative Introduction* (1982 and 1986). She has also published articles on modern fiction and on aspects of critical theory, including the work of Bakhtin, relating to fiction.

Graham Pechey is a lecturer in English at Hatfield Polytechnic. He has published articles on literary theory and Romantic writing, and is preparing a book on Bakhtin. His current research interest is in colonial discourse and third-world (mainly African) writing.

David Shepherd is a lecturer in Russian Studies at the University of Manchester. He is a co-editor of *Discontinuous Discourses in Modern Russian Literature* (1989), and is completing a book on metafiction in Soviet literature.

Clair Wills is a research fellow in English Literature at Queen's College, Oxford. She is currently working on a study of contemporary Northern Irish poetry, focusing on the work of Paul Muldoon and Medbh McGuckian. Her other research interests include twentieth-century British and American women's poetry, and feminist theory. She has published articles and reviews on contemporary poetry, including that of McGuckian, cultural politics in Ireland, Irish literary history, feminist debates and women's histories.

Index